MY AMERICAN JOURNEY

An Autobiography of Hard Work,
Self-Determination, Dignity, and Faith

LCDR Joe Walker, USN (Ret.)

Contents

Introduction

I was born and raised in a rural village of Louisiana surrounded by sugarcane fields. My family was by no means well-to-do; my father was a construction worker and my mother worked as a maid.

My parents instilled a strong work ethic in me from an early age. Before I ever set foot in a schoolhouse, I helped my father build our first house. I was a tool runner, and I kept the work area clean. As an adolescent, I worked odd jobs. Before sunrise on school days, my father and I were at the Mississippi River, raising shrimp boxes. Then I went into the fields to cut grass for feeding the animals. On weekends, my father and I built or repaired houses for people in our community and surrounding area.

In elementary school, I was an honors student. My first-grade teacher taught me two special things: (1) the power of saving when she gave me a piggy bank, and (2) how to think outside the box. However, as I progressed through the grades, I drifted and became bored with school, and my performance declined to merely average. Highly interested in music, I blew brass instruments and was a self-taught organist. I fell in love with radio and dreamed of becoming a disc jockey.

During the era of strict Southern segregation, I lived under Jim Crow Laws, and in 1967, I became one of twelve Black students to integrate an all-White high school. With reservations and a general lack of interest, I later participated in track and field, where I discovered I had natural talent.

After high school, my one goal was to join the Navy. I entered the Navy as an airman recruit and proved myself a dedicated sailor and eventually advanced to the rank of lieutenant commander. I traveled the world and collected many friends along the way.

Upon completing active-duty military service, I embarked on a career in the technology industry, maintaining mainframe computers, then graduated to software programming. I navigated my way through various jobs in the software business, finding my niche in database management.

My parents taught me the value of hard work and nurtured my sense of dignity and self-worth. Throughout life, I focused on being optimistic, with a glass-half-full perspective; and holding tight to my lifelong Catholic faith, I prevailed.

Bayou Goula, Louisiana

Louisiana is located in the South of the United States. It shares borders with Texas, Arkansas, Mississippi and the Gulf of Mexico.

Louisiana is divided into 64 subdivisions called parishes, derived from the French term, *paroisse*. Parishes are the legal equivalent of other states' counties. Louisiana is the only state in the union using a parish system.

Iberville Parish is home to more than 33,000 people. Its chief agricultural products include sugarcane, soybeans and cattle. Many of the country's largest chemical companies have plants located in Iberville Parish.

Bayou Goula is a Choctaw term meaning "Bayou People," alluding to their location on the west bank of the Mississippi River. Bayou Goula was a Mugulasha Indian village captured by the Bayougoulas (a Muskhogean tribe).

Bayou Goula is 22 miles from Baton Rouge, 80 miles from New Orleans. It's the oldest French settlement in the parish, with a population of approximately 650 nestled between Louisiana Highway 1 and the Mississippi River levee. Its two main streets are Corporal Herman Brown Jr. Street (named after a resident killed in the Vietnam war) and Breaux Street. The resident majority are Black families, with few White families.

Bayou Goula has Baptist, Methodist and Catholic churches. During its early years, St. Luke United Methodist Church doubled as a schoolhouse, where one teacher taught all the children. The church, still used today, was used in the filming of the classic film,

The Autobiography of Miss Jane Pittman. One of Bayou Goula's other claims to fame is The Madonna Chapel, built in 1905 and dubbed "The Smallest Church in the World."

Tally Ho Plantation is another Bayou Goula landmark. Also nearby is Nottoway Plantation, the largest extant antebellum plantation house in the South. Surrounding towns include White Castle, Dorseyville and Plaquemine.

The Years 1955–1959

My parents, Joseph Dave "J.D." Walker, Sr., and Julia Mae "Mick" Pierre-Walker, born and raised in Louisiana, started dating at a young age. J.D. worked in his stepfather's sugarcane field. Julia also worked in the sugarcane fields. My older sister, Audrey Mae was born in 1950.

During the spring months, J.D. went with other working adults to Albany, Louisiana, to work as a strawberry picker. On the weekends, Julia and her girlfriend would visit him. J.D. and Julia went out and, in May 1954, I was conceived on a strawberry farm.

With Julia newly pregnant, J.D. told his parents and made the decision to make Julia his wife. He asked her mother for permission to marry, and she gave them her blessing. He was Catholic; she was Baptist, but she vowed to raise their children as Catholics. J.D. and Julia were married at Our Lady of Prompt Succor Catholic Church in White Castle, Louisiana on November 13, 1954. The newlyweds moved into a two-room house; the rent was $5 a month.

Nine months after the strawberry picking, J.D. brought the local midwife to the house to assist with the birth. On January 15, 1955, at 4:30 a.m. in Bayou Goula, Iberville Parish, Louisiana, I was born. They named me Joseph "Joe" Dave Walker, Jr.

I was born with a caul. A caul is a piece of membrane that covers a newborn's head and face. A birth with a caul is rare, although harmless. The midwife assisting my mother didn't remove the caul properly, which left a permanent scar. On the right side of my forehead is the evidence of its removal.

What's in a Name?

As far as I can remember, I have always called my father "Dada." My mother's nickname is "Mick." I have always called her "Mick" or "Mickey Mouse" because that's what I heard others call her. I called my paternal grandmother, Lorenza Carter, by her nickname, "Li'l Sister." I called her husband, Riley Carter, by his first name. Both tried to train me to say Grandma and Grandpa, but I never did. Likewise, I called my maternal grandmother, Florestine Pierre, by her nickname, "Ma Flo." My mother's father died before I was born.

I called most of my uncles and aunts by their first names, except Uncle Joe, Uncle Dick, Uncle Arthur, Auntie Poncie and Auntie Dorothy Lee. Why they were an exception remains unknown.

Other adults in the community were always greeted with "Cousin" or "Mr. or Ms." before their names as a sign of respect. Replies to any adult were, "Yes, sir" or "Yes, ma'am."

As an infant, I was baptized at Our Lady of Prompt Succor Catholic Church. Bob Miller was my "Parrain" (godfather) and Arleen Miller was my "Nanan" (godmother).

I remember playful times with my parents. My mother would hold me and bounce me on her knee. I always thought it was fun to be bounced. My father would toss me into the air. When he caught me coming down, he'd rub his stubby whiskers against my face. I would laugh as I waited to be tossed again.

My parents' third child, Barbara Ann "Bobbie" Walker-Carter, was adopted by our grandparents (Riley and Lorenza Carter).

My father told me this story, and I have no memory of it. I was about three years old. Every time my father got into his car to go somewhere, I would hop in too. On this day, I was told to go back into the house.

Instead, I wandered to the rear of the car and he did not see me. There was no paved driveway and after a rainstorm, the whole yard was muddy. To avoid getting the car stuck in the mud, my father maneuvered the car to create new tracks. Because of the new tracks, the car was slightly higher off the ground. When he shifted into reverse, the rear bumper knocked me to the ground. I fell into the car's original mud tracks. I was lying on the ground in the car tracks as the car rolled over me. When it cleared me, I stood up unharmed, covered with mud. My father quickly jumped out of the vehicle and picked me up as he was crying. It was a miracle the car tires did not slide into the car tracks where I was lying.

The wood siding on our two-room house was faded, due to a lack of paint. Both front and back porches had missing boards. The roof leaked when it rained. The two wood-framed windows had no screens. Torn, faded wallpaper hung from the interior walls. The front room contained a bed for my parents. My older sister, Audrey Mae, and I shared a small fold-out couch. Many nights I was bitten by mosquitos. During the winter, the wind blew through cracks in the walls, windows, and doors. A small gas stove in the kitchen and a small gas heater in the bedroom provided heat. A bare light bulb dangled from the ceiling in the center of each room, with string attached to turn it off and on. At night, rats and roaches roamed the house and I feared they would enter the fold-out couch.

Outside, barrels positioned by the house caught rainwater from the roof. We used it for drinking, baths and cooking. We had no inside toilet. In the backyard was a falling-apart outhouse that we shared with neighbors.

When my mother had to wash clothes, we hauled water from Ma Flo's house because she had a water pump. My father loaded the trunk of his car with barrels. I was always excited on water-hauling day. At Ma Flo's house, my father turned on the valve and I held the hose over the barrels to fill them. Sometimes, I'd put my thumb over the hose because friction appeared to make the water flow faster. I enjoyed watching the weight of the water lower the back of the car as the barrels filled. Once I'd leveled both barrels with water, I hopped into the front seat and my father drove away, trying not to spill all the water before we arrived home. The road was gravel and the water that spilled eliminated some of the dust in the air.

Sitting on the steps of the two-room house. Audrey Mae, neighbor, and me.

Once home, my parents used buckets and pans to transfer water from the too-heavy-to-lift barrels into other containers. I was too young to carry water, so I made myself useful by holding the door open as they went in and out. Once enough water had been removed, my parents lifted the barrels from the trunk of the car. Even though the pump water tasted good and looked clear, the containers would be stained with a brownish color once the water settled.

At night, we bathed in a tin tub. My mother heated a bucket of water on the stove and poured it into the tub. Each morning, we washed our faces and brushed our teeth over a white tin basin. The tin tub stayed in the kitchen, along with the washboard. My mother washed our clothing in the tub and hung them on the clothesline to dry.

While we lived in the two-room house, my mother and other neighborhood women cleaned green onions for extra money during the summer. After working in the sugarcane field all day, farmers would bring loads of muddy green onions to the house and place them on the porch. The women sat on the porch in the dark, laughing and talking as they cleaned them.

The summer nights were always dark. I could hear the voices of the women, but I could barely see anyone. The mosquitos were alive and pestering. Occasionally, I heard someone slap themselves, trying to kill a biting mosquito. On the porch was a bucket stuffed with rags. Someone would set these rags on fire and when the fire was beat out, the smoke helped to keep the mosquitos away. Each time the smoke dissipated, it was my job to stir the bucket again. I can remember clearly my eyes tearing up from that smoke, as well as the smell of the onions wafting through the night air. When I wasn't stirring up the smoke bucket, I caught lightning bugs.

Brother Tony Pasqua was an Italian who lived in Bayou Goula. He was a very religious man who devoted his life to Christ. Every Thursday afternoon, he opened the church and held Holy Rosary. Every week, I was there, assisting with the opening of the church and ringing the bell. Our house was the second house down from the church. Saturday mornings, Brother Pasqua taught catechism. One week, he taught us the Lord's Prayer and the following Saturday, I was the only kid who could recite it flawlessly. I then considered myself intelligent because Brother Pasqua told me I was.

Sunday mornings, my father and I walked to Mass. Mass was celebrated in Latin, so I never understood what the priest was saying. Whenever people in the church stood, so did I. When everyone sat or knelt, I did likewise. Even though the church was large, with four rows of pews, Blacks could only sit on the right-hand side. When the Black section was filled, Blacks stood behind the Black section pews during Mass. Often there remained many vacant pews in the White section, but the Blacks still had to stand.

I was selected to be a ring bearer for a few weddings. My mother would magically present me with a perfectly fitting suit she'd borrowed from someone. Alas, the suit wasn't mine to keep. After the wedding, the perfectly fitting suit disappeared just as magically as it had come to me.

When I was three-and-a-half-years-old, my uncle (Roosevelt "Skin" Pierre) took me at Christmastime to White Castle for my first look at Santa Claus. I didn't know what to expect. The only thing I knew about Santa Claus was that he brought toys to the children at Christmas.

When we arrived, I saw loads of people standing on the street. We joined a crowd of Black people standing across the street, facing the building where the Santa Claus was. I couldn't see the building clearly because I was small and the crowd was big. So I could have a better view, Skin lifted me and planted me on his shoulders. With my little legs dangling down his chest, he held tight, and I held on to his head. As I looked around, I noticed other small children who didn't have the same wonderful view as I did. I saw the Santa Claus sitting in a chair, surrounded by White people. Little White children were greeted by the Santa Claus, one by one. I didn't say anything to Skin, but I thought, *Why can't I go and greet the Santa Claus?* After I'd had a bird's-eye view of the jolly man greeting all the White children, Skin told me it was time for us to go home. When we got home, Ma Flo asked if I saw Santa Claus and I responded that I had. She told me, "Santa Claus will bring you a new toy on Christmas."

I didn't say anything to her, but I thought, *I saw the Santa Claus, but he didn't see me. How does he know who I am, and where I live?* Plus, I'd been told the Santa Claus came into the house through the chimney. Our chimney had been closed because we had a gas heater. I was totally confused.

However, on Christmas morning, I received a toy Greyhound bus, a cowboy hat, boots and two toy cap guns with a holster. I was still confused because I hadn't talked with the Santa Claus.

Our house was so close to the Mississippi River, we could hear the ferryboats' horns as they traveled up and down the river. Skin once told me babies came from the ferryboats. He said people went to the boat and selected the baby they wanted. Every time I heard the ferryboat horn blow, I wondered who was getting their baby.

In 1959, my parents decided it was time to move out of the two-room house. My mother no longer worked in the sugarcane field; she now worked as a maid. My father worked construction and had developed carpentry skills. He was convinced he knew enough to build a house for our family. He bought two acres of land at the dead-end part of Breaux Street. Surrounded by sugarcane fields, our land had three pecan trees and was filled with weeds and wild grass.

My father enlisted me as his helper to build the house. I was four years old and didn't grasp what it really meant, but I was eager to help. I was more excited about riding in the car to Breaux Street every day. We cleared the land by chopping the tall weeds and mowing the grass. My contribution was to pick up small branches and rake loose grass.

When it was time to start the foundation, I still didn't understand how we would build this house. My father explained we would build a four-room house: a living room, kitchen and two bedrooms. He showed me the blueprints, but I still didn't comprehend. Every day, after leaving his construction job, my father stopped at the lumber yard and bought building materials. The day we started construction, he came home with his car filled with house pillars.

When we arrived at the Breaux Street lot, with the aid of his shovel, he placed the house pillars in strategic positions. I held the string line as he measured and leveled the pillars. We always worked past sunset; when it was dark, he told me to turn on the car headlights. Later I was told to start the engine to prevent draining the battery. Then I was told to turn off the engine and headlights and hold the flashlight as he measured. I alternated between holding the flashlight and starting the car and turning the headlights on and off. I felt useful and enjoyed every minute, too.

After setting the house pillars, he bought lumber and nails. Whatever didn't fit into his car, the lumber yard delivered by truck. We went to the Breaux Street lot every evening. Saturdays, we started work at sunrise. At noon, we would take a break to eat lunch meat sandwiches and drink a soda. Then we worked until sunset. We went to Mass on Sunday and then worked on the house the remainder of the day.

Weeks later, the framing was taking shape. One night a storm came through and the wind blew the frame to the ground. We had to redo work we had already done. However, I was providing support by keeping the work area clean. I served as a tool runner, retrieving hammers, levels, nails and measuring tape upon request. All our tools were manual, as there were no electrical outlets.

We did all the construction, except the electrical installation. For that, we hired an electrician. Once the electricity was installed, my father bought a power saw. I was now climbing on the ladder and on the roof. I took single sheets of shingles up to be nailed down. People would drive by as we worked. Some stopped and questioned my ability to stay on the roof without falling.

Only one person came to help us work on the house, my Uncle Wilkie Pierre. Wilkie suffered from epilepsy and my father always feared he would have a seizure on the job. We kept a watchful eye on him, and he never had a seizure while working. He was fearless and died of a seizure at age 27.

During installation of the sheetrock, I was covered with sheetrock dust. I was always busy hauling or stacking scrap sheetrock. Sweeping and cleaning up each room was my main job. We would work past midnight. I often fell asleep in the corner of a room, while my father continued working.

We painted the exterior pink, with white trim. Each interior room was painted a different color (living room pink, kitchen yellow, and bedrooms green and blue). The flooring was varnished wood, and the kitchen had tile.

We moved into the house before I started first grade. We moved our clothing from the two-room house and bought new furniture. My parents had their room and Audrey Mae and I shared a room.

The house had no inside toilet, so we built an outhouse. As Louisiana is below sea level, water quickly filled the hole my father dug. My job was to bail water out. After the hole was finished, my father built a nice outhouse and I kept it clean. Inside our house we had a covered slop jar, which we used to relieve ourselves during the night. Each morning, I had to dump the slop jar.

In the backyard, we dug a deep hole, and we had well water. My parents withdrew water from the well, which was used to wash our clothes. Only a piece of plywood covered the hole.

Audrey Mae had a bicycle with training wheels. One day she was riding her bicycle in circles around the well as I stood and watched. Suddenly, one of the training wheels hooked underneath the plywood. The bicycle flipped to the ground and she tumbled into the well. I heard a loud splash.

I ran into the house, where my mother was in the kitchen, cooking. She saw the look on my face and knew something was wrong before I could speak.

However, I did manage to say, "She's in the well!"

My mother ran outside, picked up the bucket with the rope attached, and lowered it into the well. Audrey Mae grabbed hold of the rope and was pulled out.

When she was back on the ground, she was crying and choking from swallowing water. Her crying didn't lessen her punishment; my mother grabbed her by the arm, lifted her into the air, and started whacking her buttocks with the palm of her hand. As she was spanking, she said something about not playing around the well. She covered the well again and went back into the house. Audrey Mae sat on the ground, wet and crying. I stood, not knowing what to do or say, other than feel sorry for her.

My father had a hi-fi that played 45-rpm records. Whenever we worked around the house, he would lift the handle of the player to allow the same record to play repeatedly. I knew the lyrics to all the oldies because I'd heard the songs played many times. Also, I was an excellent dancer. I slid across the floor in my socks as I danced. Whenever visitors came, my father played a record and I danced, danced, danced, and never got tired.

My Aunt Beaulah, known as Tee Nachie, and Uncle Abraham Young lived in a two-room house near us. Tee Nachie was one of the kindest and most loving women I knew. She never said "no" to me. She smoked Prince Albert tobacco and rolled her cigarettes. Often, she allowed me to roll them. I would light the cigarette and take a puff before giving it to her. When Tee Nachie sewed, she often asked me to thread the needle for her. She was always amazed I could see the tiny eye of the needle to insert the thread.

The Years 1960–1969

Every Sunday, we gathered at Ma Flo's house. My uncles and aunts brought their kids. Sometimes, there would be twenty or more of us playing in the yard. We would go wild when we heard the music of the ice-cream truck. It moved slowly down the street and we would jump on the back bumper for a ride. My uncles would give money to the oldest kids, who bought popsicles and shared with the other kids.

Sometimes, Ma Flo would babysit us when our parents went to work. One day, she told us to play in the yard. Our cousin, William Taylor, came into the yard where we were playing. Due to recent rain, the ditches were full of water, so Taylor suggested we play church and baptize the other kids. We all were barefoot and wearing shorts. Taylor and I entered the knee-deep water and stood waiting for our first "victim" to come forward to be baptized.

No one wanted to volunteer, so we coaxed the little redhead boy to come into the water. The other children stood watching as Taylor and I dipped Pooche Boy beneath the water, as we had seen the Baptist minister do. Pooche Boy came up crying and when we let go of him, he ran into the house to tell Ma Flo.

Ma Flo had a vibrant cursing vocabulary. When she was angry, curse words flowed out of her mouth effortlessly. She came out of the house, cursing and not asking any questions. She had a belt in her hand and started whipping every child in sight. Taylor ran home and escaped the whipping. That was the end of our playing church.

At noon, Ma Flo would call all the children into the house to eat. We sat on the floor next to each other as she dished our plates. Usually, we ate red or white beans and rice. She always cooked her beans with salt pork.

All my cousins were Baptist; I was the only Catholic. Catholics weren't allowed to eat meat on Fridays. She would serve dinner while constantly cursing at me. She would rant about all the other children eating what she had cooked, but I had to be the special one. I sat quietly on the floor as she continued her diatribe. Then she would lovingly give me a plate of fried egg and rice.

Mr. Thimble walked past Ma Flo's house daily. He was a short elderly man who walked with a limp. I used to follow him to the pecan tree, where he sat to play his harmonica. I had never seen a harmonica. I was captivated by his playing. He blew the tune of a freight train and occasionally would remove the instrument from his lips and say, "The train is coming down the track." I wanted to blow his harmonica. But I never asked, because he was a wine drinker, and he was always a little on the tipsy side. Even as a child, I knew my limits. I don't remember where and how, but years later, I was given a toy harmonica. I blew the harmonica the same way I saw Mr. Thimble blow. I'd also occasionally say, "The train is coming down the track."

Daily delivery trucks drove through the community, selling wares. The milkman came early in the morning. He delivered the milk in one-gallon glass jars. The fruit man drove slowly down the street, tooting his truck horn and yelling, "Watermelon, red to the rim." He would sell the freshest fruits and vegetables (bananas, berries, apples, oranges, grapes, beans, potatoes and more). The pecan man tooted his horn and shouted, "Pecan man." He bought and sold pecans. Pecan trees were plentiful in our area, and we earned money picking and selling pecans. The fish man sold fresh catfish, shrimp and crawfish. The bread man sold fresh sliced white bread and doughnuts. The dry cleaner delivered and picked up clothing.

The life insurance man went door to door. He was an overweight man, profusely sweating and breathing heavily. My mother left cash to pay for the insurance policy, then he would stamp the insurance book to indicate the policy had been paid for the month.

Before long, we outgrew our little pink four-room house. My baby sister Josie was born, and she slept in a crib. Still believing what Skin had said about babies, I was sure she came off the ferryboat. I'd been sleeping in the bed with Audrey Mae. I slept at the bottom of the bed and she slept at the top.

My father drew plans to enlarge the kitchen, add an extra bedroom, and an inside bathroom. I'd have my own room. I help paint the interior and exterior. We had never built an inside bathroom, but we did all the plumbing. After we dug the septic pool, we installed cement blocks around its walls. I mixed the cement in a wooden box. While my father was laying bricks, I lugged buckets of cement to him as he installed the brick walls. I was constantly mixing cement and lowering cement blocks into the hole.

Everyone was thrilled to have running water coming into the house. Sometimes the electric pump would stall, but my father taught me how to re-prime it. When Audrey Mae had to wash the supper dishes and there was no water, I would take my time restarting the pump, just to get her angry. It made me feel as though I had power—until my mother made me go and restart the pump.

1961–1962 (First Grade)

On my first day of school at Bayou Goula Elementary School, I was unclear what to expect or do. All I knew was, Audrey Mae went to school and I was told I could go, too. I was excited because my mother had bought me shirts, jeans, shoes, a red raincoat and galoshes. I had a new tablet, a new pencil and a new flattop haircut. As I got dressed for school, I put on all my new clothing, including the raincoat and galoshes. My mother made me take the rain gear off because it wasn't raining.

Audrey Mae was in sixth grade. As we left for school, my mother stood in the doorway and yelled to me, "When you need to go to the bathroom, ask the teacher to be excused."

I felt good, dressed in my new clothing, walking and gripping my first-grader brown writing tablet and wooden pencil. Now I was going to finally find out what they did at this school!

Because our house was the last one on the street, we were the first to leave. When we arrived at our neighbor's house, the Bracken kids joined us and we walked together. These were the only people I knew, other than my cousins. Rather than walk the length of Breaux Street to get to school, we took a shortcut through the sugarcane field. In the sugarcane fields "head lanes" are used by tractor drivers to make U-turns in the field. The head lanes were our traveling routes to get to another street. We still had to walk through brushes of grass wet with morning dew. When we arrived at school, our new school clothing and shoes were soaked, but with the climate, our clothing dried quickly.

My first impression of this school was the large numbers of children. I had never been up close with this many kids, other than my cousins and neighbors. Plus, I didn't know so many children the same age as me existed.

I wasn't afraid, but I didn't leave Audrey Mae's side. I didn't want to get lost. When I heard the school bell ring, everyone started going inside. Audrey Mae led me to my first-grade classroom.

As we approached the door, a beautiful light-complexioned woman stood in the doorway. Audrey Mae said something to her, and the woman gave me a smile. She told me to be seated at one of the desks. Audrey Mae left and went to her class.

As I looked about the classroom, I was still amazed to know there were so many children the same age as me. Some were crying and I didn't know why. I was still wondering why I was there and what I was going to do in this school.

I learned the beautiful light-complexioned woman's name was Miss Wisher, and she was the first-grade teacher. I immediately took a liking to her and felt a sense of security. She was busy trying to console and stop the many children from crying. Even though she wasn't speaking directly to me, I felt as if she was.

Miss Wisher sat at her desk and started calling names. I thought she knew all our names, and I was even more impressed when she called mine.

I noticed a cute little girl sitting in the row next to me. She sat quietly, the same as me, and she wasn't crying. I liked this little girl already, and I learned her name was Julia Faye Harris.

Soon the bell rang, and we went outside to play. The first day of school, we weren't required to stay all day. We left at noon, but my parents were working, so we walked to Ma Flo's house.

When I arrived, Ma Flo asked me, "How did you like school today?"

I told her, "I saw a pretty girl and her name is Julia Faye Harris. She is my girlfriend."

Ma Flo ignored what I said and continued her house cleaning.

The second day, I wore my same new clothing. I was eager to go back. At the beginning of class, we were taught to stand by our desks, face the flag in the corner of the classroom and place our right hands over our hearts. We recited the Pledge of Allegiance. We did this every morning. It took us days to memorize all the words.

Miss Wisher explained the days of the week. On the blackboard, she wrote the month, date and year. Each day, it was updated as we learned the days of the week. Still, some students cried. She dismissed those who wouldn't stop crying. I assumed they went home because they didn't come back to the classroom.

We ate lunch in the cafeteria. It cost 45 cents a week. Every Monday, Miss Wisher collected lunch money for the week. When a student's name was called, we walked to her desk and paid for our lunch. Some students didn't pay because their parents were lower income. Also, each morning older boys came into our class and sold small cartons of milk for two cents.

Miss Wisher taught us the grace prayer. Before lunch, we stood next to our desk and recited it. Then single file, we walked to the cafeteria. We washed our hands before entering the cafeteria. Today, I sometimes still say the God is great prayer I was taught in first grade.

I thought I had learned all the numbers, until Miss Wisher introduced us to the numbers 10, 11, 12, etc. She taught us the alphabet by singing the ABCs. Once we memorized the letters, she wrote "A a" on the blackboard. I had difficulty writing within the thin blue lines on my tablet. Miss Wisher guided my hand to form the letter within the lines. At home, I practiced as I was taught. Each day Miss Wisher graded our work. She had a red marker, and she'd mark "A+" on my paper when I'd done a good job. My goal was to get an "A+" every day. I was soon identified as an honors student.

We were taught nursery rhymes and to draw. Miss Wisher drew a stick woman on the blackboard. The stick woman wore a dress. She told the class to draw everyone in their family. I drew all the members of my family the same as the teacher had (a stick woman in a dress).

When Miss Wisher came to check my work, she said, "Women wear dresses and men wear pants." With her red pen, she drew pants on my stick man.

At that moment, she taught me to think outside the box. We wrote words, beginning with our names. I was excited about first grade. Each day I knew I'd learn something new.

By now, I figured out that some of the students cried because they didn't want to be there. When crying didn't work, urinating at their desk was a guaranteed ticket home. Leaving the classroom with teary eyes, sniffling and wet, the student was supposedly going home to change. But they didn't return until the next day.

I had my first fistfight that year. I was on the playground and saw a boy make another boy cry. Then the bully walked over to me. He removed the towel from his back pocket (boys carried washcloth towels instead of handkerchiefs). He wrapped it around his fist as he mumbled under his breath. I knew he was going to hit me, and I blocked his swing. We fell to the ground, and I punched him in the face. His nose started bleeding. I let him up and he ran, crying, to the principal's office. Later, I saw the principal on the playground. I ran and hid underneath the school music building and stayed there until the bell rang. I returned to the classroom, and the boy I hit sat with tissue up his nose. I was sure the principal would come into the classroom for me. However, nothing was said. And the bully never bothered me again.

A professional photographer came to the school to take our photos. We were told to take the photos home for our parents' selections and return with the fees to purchase them. My mother said we had no money in the family budget for photos. I was told to return them to the school. However, I inadvertently left the photos on the kitchen table, within reach of my baby sister (Josie), who grabbed one and tore it. Because of this, my mother was forced to buy the photo. My first-grade photo shows a ripped top right corner.

Miss Wisher made Christmas special for all her students. She gave each of us a gift (a small piggy bank). I was thrilled to receive mine and challenged myself to fill it with coins.

Miss Wisher had a profound impact on my learning. I wanted to learn everything she could teach me. I listened intently and followed all her instructions. Undoubtedly, she was my favorite teacher, and she provided me with a solid foundation for my future education.

When I was about four, I'd sit in my father's lap and steer the car as he drove. At six, I watched his every move. I knew I could drive. I was just waiting for my opportunity.

My father knew I was eager to drive. Finally, the day came. He stopped the car on the river road and said he'd let me drive. When he slid into the passenger seat, I scooted behind the wheel and shifted the car into drive. My foot barely reached the gas pedal. I had to sit on the edge of the seat and peek through the steering wheel to see the road. I started slowly down the gravel road, both hands on the wheel. My father sat with one arm around the seat and his right arm hanging out the window.

I was responsible for mowing our lawn. I carried a plastic gallon jug and walked many times through the sugarcane fields to the store (about two miles away) to buy gas for the mower. We had a large yard and a push mower. In shorts, a T-shirt and beach slippers, I pushed and pulled that mower all over the yard. Then, on my hands and knees, I edged around the pecan trees, the house pillars and the sidewalk/driveway with a cane knife. It was hot and humid in summer, and it took me hours, but I kept our yard well manicured.

After the yardwork was completed, I washed the cars. We had a brown 1954 Mercury and a pink 1959 Mercury. I drove both cars in the yard. I liked driving the pink one because it was a push-button car. You'd push "drive" to go forward, and "reverse" to go backward.

I disliked working on the cars, but anytime one had a flat tire, I had to assist. My father often had to replace parts on the cars. At night, it would be on a jack with my father underneath, replacing a generator. I held the flashlight, kept mosquitos away from him, and retrieved from the toolbox whichever wrench he requested. Touching greasy wrenches irritated me badly. I hated getting my hands messy.

I had faithfully attended Saturday-morning catechism. Brother Pasqua prepared us for First Communion. We practiced over and over the proper way to receive Holy Communion. Brother Pasqua went to each home to inform the family of the date and time and proper attire. Girls wore white dresses, veils and shoes. Boys wore white shirts and black trousers, neckties and shoes, with a fresh flattop haircut.

That Sunday morning, I arrived at the church dressed in the proper attire. As we entered, Brother Pasqua stood at the door to greet us. He'd reserved the center aisle front pew. We sat in the White section of the church. At communion time, Brother Pasqua brought all the First Communion kids to the altar, where we knelt. He explained to the priest we were receiving Holy Communion for the first time. After the priest placed the host on my tongue, I made the sign of the cross and walked back to the pew in the White section. The next Sunday at Mass, we returned to sitting in the Black section.

Brother Pasqua taught us the procedure for confession. I never felt I needed to go, because I hadn't done anything to confess. So, when I went, I confessed what I'd heard him use as examples in class, such as, I missed Mass through my own fault, I lied to my parents, etc.

One Saturday morning, Brother Pasqua had a bag full of rosary beads and he gave each child in class a set. When he came to me, he had one white rosary left in the bag. Its crucifix was broken.

He told me, "I'm sorry, but this is the only rosary I have left." I graciously accepted the broken rosary. I still have my rosary with its broken crucifix.

As Christmas approached, I remained uncertain about Santa Claus. The previous year, I'd gone to see this Santa Claus, who only talked with the White children. I was convinced the Santa Claus didn't know me. I never talked with him. Plus, we'd moved into our new house—with no chimney. If Santa Claus came down the chimney, how would he get into our house?

However, I was amazed on Christmas Day when I received a black-and-white Mickey Mouse guitar. I had the best time with that little guitar. That's when I first discovered my interest in music.

Fortunately, I was generally a healthy child. If I got sick, I had to be almost dying before my mother would take me to the doctor.

During the Jim Crow Era, Dr. Musso's office entrance signs were posted with "White" and "Colored." In the office, Whites sat in one waiting room and Blacks in another. We could hear the White people in the waiting room talking, but we couldn't see them; they couldn't see us, either. In the Black waiting room, people spoke in whispers. I believe they were too sick to speak loudly.

After signing in, we'd wait to be called. Soon, a parent left the doctor's exam room with their child. The child would be sniffing, with tears in their eyes. I knew the child had gotten a shot with the big needle. Dr. Musso had a large needle. Whatever ailed you, Dr. Musso gave you a shot of penicillin with the big needle.

Dr. Musso was mean and intimidating. He wore a white hospital jacket, white shirt, black trousers and a black necktie. Attached to his head was a medical head-light device he used to inspect the throat and other body parts. Just the sight of him scared me.

A White nurse served the Whites, and a Black nurse served the Blacks. The Black nurse came into the waiting room and called us into the examination room. As I entered, I felt weak because I was sick, and I was shaking because I wasn't looking forward to seeing Dr. Musso. The nurse told me to sit on the exam table and my mother sat in the chair in the corner. After a short time, Dr. Musso walked in and I began shaking even more. He never looked at me and instead walked to the desk to read the notes the nurse had written. While still not looking at me, but in his intimidating voice, he asked, "What's the matter with you, boy?" I was too weak and too scared to speak.

My mother replied, "He has a cold and a sore throat."

I thought, *It doesn't matter what ails me, he's going to give me a shot of penicillin with that big needle.*

I believe he had no compassion for Blacks.

Dr. Musso had the nurse remove my shirt while he prepared his big needle. When he grabbed my little arm and stuck me with that big needle, I started crying.

Dr. Musso walked out of the room, unfazed. The nurse tried to comfort me by saying she had a candy sucker for me at the front desk.

I didn't respond, but I thought, *That candy sucker won't take the pain away.*

I can't recall ever going back to Dr. Musso's office after that one time. And I never knew why until years later.

My parents' fifth child, Belinda Marie Walker, was born November 17, 1961. None of us could sleep because she constantly cried. My mother would walk the floor, holding her, trying to get her to stop crying. Audrey Mae would relieve my mother, but still Belinda wouldn't stop.

Two days after Christmas, my parents took little Belinda to Dr. Musso, who gave her a shot of penicillin with his big needle. But there was no change in her condition. She'd cried for so long, her voice was faint, but her crying continued. Not knowing what more to do, my parents took her back to Dr. Musso.

In the middle of the night, they knocked on the doctor's door, begging for assistance.

Dr. Musso came to the door furious. He called them all kinds of names, belittling them for disturbing his sleep. According to my father, the doctor complained, "Stupid niggers come waking me in the middle of the night with a damn crying baby."

The doctor treated the baby by giving her another shot.

My parents paid Dr. Musso and thanked him for his service. By the time they arrived home, Belinda had stopped crying. My mother put her into the bed between them. The house was quiet for the first time, and my mother was relieved to get a good night's sleep.

At daybreak, my mother awoke, pleased to hear silence. She gently shook Belinda, thinking she was in a deep sleep.

When she got no response, she yelled out to my father. "I think this baby is dead!"

He jumped into action to assist in trying to wake her. But my baby sister was lifeless.

Neither of my parents had ever had to deal with the death of a child. They called my uncles and aunts for advice. The mortician came and took Belinda's body away.

That was the first time I saw my father cry. After the burial, he wept for hours. That night, the house was quiet, and my ears missed the sound of Baby Belinda's cry. It was then I realized she was never coming back.

We learned Belinda had colic. Some babies are born with it. Colic typically goes away by six months of age. Baby Belinda died on December 28, on her 41st day in this world. I always wondered what could have been if Belinda had lived a full life. May she forever rest in peace.

One Sunday morning, at the end of Mass, the priest announced there'd be a nurse's station at the back of the church. Nurses would be administering the polio vaccine. It was likely part of a government-directed order. I had no idea what polio was, and no one ever gave me an explanation. In the back of the church, all the Whites queued up to receive the vaccine. After all the Whites had been served, the Blacks queued up.

When I approached the table, a nurse gave me a small sugar cube. That was a surprise; I was expecting a shot with a needle. I said nothing, just downed my sugar cube and walked away.

29

1962–1963 (Second Grade)

It was a new school year and I had a new teacher. Miss McCoy was a tall, attractive brown-skinned woman. I was excited to be back in school. I decided I would be an honors student again. Amazingly, in second grade there were no crying students wanting to go home.

I knew almost everyone because most of the students had been in first grade with me. I learned later that those students I didn't know were repeating the grade. After roll call, Miss McCoy asked everyone to stand at their desk and tell the class about their summer vacation. None of us had anything exciting to share other than we'd played softball, marbles, hopscotch, hide-and-go-seek, hula hoops and other games all summer long.

I could have talked about how I had to mow our lawn every other day. In our large yard, the grass grew fast. By the time I finished one side of the yard, the other half had grown. But I didn't think anyone wanted to hear about me mowing our lawn.

Julia Faye Harris was the only one who had an interesting summer. She'd gone to Colorado to visit relatives. The new dress she wore had been purchased in Denver. It had a chain that was linked to an ink pen. The pen went into the pocket of the dress. Everyone in class admired her new dress because they had never seen such a combination. I was impressed with her new dress, too.

My new school clothing was one pair of jeans, two shirts and shoes. Monday through Wednesday, I wore the same clothes to school. When I came home, I hung them for the next day. Thursday and Friday, I wore a different shirt. Sometimes, I'd play in the grass or shoot marbles in the dirt with the other boys. The knees of my jeans would be dirty, or green. Still, I wore the same jeans to school the whole week. On the weekend, my school clothing was washed.

My new shoes were shiny, but cheap, and fell apart within weeks. When the soles developed holes, I inserted cardboard inside the shoes. On rainy days, the cardboard would get wet, making my socks and feet wet, too. Soon, the soles of the shoes would separate from the uppers and I'd slide my feet when walking to prevent making a flip-flop sound.

Some things we learned in first grade were repeated in second grade. Every morning, we said the Pledge of Allegiance. We recited the grace prayer before lunch and walked single file. We built on the numbering system we'd learned in first grade and learned to add and subtract. We formed words with the alphabet and learned new words by reading aloud. I was excited to learn each word. After school when I went home, I'd communicate by spelling rather than speaking words.

Miss McCoy had a red marker, same as Miss Wisher. When I did good work, she marked my brown tablet paper with an A+.

One November day, the principal came into the classroom and announced, "The president has been shot!"

She went from class to class to deliver the news. We had no PA system, and it was common for her to come into each classroom with messages. She'd heard the news on the radio in her office.

Miss McCoy's eyes got teary. The class sat in silence. I didn't understand what had happened, but whatever it was, it was serious. Miss Wisher came to our room with a sad face to talk with Miss McCoy.

That day we learned who John F. Kennedy was and that he was the president of the United States. We learned he had been shot in Dallas, Texas. We also learned about the vice president and that he, Lyndon B. Johnson, would become president of the United States.

Rarely would the cooks at school make something I didn't like to eat. However, one day they served sauerkraut. I'd never heard of or seen sauerkraut. Miss McCoy always encouraged us to at least taste everything on our plate and then decide if the food was good or bad. I could tell by looking at the sauerkraut, I wouldn't like it.

Miss McCoy insisted I had to at least taste it before I could leave the table. All the other students stood outside the cafeteria in single file, waiting for me to taste it.

I thought if I waited long enough, Miss McCoy would tell me to join the others. But she was determined that I taste the sauerkraut before I left the table. She stood over my shoulder, waiting for me to taste it. Finally, I dipped my fork into the sauerkraut and scooped up a small amount. Slowly, I raised the fork to my unwilling mouth. The moment the sauerkraut entered my mouth, I hated it. I knew I would.

Miss McCoy told me, "You may leave the table and join the other students in line."

Now that the sauerkraut was in my mouth. I refused to swallow it. I went into the classroom and held that nasty stuff in my mouth the entire period. When the bell rang for recess, I was the first one out of the classroom. I ran into the bathroom. To my surprise, very little sauerkraut remained in my mouth. I must have unknowingly swallowed some of it. I spit out whatever was left. To this day, I refuse to eat sauerkraut.

Throughout elementary school, Mr. Castelle came to our school to teach music. He was a tall, light-complexioned mixed-Indian man with straight black hair. His regular job was teaching music at Dorseyville Junior High.

I took an immediate liking to him; he played piano and taught us to sing nursery rhymes. He even taught us to square dance. We formed a circle, alternating boys and girls. We learned to swing our partners to the left and right. Then cadence was called to change partners. Each boy alternated dancing with the girls. I didn't particularly like to dance with some of the girls. But when we changed partners and I got to dance with Julia Faye Harris, I was always happy. She was my girlfriend—but the only person who knew that was me.

Department stores in the South had a strict policy that Blacks couldn't try on clothing before a purchase. When my mother bought me shoes, she would measure my foot with a piece of string and take the string to the store. She'd place it against the bottom of the shoe to determine the correct shoe size for me. Most of the time, she would buy a perfect fit. Whenever a purchase wasn't quite right, the shoes were resold or given to my cousin. Blacks couldn't return any items; all sales were final. Shirts, trousers and other clothing were all purchased by guessing the size.

Many Blacks couldn't afford to make same-day purchases, so stores allowed customers to buy clothes on layaway. The store kept the clothing in the warehouse while the customer made monthly payments. When the balance was paid in full, the customer got to take the clothing home. People also purchased clothes through mail-order catalogs.

Before we went on a road trip, my father would drive to the gas station. The attendant came out and asked how much gas we needed. He'd pump the gas, check the tire pressure, the water and oil, and clean the windshield. When he washed the windshield, the whole car rocked back and forth. In my mind, I thought he must be a strong man to make it rock. Later, I learned my father's car bounced because it needed shocks. When the attendant was finished, my father would give him the money and he'd bring back the change. Depending on the amount of gas purchased, we received S&H Green Stamps, which my mother collected. When she had a full book of stamps, she mailed it in for a household item, such as a toaster or silverware.

At that time, gas-station toilets and water fountains read, "White" and "Colored." As a child, I had no problem with the toilets, but I couldn't understand "White" versus "Colored" water fountains. I had drunk water all my life and knew what it tasted like. I figured White people were drinking a different water, and I desperately wanted to taste the "White water." But I never did.

We were always excited when we got to ride the ferry. As my father drove up to the ramp, the ferryboat workers directed cars to specific parking.

The White children got out of their parents' cars to stand at the rail. They watched the ferry cruise across the river. Black children couldn't stand on deck. We were only allowed to get out to use the "Colored" bathroom; we went directly to the bathroom and back into the car.

My father bought me a red-and-white Philco transistor radio, in the shape of a rocket. It had an earplug and a clip that had to be grounded to some sort of metal to play. While riding in the car, I clipped it to the window frame. With the plug in my ear, I listened to music on the local station. I fell in love with radio. The more I listened, the more I wanted to be inside the radio. I liked the excitement I heard.

A cousin from another town came to Bayou Goula weekly to cut the hair of all the men and boys. Every Saturday, my mother gave me 25 cents and I walked to the barbershop. All the boys came to school on Monday with fresh flattops that had been completed with a razor line.

The barbershop was first come, first served. I went early to be in the queue. However, some elderly men would come in, wanting their haircuts immediately. They'd ask for my position in the queue; normally, I was at the top of the queue. Because they didn't want to wait, I'd sell my chair in the queue for a nickel. Sometimes, I was at the barbershop all day, selling my chair. I made as much as 25 cents. It would be late evening when I finally got my haircut.

Church ladies would come to the barbershop to sell meals for their church fund. They sold fried chicken and fried fish dinners for 50 cents. Each plate included a side of sweet peas, potato salad, sliced white bread and a slice of sweet-potato pie or pound cake. The dinners were served on paper plates covered with aluminum foil. Plastic forks and a napkin were included. Also, they would sell pies (coconut, lemon or sweet potato), still warm, right out of the oven. Pies were 10 cents apiece. I often made enough money selling my chair in the queue to buy two pies.

One Saturday, I was at the barbershop all day selling my chair and playing marbles in the yard with the other boys. I always walked around with my pockets full of marbles. I kept my favorite shiny marbles separated from my regular ones. I'd been so busy playing marbles that Saturday, I didn't realize the barbershop was closing, and I hadn't gotten a haircut.

Instead of going home to tell my mother I didn't get a haircut, I went to Abraham's house. I knew he had a pair of clippers because I'd seen him cut another man's hair. So, I asked him to cut my hair. I had no idea he didn't know how to do a flattop. He only knew how to give a bald haircut. As I saw hair fall into my lap, I became nervous and asked for a mirror. I saw nicks all over my head. I started crying and Tee Nachie gave me hair grease to put on my hair. I thought it would make my hair grow instantly.

Monday morning, I went to school with a bad haircut.

The following Saturday, I was back at the barbershop. Like the prior Saturday, I was busy playing marbles and selling my chair. Then the barbershop closed and I didn't get my haircut again. I was scheduled to be in a school play and my mother had insisted I get a haircut. I didn't want to go back to Abraham, so I went home and admitted to my mother I didn't get a haircut because I was busy playing marbles.

She told my father to take me to his barber. Neil was an out-of-town cousin, who lived in a one-room house that doubled as his barbershop. People sat on his cot bed to wait. He called everyone who walked into his barbershop "Shot."

Neil wore leg braces due to polio and always kept a pocket

full of money. He'd take loads of paper bills from his pocket when exchanging money for haircuts. He kept his pistol handy, too. Neil would take it out and show it to people. I was always afraid he might accidentally pull the trigger and shoot someone.

When my father told him I was going to be in a school play, Neil said, "I'm going to give you the best haircut you ever had. When I'm finished, the flattop shape will be permanent."

When he was done, I tried combing my hair forward, to the side, and to the back, and the flattop shape remained. There were no wild hairs to be seen. That truly was the best flattop haircut I ever had.

My least favorite holiday of the year was Mardi Gras. All the public schools in Louisiana were closed. My parents went to work and I had to stay at Ma Flo's house with all my cousins. There were many children and Ma Flo would tell us to play in the yard. But it was Mardi Gras and we knew it was safer to be in the house. When we were outside, the Mardi Gras people would appear when we least expected. Suddenly, we heard the sounds of their approach. We all ran inside; the only safe place we knew was under the bed. Sometimes eight or more children tried to hide under one bed. We had tears in our eyes and hoped the Mardi Gras people wouldn't hurt us.

They burst into the house with sticks and whips, making weird sounds. Reaching under the bed, the Mardi Gras people would grab for a leg and drag a child from beneath the bed. One by one, we were dragged out and beaten by the Mardi Gras people with their sticks and whips. Each child was screaming and crying. Ma Flo was no help; all she did was stand there and look on as the Mardi Gras people beat us. They didn't whip the adults, only the children. We never knew who the Mardi Gras people were, because they were dressed in costumes, their faces covered with ugly masks. However, they knew us and called us by name. Hours later, after the Mardi Gras people had left and we'd calmed down and stopped crying, another group of them came along and terrified us all over again.

Most of my day was spent hiding under the bed. I hated Mardi Gras and wished I were in school.

The day after Mardi Gras was Ash Wednesday, the beginning of Lent. On Ash Wednesday, we went to Mass to receive ashes on our forehead. The Baptist children were always confused to see Catholics walking around with ashes on their foreheads. Also, we were taught to do a penance during Lent. My penance was normally refraining from eating sweets (particularly cake and cookies). Over the years, I graduated to thinking outside myself and chose as my penance the saying of a daily prayer for someone.

1963–1964 (Third Grade)

My third-grade teacher was Miss Fulton, a middle-aged woman with eyeglasses who always smelled fresh, like the scent of an apple. She tended to chew on her tongue. During the week, she stayed with a cousin and walked to school each day. Every Friday she went home to Baton Rouge.

Miss Fulton introduced us to multiplication. We had to memorize the multiplication tables from 1 through 12 and recite the table on command. If Miss Fulton caught any students counting numbers on their fingers, she'd whack their knuckles with her Westcott ruler.

Students cried in third grade. They weren't crying to go home, but rather, they were crying after being whacked for giving an incorrect answer or counting on their fingers.

Miss Fulton taught us geography, and I was intrigued by the world map. She also introduced us to the dictionary and I learned how to look up the words I was learning. Not only were the words listed alphabetically, there were definitions next to the words. The dictionary fascinated me, and I knew whoever came up with this idea must have been a genius.

Returning to school after the Christmas holidays, I wore a new Royal wristwatch my father had bought me for Christmas. I was the only student in class with a watch. When Miss Fulton saw me wearing it, she asked if I knew how to tell time. I didn't.

She took that opportunity to teach us to tell time. She drew a large clock on the blackboard and explained hours and minutes. She discussed the long and short hands on the clock.

When we went out for recess, other students on the playground came to me and asked, "What time is it?"

I looked at my watch and immediately gave them the exact time. Later, I realized, I was constantly giving the time of day to students who had neither appointments nor deadlines to meet. But it still made me feel important to know I could give the exact time on request. That Royal watch still works and is stored in my safe-deposit box.

Audrey Mae and I walked through the sugarcane field many times to go to the store. One day, Miss Iona, our neighbor, asked us to buy something for her. She said, "Do you want me to write my order?"

We replied, "No, we can remember."

As we walked, we played tag. Then we started skipping and singing. When we reached the store, we couldn't remember what we were supposed to buy. Walking back, we were not in a playful mood, as we knew she would be angry with us.

When we approached the house, Miss Iona was sitting on her porch. With no bags in hand, she knew what had happened. She yelled, "Give me my money! You stupid kids." We did not receive the usual nickel we would have for doing her a favor.

Whenever anyone in our family had a birthday, the birthday person selected the kind of cake they wanted my mother to bake. After she mixed the cake, I always asked to lick the bowl. When the cake was served, the birthday person got the first slice. On my birthday, I always asked for a lemon coconut cake.

That year, my mother bought me my first two-piece dress suit. It was dark blue, with a glossy wet look. When I stood in the sun, the material appeared shiny. I only wore it to Mass on Sundays. After church, I carefully hung my suit on a hanger until the next Sunday.

When I started to grow, the suit appeared to shrink. I started raising my shoulders when I wore it so the sleeves would seem longer. I wore the trousers as low as possible around my waist, so they wouldn't be above my ankles. It was my only suit, and I didn't want to give it away or stop wearing it, so I asked Tee Nachie to lengthen it. When she was done, the suit fit perfectly and I could enjoy wearing my favorite suit again.

Building our house gave my father and me credibility as builders. Our first real customer was Tee Nachie, who purchased the lot next to us. My father drew the blueprints for a house with three bedrooms, living room, dining room, kitchen and bathroom.

Before we could start construction, we cleared the lot of weeds and grass. Then we leveled the land for the laying of the house pillars and foundation.

This was our second house, so the foundation and framing were less difficult to construct. I was nine years old now, stronger and able to contribute more manpower. My father gave me specific projects to complete on my own. After school, I went directly to the house and started working. My father would come home with stacks of lumber in his car. I'd unload it while he ate supper. Then we worked together into the night.

Our first customer, Tee Nauncy's house

Installing sheetrock was a challenge. I couldn't lift it for the ceiling installation, so my father built a T-shaped 2-by-4 lifter for me. He set one end of the sheetrock on the stepladder and, aided by my T-shaped bar, I guided the other end. As he climbed onto the ladder, he'd lift his end of the sheetrock to the ceiling and I'd guide the opposite end. Once it was nailed in place, I removed my T-shaped bar and the process started again.

We did all the carpentry, plumbing and installation of the septic tank. We hired an electrician to complete the electrical installation. I assisted with varnishing the floors. We installed tile flooring in the kitchen and bathroom. I assisted with painting the interior and exterior of the house and on moving day, I helped transport their furniture into the new house.

I took my Catholic faith seriously. I'd been to Mass so often, I knew all the parts of the Mass by heart. I played church with my little sisters. I was the priest and they were the congregation. I'd go through the entire Mass, using a piece of white bread as communion. I closed Mass by singing a hymn. I thought I might become a priest someday.

During Sunday-morning Mass, when we received communion, we knelt at the altar. The priest came to each person and placed the host on their tongue. Our neighbor, Mr. Anthony Williams, was elderly, and practically blind. One Sunday, we were the last two in line. As we knelt there, the priest headed back to the altar. I assumed he was going to retrieve more communion. Everyone else was back in their seats. Finally, when I saw the priest start clearing the altar and preparing to end Mass, it became clear we weren't going to receive communion.

I leaned and whispered, "We're not going to receive communion because the priest ran out."

I was disappointed the priest didn't even acknowledge us. The least he could have done was tell us he had run out. As I stood, I took Mr. Anthony's arm and walked him back to his seat. When we passed the elderly ladies in the Black section, their heads nodded and they mouthed, "Thank you."

My parents' sixth child, Judith Ann "Judy" Walker, was born in 1964. I would often babysit my siblings and cousins. I've changed and washed more diapers than I care to remember.

At the beginning of spring, my father started a garden. We tilled the soil with a shovel and hoe. Audrey Mae and I were awakened before sunrise to plant many kinds of beans and peas. My father dug the holes, we planted the beans, and he covered them with soil.

When the beans sprouted, I ventured into the woods with a cane knife for bean poles. I had to haul the poles back to the garden, about a half mile away. Once I had them all set in the garden, I wrapped each vine around a pole.

When the beans were grown, I picked them. While we watched TV at night, each of us had a bowl in our lap as we shelled beans. My mother cooked some and froze others. When we weren't shelling beans, we shelled pecans.

My Uncle John "Plute" Pierre raised hogs and whenever a hog killing was announced, I was always there. Everyone arrived at 5:00 a.m. I'd gather wood to boil the water. I wanted to be involved in the whole process, but they only used me as a runner.

Almost every part of the hog was eaten. When the skin was chopped into small pieces and put into a large black pot, I finally had a job. I got to stir the pot while the skin cooked. Soon, we had golden-brown hog cracklings, which we sprinkled with salt. Once all the meat was butchered, it was taken into the house, where the women sorted it for families. They made blood sausage, boudin sausage and head cheese. About noon, someone would yell out that dinner was ready. I always looked forward to fresh liver and rice. All the working men, including me, were dirty and smelled of smoke from the fire. We sat in the yard with plates of liver and rice. By now all the hard work had been completed and it was time for cleanup.

I was now the most valuable person in the yard and usually the last one to leave with Plute.

My father decided we should have a pig, which I also thought was a good idea. First we built a pen, then we bought a pig from a farmer. We brought it home and it ran around the pen, and I was happy to have a pig. Later, after we went into the house, I noticed the pig running in the yard, so we chased it. When it ran under the house, my father went to one side of the house and told me to go to the other side. He'd force the pig to run in my direction and I was supposed to catch it, but I had no intention of catching it. When the pig ran toward me, I told my father it ran too fast and I couldn't catch him. After scampering around the yard chasing the pig, he finally caught it with his bare hands.

We figured out the pig had dug into the ground with his snout and escaped. After that, my father put rings in the pig's nose to prevent him from digging.

As much as I'd initially wanted a pig, that animal became my worst nightmare. I didn't know it'd require so much work! I had to get up every morning at 6:00 a.m. to feed it. I went into the fields and cut two kinds of grass to feed the animal: blood weed and Johnson grass. Some days, I would walk a half mile into the field for grass. Then I had to drag it back to the pig pen. Some mornings, there would be dew in the field and my clothing would be soaked before I got back.

By now, our cute little pig had grown to be a hog—and I didn't like this hog. When I came home from school, I had to go back into the field to cut more grass to feed it. Even on rainy or cold days, I still had to go and cut grass. On Sundays I didn't have to cut grass; instead I put grain mix in the trough. In summer, I carried buckets of water to pour into a hole I'd dug. The hog would splash in the water to keep cool. I really disliked this hog. I would constantly ask my father when we were going to kill it. His answer was always that the hog was too skinny. He'd tell me I had to feed the hog more to fatten it up.

I was always out in the cornfield with Abraham. We planted corn and he allowed me to ride his horse. I would drive the horse cart through the cornfield. We planted sweet potato vines and when it was time to dig the sweet potatoes, Abraham used his horse and plow to dig them up. I'd retrieve the sweet potatoes and load them into the cart.

Abraham was a hard worker. Then one day he suffered a mental breakdown. Because he said he wanted to kill everyone, he was tied to his bed, and with an evil look in his eyes, he sweated and cursed at everyone. Someone had to sit and watch over him nightly, afraid he'd hurt himself if he were left alone. Finally, Tee Nachie sent Abraham to a mental hospital in northern Louisiana.

My father took us to visit him. It was my first time seeing mentally disturbed people. I remember walking past locked cells, with people yelling and cursing for no apparent reason. Others sat and talked quietly to themselves.

Abraham stayed in the hospital a few months until he was cured. Finally, he was released and went home. I could never totally trust myself being alone with him after that. I always thought he might have another breakdown.

That year, Abraham had planted corn and the corn was just sprouting. I was walking through his cornfield on my way to cut grass for the hog. I had just sharpened my cane knife and, as I passed by, I chopped at each stalk. By the time I realized what I had done, I'd already hacked several rows. Later that day, Abraham went into the cornfield and saw the destruction. He was furious! He knew I was the only one who'd gone into his cornfield. I saw him storm out of the field. My first thought was he might have another breakdown. I knew he was coming for me.

I ran inside and told Tee Nachie that Abraham was coming for me. I knew she'd protect me. When he came in, he wore the same wild expression he'd possessed while tied to the bed. And that terrified me.

The two of them started arguing as I stood behind Tee

Nachie, holding on to her dress. She finally calmed him down and told me to apologize.

I said I was sorry and would never do it again.

Abraham said nothing, nor did he accept my apology.

Later that day, on my way back from the store, I saw him coming toward me. We were the only two on the road. As he got closer, I crossed to the opposite side. I didn't know what to do or say. As we approached each other, I could see he was still angry.

I smiled and said, "Hi, Abraham."

I believe the smile is what did it. He crossed the road, grabbed me by the arm and spanked me. He wasn't hitting hard enough to hurt. But I was yelling and pretending to cry. I was thinking about his time in the mental institution and was afraid he would lose his mind again. He finally let me go, and I ran home. It took a long time before he fully forgave me. But when he did, we were good friends, and I never disrespected his property again.

1964–1965 (Fourth Grade)

My fourth-grade teacher, Mrs. Davis, was a tall woman with thick, straight salt-and-pepper hair. She was strict and seldom smiled. I had heard about her and wasn't looking forward to fourth grade. Her classroom was so quiet, it was almost spooky.

My eagerness to learn ceased when I entered her class. My goal was to answer every question she asked me correctly, do my homework on time and make passing grades. We learned division and fractions. Her teaching method was fast-paced and I was afraid to ask questions. I had to ask my mother to explain numerators, denominators and reducing fractions.

Mrs. Davis paddled students for not doing their homework, giving incorrect answers, or misbehaving. I never volunteered for anything in her class. When I was called upon, I provided the correct answer and nothing more. About this time, I learned cursive writing—and how to forge my mother's signature. Any time I was given papers to bring home, I signed the papers myself, including forging my mother's signature on my report card. I had good grades, but no one ever asked to see my report card. The only time I requested my mother's signature was when money was involved.

For the fourth year in a row, I received an award for perfect attendance. I was just happy to be out of fourth grade.

That year, Hurricane Hilda was predicted to come ashore along the Louisiana coastline as a Category 4 storm. Normally, we stayed home when a hurricane was forecast, but the news broadcast said everyone should seek shelter. Our neighbors were packing up and leaving for the elementary school, which was set up as a shelter.

I helped my father cover our windows with plywood. We nailed down anything that could be lifted by the wind. My mother and Audrey Mae saved water in containers, buckets and even filled the bathtub. We knew when we got home, the power would be off for weeks, so we took any food we could eat out of the refrigerator.

After the house was secured, we got in the car with our blankets, flashlight, battery-operated radio, tuna, crackers, snacks, and jugs of water. The weather was cloudy, with showers and little wind.

When we arrived at the school, all the desks had been removed and people claimed space in specific classrooms. We found our cousins and occupied a corner near them. My mother spread our blankets on the floor. Each family sat on blankets. The room was noisy; people talked, laughed and socialized. Kids played games they'd brought with them. Some had transistor radios on, tuned to the weather reports tracking the eye of the storm.

By nightfall, the rain was heavy, with extreme winds, thunder, and lightning. No one seemed to be afraid. People's only concern was whether their houses would be standing afterward.

When the children were tired of playing, they fell asleep. The room was dark, and some people had lit candles. Everyone removed their shoes. The room was smelly, and it became even warmer because there was no ventilation and the windows couldn't be opened.

I told my mother I was going to the bathroom and left the classroom barefoot. As I walked down the sidewalk, rain pelted my face, and I struggled not to get blown away. In the bathroom, I could hardly see because it was so dark. It was full of cigarette smoke; men stood together, talking. I didn't see my father, but some of the men knew me. One commented that if I wanted to be a man, come hang out in the bathroom with them.

It was smelly; the toilets were clogged due to the sewer overflowing and flooding. I did my business and maneuvered out of the crowded, smoky bathroom.

On my way back, fighting the wind and rain, I stepped on the cut edge of a discarded sardine can on the sidewalk. Back inside, when I asked for a towel to dry myself, I saw my foot was bleeding from a deep cut. Blood was gushing out. People scrambled for rags to stop the bleeding. The rest of the night, I was in pain and my foot throbbed. Nobody could do anything. We had to stay put until the storm was over.

The next morning, the storm had passed. It was daylight, and the sun was shining. Everyone started packing for home. My foot still hurt, and I couldn't put my shoe on, so I hopped to the car. When we turned onto our street, we saw fallen trees and power lines across the road. Some roofs had been blown off and pecan branches were everywhere. I realized I'd be working for weeks picking them up.

We parked on the road and saw that some of our roof shingles were on the ground. Inside, the house was dark because of the plywood over the windows.

I thought I'd get to rest, because I'd hopped on one foot the whole way. Plus, I was in pain. But that was wishful thinking. My father needed me to help remove the plywood from the windows. He warned me to avoid the live power lines while I picked up tree branches. My mother and Audrey Mae started cleaning out the refrigerator and defrosting the freezer.

I jammed my cut foot halfway into my shoe and hopped around the yard, dragging branches and picking up debris. Any yardwork I did always included Tee Nachie's yard. And before dark, I still had to feed the hog.

Tee Nachie always had a home remedy for any illness or injury. She gave me a piece of salt pork and said to attach it to a rag and wrap the salt pork around my cut foot. I don't know why, but I never questioned her remedies. Within days, my foot was healed.

After we completed our cleanup, we helped neighbors repair their roofs. The only thing we couldn't control was restoring electricity. We had to wait weeks for power to be restored.

My father bought a powder-blue 1959 Mercury. We had two Mercurys (pink and blue), and I had to wash them weekly. My reward was getting to drive to church on Sunday morning. My father sat in the passenger seat and Josie sat in back. Audrey Mae was a Baptist and didn't go to the Catholic church.

Every Saturday, I went shopping with my mother and her sister, my Aunt Emma Mae. But at Christmas, my mother told me I couldn't go with her. I was angry as she drove away without me.

After shopping, I always brought the bags into the house. I lugged them all from the backseat of the car. Then I asked my mother for the keys to the trunk. She said she'd carry those bags in later and I became suspicious. An hour later, when she thought I was busy, I saw her run across the yard to Tee Nachie's house, pushing a bicycle. I didn't say anything, and she wasn't sure I had seen her pushing it.

Later that day, I went to Tee Nachie's house. Normally, I could go into any room I wanted. But she had her back bedroom door locked and informed me I couldn't go inside. I kept asking why and she wouldn't give me a straight answer. I knew the bicycle was in there, and she knew I knew.

Christmas morning, I received a bright, shiny red 26-inch bicycle with silver fenders. I was excited to have my first new bike. It was the last time my mother tried to fool me about Santa Claus. Anyway, years earlier, I had concluded Santa Claus only knew White children.

I always looked for ways to make extra money. I befriended a boy who worked for an elderly White family. He was going away to college and said I could have his job. The White family lived in a large old-fashioned plantation home with no inside plumbing. They had a large cistern next to the house that provided all their water. The boy's job was to fill their water containers in the kitchen daily. He introduced me to the family, who agreed to hire me. After school, I rode my bicycle to their house to work and was paid 10 cents a day.

Our neighbor, Miss Iona, had a 1963 Ford Fairlane, white with red interior and a red top. She asked me to wash her car. I washed my parents' cars weekly and never received a complaint. I knew Miss Iona was demanding and strict; everything had to be done to perfection. But I needed the money and believed I could wash the car to her satisfaction, so I accepted the job.

I arrived early Saturday morning. Miss Iona parked her car under a pecan tree and provided a bucket, soap, rags and a hose. I took my time and cleaned the car thoroughly, because I knew she'd inspect my work. When I finished, I looked it over and thought I had done a good job. I stored the rags, bucket and hose and went to tell her I'd finished washing the car.

When Miss Iona came out, she pointed to water spots on the windows. Then she opened the doors and pointed out dirt inside the door jambs. She opened the trunk and hood and indicated dirt inside the grooves. She said, "I thought you knew how to wash a car."

I cleaned all the areas she noted and more. I knew she'd find something to complain about, but once I'd finished the second round, I took my chance and told her the car was clean.

Miss Iona inspected it a second time. Still, I hadn't cleaned it to her satisfaction. She threw a fit and started yelling. She said I knew nothing about washing cars and I'd never wash her car again.

I had no desire ever to do so. I just wanted to get paid, but I was pretty sure she wouldn't pay me. It was past noon, and I'd been washing that car all morning. Finally, she reached into her brassiere and gave me a $1 bill.

Weekdays, I ate cereal for breakfast. My mother always monitored the milk, because there had to be enough for the baby. We poured a little milk into the bowl, then added water and sugar.

On Sunday, we fasted before Mass. After Mass, my mother would cook a big breakfast. It consisted of grits, eggs, sausage, bacon, toast or biscuits. Sometimes she served pancakes with syrup and butter, too. At the same time, she'd be cooking Sunday dinner. Dinner was eaten at noon and always included fresh yard chicken (meat was a luxury for us). A typical Sunday dinner could be stewed or smothered chicken, with thick gravy, white rice, sweet peas, macaroni and cheese, potato salad, and Kool-Aid. Dessert was always some sort of cake (pound cake, jelly cake or lemon cake). My favorite weekday meal was red beans and rice or succotash.

Even though my mother was Baptist, she knew all the Catholic protocols and ensured we abided. She reminded us to observe a holy day if we forgot. Every Friday, we were usually served fish. Saturday morning, she sent us off to catechism, even when I would have preferred to stay home and watch cartoons. Sunday mornings we were always dressed and at church before Mass started.

Sometimes, I attended services at the Baptist church with my mother. My uncles sang in a gospel group. I especially enjoyed seeing my uncle play the guitar.

The Baptist church gospel singing was usually during the summer on Saturday nights. When we arrived, I immediately went under the pecan tree where the elderly men sold sodas. They'd let me sell sodas covered with ice cubes in a tin tub. I liked popping the cap off the bottle and making the sale. The men engaged in conversation with each other and were always glad I had taken over. In between sales, I slapped at mosquitoes because I wore my matching Sunday short pants and shirt. When the singing started, I wanted to be in both places.

I'd go into the church to find everyone standing, clapping and singing along with the gospel group. I would focus on my uncle playing guitar. Often, and unexpectedly, a woman would start to shout. When receiving the Holy Spirt, it's hard to hold it in. The church had wooden benches and the shouting woman would knock the benches onto the floor, because she was out of control and unaware of her surroundings. Two or three men would rush over and try to calm her. Sometimes they even had to wrestle her to the floor. After the shouting woman calmed down, she would be given a cup of water. The men would pick up the benches and try to identify the rightful owners of shoes, hats and whatever else had fallen to the floor. In the meantime, the singing and clapping never stopped. I was always concerned the women would hurt themselves during the shouting.

Every Sunday afternoon, the local store converted into a dance hall for teenagers. Before the dance, red sawdust was sprinkled on the wood floor. In the corner was a jukebox that played five songs for a quarter or one for a nickel. Some of the dances that were popular were the monkey, the swim, the jerk and the mashed potato. There was so much dancing, the wood floor would shake. Even though the windows were open, the teenagers would sweat profusely. I was always the youngest kid there. I knew all the dance moves, but the girls wouldn't dance with me because I was too young. I stood in the corner, sipping my orange soda, eating cookies and potato chips.

American Bandstand came on TV every Saturday. I learned the latest dances by watching that show and sometimes, Black people danced. Whenever the camera showed a Black person, I'd get excited to see a Black person on TV.

Saturday evenings, I religiously watched *The Lawrence Welk Show*. I enjoyed watching the fiddle players and dreamed of becoming a band director like Lawrence Welk.

Sunday afternoons, *The Ed Sullivan Show* came on. The first time I saw the Jackson Five perform was on his show. I thought they were superb. When James Brown appeared on the show, I was speechless. It was the first time I saw him do the splits. He danced so hard he'd sweat. Then his sidekicks came on stage and wrapped a cape around him. As they led him off the stage, he threw the cape on the floor and resumed dancing. He gave the best performance! I also thought Richard Pryor and Red Skelton were geniuses.

I remember the first time I saw a ventriloquist on *The Ed Sullivan Show*. After watching the show, I took a white sock and used a black marker to make the eyes, nose and mouth. I slipped the sock on my hand and tried not to move my lips as I worked the magic with my hands. I thought I was doing rather well, so I ordered a ventriloquism kit. It wasn't what I expected, and I immediately lost interest in being a ventriloquist.

As a construction worker, my father was rarely unemployed. He was a member of the local union. When a construction job he was working on ended, he would go to the union hall to be assigned a new job.

One day, I went there with him. When we arrived, men were out on the sidewalk, drinking and gambling. Inside, a man with a microphone on stage called out available jobs. My father listened intently. When he heard one that suited him, he yelled out, "I'll take the job."

Just like that, he had a new job. We left the union hall, walking past the gambling and drinking men on the sidewalk. The next day, my father went to his new job. That was a teachable moment for me without him having to say a word.

Morning and night, we went to the Mississippi River to raise our shrimp boxes. My father woke me at 5:00 a.m. and, within minutes, I was ready to go.

We unloaded our buckets and bait. We waded into the river, toward the shrimp boxes. My father would be in water up to his waist, and it was almost to my shoulders. He dumped the shrimp into the bucket. As he rebaited the boxes, I would float the bucket of shrimp to the riverbank and pour them into a croker sack. I'd carry the empty bucket back to my father for refill. About the time I'd reach him, there'd be another bucket of shrimp waiting for me. I would repeat the process until all the boxes had been raised and rebaited.

We finished about sunrise. It was always beautiful to watch the sun come up. The smell of the river in the early morning was pleasant. Sometimes a boat pushing barges would pass us, and the crew would wave to me. After we finished hauling in the shrimp, my father would swim. He was a good swimmer and wanted to teach me, but I would panic when my feet didn't touch bottom.

Sometimes on weekends, we would go crawfishing. We had many crawfish nets. We'd leave early Saturday and bring our lunch. We wore boots as we waded in the knee-deep water, and he'd insert the baited nets in the water. I came behind him, lifting nets and removing the crawfish. I'd carry buckets of crawfish to the car and dump them into a croker sack. At the end of the day, we had several sacks filled with crawfish and we gave some to our relatives and neighbors.

That year, my father came up with another bright idea. He suggested we raise rabbits. We started building a rabbit cage and told me we were going to get two rabbits. I didn't understand why we built six cages for just two rabbits.

We went to a farm and bought a pair of rabbits. We brought them home and put them in the cage. My father trained me how to care for them. The idea of *us* raising rabbits changed to *me* raising rabbits. I fed the rabbits daily and ensured they had water. Within a few days, when I went to feed them, I was shocked to see baby rabbits. I learned they multiply fast and the six cages we built were soon filled. Our Sunday dinners now included rabbit.

At first, I thought caring for rabbits was fun. But soon, same as with the hog, I grew to dislike the job. I was now cutting and hauling grass for the hog and rabbits. I had preferred remodeling houses. When remodeling a house, I could see the result, and I felt a sense of accomplishment. Feeding the rabbits and hog was a never-ending chore.

Tee Nachie and Abraham raised chickens in a fenced yard with chicken coops. Sometimes, I assisted with feeding them corn. The chickens provided eggs and Sunday dinner's main course.

I loved radio! Whenever I listened to the radio, I visualized the behind-the-scenes process for sending out the music over the airwaves. I went to bed listening to the radio. When I woke up, I listened to the radio. My favorite local station was WXOK in Baton Rouge. I knew all the DJs' names, and every day I practiced imitating their voices and patter.

One day, while my father and I were in Baton Rouge, he drove to the radio station. We went inside and sat in the lobby. Through a glass window, I saw the DJ at work. The red "On Air" light was flashing, and he'd talk before cueing up the next song. I didn't speak with the DJ, but I was excited and satisfied just to be inside the station. I was living a dream.

When we left the radio station, we went to our favorite soul-food restaurant, Every-Ready Café, for smothered chicken with rice, mustard greens and corn bread. When we left, my stomach was full and my mind was bursting with visions of working in radio.

After visiting the station, my love for radio deepened. At night, I continued going to sleep with my transistor radio ear plug in my ear. When the local station signed off, I searched the dial for a late-night station in Tennessee. The out-of-state signal wasn't clear, but if I positioned my antenna just right, the station came in clearer. I loved listening to the DJ jive talking. I'd listened to so many songs on the radio, I could identify the title and artist within a few beats at the beginning of the song.

I had been practicing my DJ voice and wanted to record it. I went out into the field and picked pecans for money. Money in hand, I went to the Western Auto store in White Castle and bought a miniature reel-to-reel tape recorder for $10. I recorded songs off the radio. Using my radio voice, I talked over the songs, just like I'd heard the professional DJs do. I emulated everything they did, then played the recording back and listened to myself. I developed my own style and constantly worked to improve as a DJ.

Every Friday night at midnight, a musical program came

on TV, *The Midnight Special*. I stayed awake to watch my DJ idol, Wolfman Jack.

I watched many favorite TV shows religiously: *The Gomer Pyle Show, Bonanza, Gilligan's Island, Leave it to Beaver* and *The Andy Griffith Show*. But I was obsessed with *The Rifleman*, which portrayed a strong bond between a father and son. Their honesty and trust for each other came through loud and clear. The relationship between Lucas and Mark McCain was similar to the relationship I had with my father. The years I spent with him, building houses, fishing, and enjoying other father-and-son things, developed an unwavering mutual trust and respect.

My Saturday-morning TV favorites were *Popeye The Sailor Man, The Three Stooges, Road Runner, Bugs Bunny, The Jetsons, The Little Rascals* and *The Flintstones*.

1965–1966 (Fifth Grade)

Miss Thompson was a nice lady who taught two grades simultaneously. Half of us were fifth graders, and the other half were sixth graders. The classroom was mostly filled with chaos, with never enough time devoted to learning the subject matter. Even though she had a paddle in her classroom, she didn't get the respect she deserved.

Geography, one of my favorite subjects, never got enough attention. What we didn't cover in class, I studied on my own. I knew all the states and their capitals. I knew all seven continents and bodies of waters. I dreamed of visiting all the different places in the world. I wanted to know how other people lived.

Mr. Castelle brought a tonette into music class. He played "Twinkle Twinkle Little Star" on it, then asked who wanted to learn to play the instrument. I believe mine was the first hand to go up. He said a tonette cost $1 and told us to ask our parents for the money. After he mentioned the money, my heart sank. I knew I'd have a problem getting $1 from my mother. It wasn't pecan season, so I couldn't earn the money myself.

I told my mother I wanted to learn to play the tonette. She had no interest after I told her I needed $1. But, after a few days of begging and pleading, she gave me the money. Because I wanted to play the instrument, I practiced constantly.

That year, we were introduced to the 4-H Club. It was explained that each student must complete a special project to submit at the end of the school year. They presented us with various types of acceptable projects.

I signed up. Because there was no follow up after that initial meeting, I never gave 4-H Club a second thought.

At the end of the school year, I saw students coming to school with their 4-H Club projects—projects they'd worked on all year. Boys had completed carpentry projects and girls had completed sewing and baking projects. But I had *nothing*!

Because school hadn't yet started, I took off running through the sugarcane field. Arriving at home, I found a broken lamp that had been thrown into the garbage. I went into the tool shed and removed the lightbulb socket from the lamp. I cut a 2 x 4 wood block and drilled a hole into its center. Then I inserted the socket into the hole and applied glue to secure it. I plugged it in to ensure the lightbulb was good. Then I grabbed my makeshift project and ran back through the sugarcane field, making it back before the school bell rang.

I turned in my project: a lightbulb socket glued to a 2 x 4 block. It wasn't my proudest moment—especially when my project was placed next to the other students' projects. The lightbulb glued to a wood block looked pathetic.

During the summer, my cousins, Roosevelt and Nathaniel, would ride their bikes to my house to get me, to spend the night at their house. I had no suitcase, so I put my hand-me-down clothes in a paper bag. We took an eight-mile bike ride on the gravel river road along the Mississippi River. Passing cars blew dust into the air.

Every day, we rode our bikes all over their neighborhood. We played behind the levee near the river. Their vegetable garden was behind the levee. Sometimes we had to pick beans, blackberries, figs and pears. At the end of the day, after the sun went down, my Aunt Helen called us in. We took baths in their large tin tub with water carried in a bucket from the hand pump and heated on the stove. I was the youngest, so I bathed first. Afterward, my cousins took baths in the same water. In jockey shorts and T-shirts, we played games in the bedroom until bedtime. We knelt, said our prayers and went to sleep.

One of my most memorable Easters was spending the weekend at Roosevelt and Nathaniel's house. On Easter Sunday morning, their tradition was to go to sunrise service. We were awakened when it was still dark. I had no dress clothing, so my Aunt Helen let me wear my cousin's white suit jacket, black trousers, white shirt and black necktie.

We left early, walking with flashlights. Before sunrise, the minister led the congregation out of the church, across the river road and up the levee. Once there, everyone joined hands and sang "He Rose," along with the choir. Sunrise over the Mississippi River was a beautiful sight.

Further up the road from the church was the cemetery, which could be seen from the river road. A chain link fence surrounded the entire cemetery. The grass was well manicured and all the gravesites were snow white, with some tombstones above ground. Only Whites were buried there. Alongside the White cemetery was a dirt road. Following the dirt road through bushes, in the back, was the Black cemetery, where many of my relatives are buried. The cemeteries are still separate to this day.

Door-to-door salesmen were always coming around, selling something. I enjoyed watching them demonstrate products. I would volunteer to assist as needed for a demo. My parents' most valuable purchase from a door-to-door salesman was our *Encyclopedia Britannica*, the only educational books we had. I read all about the Navy, memorizing every rating and rank. Another page displayed a photo for each letter in American Sign Language. I studied the hand positions and taught myself to sign the alphabet.

Living on Breaux Street, we could hear the church bell ring on Thursday for the rosary and Saturday for catechism. In the winter months, Brother Pasqua would have us all huddle around the large heater in the back of the church in our coats and gloves. As a young boy, the Catholic Church kept me balanced spiritually.

I'd only ever seen White boys serve as altar boys. But one day, Brother Pasqua invited me to be an altar boy. He taught me all the procedures, then went to the priest on my behalf. He said he had trained me, and I was ready to be an altar boy.

The priest's response was, "We cannot have a Negro boy as an altar boy."

Brother Pasqua delivered the news with tears in his eyes. I was disappointed, but I think he took it harder than I did. Later, he told me, "You're going to be the first priest from Bayou Goula."

Even though I couldn't be an altar boy, I felt I did help with changing minds in the church. Years later, as an adult, I attended Mass at this same church, and a little Black boy was serving as an altar boy. He was doing something I'd not been allowed to do.

On a visit at my cousins', their parents had bought them a portable organ. They couldn't play it, so I did. I enjoyed playing their organ, but I wanted one of my own. I went into the fields and picked pecans to sell. With $20 in hand, I went to the Western Auto store and bought the same portable organ my cousins had.

With my limited music lessons from Mr. Castelle, I started teaching myself to play the organ. Practicing every day, I learned the notes and played the songs in the organ song book. I wanted to develop my own style and not mimic anyone.

Brother Pasqua came to our house often. During one visit, he was talking with my mother and heard me in my bedroom practicing the organ. He asked my mother who was playing the music. When she told him it was me, he said he wanted me to bring the organ to church. He told me we'd start a choir and I could play my organ. He was so excited I could play, he didn't bother to ask my skill level. I didn't want to disappoint him, so I agreed to play. He gave me a hymn book. I didn't know the melodies, but he'd hum the tune and I taught myself to play the hymns. After I learned them, he taught our catechism class the songs.

Not wanting another rejection, he told the priest we were the junior choir. At Christmastime, we expanded our repertoire to include Christmas carols. For Christmas midnight Mass, I brought my organ to the church. I set it up in the front of the church. When it was time to perform, the children left the pews and gathered around me. I played and signaled them when to sing. The sound wasn't loud enough because we had no speakers. But the singing was loud and clear. Playing in the church gave me confidence.

When I played my organ in the church, I wore my glossy two-piece suit. I'd outgrown it and Tee Nachie had maxed out the sleeves and trouser length. When I sat down to play, the trousers came above my ankles and the sleeves were past my wrists. Finally, I had to give my favorite suit to my cousin.

The church organist was an elderly White woman in poor health. Whenever she missed Mass due to sickness, we had no music. Brother Pasqua had confidence in my playing ability and asked the priest if I could play whenever the elderly White woman was absent.

The priest's answer to Brother Pasqua was "No."

Once a month, after the rosary, Brother Pasqua asked us to stay and help sweep and dust the church. I always volunteered to clean the choir loft. This enabled me to play the church organ. It had foot pedals, which I'd only seen on the *Lawrence Welk Show*. I played quietly and taught myself to use them.

Audrey Mae and I used to clean the house. We swept and mopped each room. Once they were dry, we applied paste wax to the wooden floor. Lacking a floor buffer, we used rags to shine it. We did extra shining by sliding across the floor in our socks, which was the fun part of the job.

Our washing machine had an attached wringer. After washing, clothing was inserted between the wringer rollers one by one. Then we rinsed the clothes. After rinsing, we fed the clothes through the wringer again, then took them to the clothesline (a wire line strung from a pecan tree to a corner of the house) to be hung to dry. As I hung the clothes, I'd hide behind the house whenever cars passed. I didn't want anyone—especially my friends—to see me hanging out clothing.

Audrey Mae and Josie had to store the leftovers in the refrigerator after supper and wash the dishes. Sometimes, I came in to eat after they'd finished. With no microwave, we reheated food on the stove. The rule was I had to wash any kitchenware I used. I ate a lot of cold food because I didn't want to wash dishes.

As a maid, sometimes my mother brought clothing home to iron. Ironing fascinated me. Whenever she brought a basket of clothes home from work, I'd iron them, then hang the shirts and dresses, just like my mother did. I'm sure she never told the owner her son had ironed their clothing. She just collected the money.

My mother started asking me to iron her dresses. Before long, my father stopped sending his dress shirts out to the dry cleaner. I hand washed and ironed them. Of course, I ironed my hand-me-down clothes, and when I saw a rip in my pants or shirt, I brought out the needle and thread.

My mother worked for a White family part-time on Saturdays. I was hired to mow their lawn and trim the hedges. At noon, the owner gave me a sandwich and a Coke. I sat underneath a pecan tree to eat my lunch. Then I continued working in the yard. At the end of the day, the owner paid me $5.

Because I'd done such a good job, she asked me to come back the next Saturday to wash and clean the windows. She provided a ladder, bucket, rags, soap, hose and a screwdriver to remove the screens. After I cleaned the outside windows, she decided I should do the inside, too. I also scrubbed the baseboards.

As I cleaned every room, I had to move furniture. When I moved the first piece, I noticed a quarter on the floor. I ignored it. In the next room, I found more coins. I assumed it was because White people were rich. When the owner came into the room, I told her I'd found coins on the floor. She thanked me and collected the money from the floor. At the end of the day, she paid me $5.

On our way home, I told my mother about the many coins I'd seen on the floor as I cleaned. She told me the owner put the money there to see if I'd steal. I later thought, *I passed the owner's test without knowing I was being tested.*

Although I was doing other jobs, I couldn't avoid feeding and caring for the rabbits and hog. I still had to go into the field morning and night to cut grass. I didn't mind feeding all those rabbits, but I never developed a liking for the hog. I wished it would escape from the pen and never be found.

On leave from serving in the Navy, Uncle Joe drove to Louisiana in a new navy-blue 1965 Chevrolet Impala. While it was only my second time seeing him, I felt I knew him because his photos in his Navy uniform were displayed in Ma Flo's house.

I volunteered to wash his car. When he wanted to visit other family members, he let me chauffeur him and his family to each family's home. At 10 years old, I didn't have a license, but I was a good driver.

Beyond our house on Breaux Street was an abandoned baseball field. At the beginning of summer, people came with lawnmowers to cut the wild grass that had taken over the ball field. I wasn't a baseball fan, but when I saw people working on the field. I offered to help. I cut grass, raked, and helped chalk the field. When the concession stands and bleachers were repaired, I helped. When they finished, it was a professional baseball field again.

My main reason for helping with cleanup was to gain access to the man who operated the broadcast system. A section of bleachers was reserved for his equipment, and I watched him connect wires and do sound checks. Before each game, he'd mount speakers on his car. Inside was a mobile studio. He'd drive slowly through Bayou Goula, promoting the baseball game and I followed him on my bicycle. Between announcements, he played records and kids would dance in the street.

Because I'd made myself known and been helpful to everyone, they told me if I volunteered as a ball boy, I'd get into the games free. As ball boy, I retrieved foul balls hit into the sugarcane field.

During games, I would stake out a spot in the bleachers near the announcer. I observed his every move as he called the game. When he spoke into the mic or cued a record, I watched. I saw the joy he brought the fans when he played their favorite song, and they couldn't keep from dancing in the bleachers. I only wished I could do what he was doing.

When a foul ball went into the field, I'd hear calls for the ball boy. If I didn't see where it landed, I rarely found them. Sometimes an older man would tell me to go back to the field, with specific directions to where I'd find the ball. He'd claim he'd seen exactly where it landed. But I had no interest in finding lost balls. I wanted to stay in the bleachers with the announcer.

1966–1967 (Sixth Grade)

Miss Gant, our principal, was my sixth-grade math teacher. She was a tall woman who wore high-heeled shoes, which made her look even taller. A no-nonsense woman with a serious face, she seldom smiled. She had in her office a wooden paddle she used for misbehaving students. The first half of the day, we were in Miss Thompson's class, and the second half we were in Miss Gant's class.

Miss Gant maintained an orderly classroom. She'd start with a quick lesson review, then gave a new assignment. The rest of the period, she was in her office, next to our classroom. Even the most unruly students from Miss Thompson's class behaved like model students, unsupervised, in Miss Gant's class. I found this amazing.

During that year, I learned to read music and advanced in my proficiency on the tonette. Mr. Castelle invited six of us to play in the concert at Dorseyville Junior High. The boys wore white shirts, black pants and black ties; the girls wore their Sunday dresses. He drove us to the school where we sat in concert with the Dorseyville Junior High students. We played the two songs we had learned, "Twinkle, Twinkle Little Star" and "Long, Long Ago" and received an ovation from the audience.

In August of that year, my mother gave birth to her last baby, a boy. She told me I could name him. I named him William. Because my maternal grandfather's name was Samuel, she named the baby William Samuel Walker.

At our house, the Thanksgiving holidays were time for

"spring" cleaning. Our parents were home from work on Thanksgiving Day, so early that morning, my father woke Audrey Mae and me. As soon as we were dressed, we were given our duties. I filled a bucket with water for washing the outside windows and a broom to sweep away cobwebs, while Audrey Mae cleaned the inside windows. Everything had to be clean because we'd also touch up the paint on the windows. When the windows were completed, we repainted the inside of the house.

By early afternoon, the house smelled of turkey, dressing, greens, rolls, pies and other dishes. The aroma of food made us even hungrier. We were only allowed to drink water and go to the bathroom during cleaning. We couldn't complain because our parents worked alongside us.

Finally, by late evening, we had almost finished our cleaning, and it was time to eat. As we sat down, we were thankful for our meal. We were so hungry, we stuffed ourselves as if it were our last meal. The house was clean, inside and out. Audrey Mae and I looked forward to going back to school to avoid the hard labor.

Li'l Sister and Riley bought an older house that needed renovation. We installed a new roof, windows, siding, sheetrock and new flooring. Weekdays, we worked until late into the night. On weekends, we worked from morning until midnight. When the house was completed, we helped them move in and get settled.

My father became known as an excellent carpenter, so we had more work than we wanted. We built several new houses and performed countless repairs on houses in Bayou Goula and other towns.

Brother Pasqua bought a house and asked my father to add a patio. We built a concrete slab and added brick flowerpots. I mixed the concrete by hand and carried buckets of it to my father as he smoothed and leveled the patio.

Brother Pasqua also hired us to install a concrete platform at the front entrance of The Madonna Chapel. We dug out the grass and built a raised platform. My father completed the smooth finishing as I poured concrete into the frame. I feel proud to know our work is still appreciated after all these years.

Brother Pasqua hired us again to build a manger for the nativity display in St. Paul Catholic Church. My father and I built the manger at night, after returning home from his construction job. Brother Pasqua sat in a pew, watched and sang hymns as we worked.

Brother Pasqua wanted my friends Leonard Bracken, Jeffrey Randolph and me to meet a Black priest, so he got our parents' permission to take us to New Roads, Louisiana. When we arrived, he introduced us to the Black priest and the nuns. We had never seen a Black priest; it was an eye opener for us. The priest invited us to Mass. After Mass we had lunch with him.

One day, Brother Pasqua told Leonard, Jeffrey and me we didn't have to sit in the Black section of the church. He said we could sit anywhere we wanted. We decided to sit in the White section. Mass started at 8:00 a.m. When the doors opened at 7:00 a.m., we each sat in a pew by ourselves in the White section, waiting for Mass to start.

As the Whites came into the church, they pretended we weren't there, and no one sat next to us. During Mass, I glanced at Brother Pasqua, who sat at the altar with the priest. I could see a smile in his eyes.

Brother Pasqua believed I would become a priest. One day, he asked if I wanted to enroll in the Catholic school. Not knowing much about the Catholic school, I replied yes.

I did know it was an all-White school; the public schools in the South weren't integrated, either. Brother Pasqua, who worked at the Catholic school, told them about my character and inquired about my enrollment. He must have given them a good sales pitch, because the school gave him approval to bring me over.

Extremely excited, he came to our house to deliver the news to my mother. We sat at the kitchen table as she cooked supper. He told her he had spoken with the principal and received approval to enroll me at the Catholic school. He brought the paperwork and explained the details of my enrollment. He had the forms spread on the table and said the only special requirement was that I had to wear a khaki uniform and there was a monthly charge. That was the breaking point. My mother said she didn't have money for a khaki uniform or monthly fees. Brother Pasqua begged her to enroll me in the school. But no matter what he said, her answer was the same: She didn't have the money.

He left our house brokenhearted. I would have been the first Black student to attend White Castle Catholic School. Brother Pasqua was a God-loving man and a hero for the Black community, and he was always seeking opportunities for me.

My Uncle Arthur and Auntie Elizabeth "Poncie" Jones were like my second set of parents. Uncle Arthur normally had a low tolerance for children and most of my cousins were afraid to even talk with him. But he always wanted me around and I enjoyed being with him and driving his car. Auntie Poncie was one of the kindest people I knew. I never heard her use a curse word or speak ill of anyone. Also, she could recite her ABCs backward.

Uncle Arthur built a store, the Sweetshop, next to their house. Each evening, it converted into a restaurant. Auntie Poncie managed the store and was an excellent cook.

Sometimes, I stayed the weekend at their house and worked in the Sweetshop. My cousins Carolyn, Herbert and Herman worked there, too. They were older and when I was there, they were free to go and see their friends. Herbert was my idol. He wore his hair in a huge afro, and I wanted to be cool like him.

Across the street from the Sweetshop was St. John Baptist Church. Every Easter, they held a baptism ceremony. That was a busy day for us. We made snow cones and sold sweets at top speed. I felt privileged to work there. Sometimes Auntie Poncie would pay me $5. I never expected any pay. I worked there because I enjoyed it. Also, I was learning a skill, which was more valuable than money.

Once, Uncle Arthur and Auntie Poncie planned a weekend trip to New Orleans to visit his sister, and they invited me. We'd been riding for a while and Uncle Arthur asked why I was so quiet. I said I had a stomachache. He told me to lie down on the backseat, which is how I spent the rest of the ride.

Finally, we arrived in New Orleans. This was my first time meeting Uncle Arthur's sister. She had a son about my age. The older folks started talking and I was told to go play with their son. He showed me his drum set. I was in heaven. It was my first time being this close to a drum set. This kid had the works: snares, cymbals, tom-tom and a bass drum. I planted myself on the stool and started beating. Drumsticks in hand, hitting snares and cymbals, my foot worked the bass drum. Finally, I had a chance to hone my drum skills! I was beating on them, having a good time.

Uncle Arthur came in the room and told me to get off because I was making too much noise. Then he added, as he closed the door, "I thought you were sick with a stomachache."

I didn't respond, but I was thinking the drum set healed me.

Skin played electric guitar in the family gospel group. He taught himself to play and only knew how to play religious songs. Sometimes, he'd go to the barbershop and entertain the men as they waited for haircuts. One day, I was in the yard playing with the boys when he called me inside. He told the men I could play guitar. He handed me the guitar and I started playing the one song he'd taught me. When I finished, everyone clapped. What they didn't know was I only knew that one song. But my performance gave the impression I was a great guitar player.

I always wanted to play soul music. While Skin was at work, I'd sneak into the room where his guitar was kept, connect the amplifier and play. Ma Flo would come in and threatened to tell Skin I was playing his guitar. She never did, but he'd often complain it was out of tune, indicating someone had been playing with it.

My father exposed me to many experiences. One night, he told me we were going hunting. Hunting didn't excite me, and I didn't know why we needed to go. Beyond our house was wilderness. There was no moon; it was totally dark. He brought out his shotgun and attached a head light to his work hat. He gave me a flashlight, and we walked toward the dead-end of the street.

As we entered the wilderness, I was scared, but I didn't tell my father. I followed behind him, not knowing what to expect. I believe we were hunting possum. An hour after hearing all kinds of weird sounds and no possum in sight, he said we should head home. I was thrilled to go home and glad we didn't find a possum.

The White owner of the sugarcane fields didn't approve of our walking through the head lanes. One day, I was walking on the head lane alone and the farmer started following me in his truck. As I ran, he followed me, keeping about six feet behind. I ran as fast as I could, turning to look back at him occasionally. He was smiling as he kept up with my pace. If I'd stumbled and fallen, he'd have run over me. We were the only ones in the field and I wondered, *If he ran over me, would he tell anyone or just hide the body?* When I got to the end of the head lane and out of the field, he stopped, turned around, and drove back into the sugarcane field. I was scared and out of breath.

During the summer, I often went to my cousin's house, and I saw a girl next door I'd never seen. That summer, I met Ida Washington, and I was at my cousin's house every day.

At a friend's house, elderly men had set up a boxing ring. Two boys started boxing and it was clear one boy was a better boxer because the other boy started crying after two punches. The gloves were strapped on another boy, who soon cried, too. The boy who made them cry was now the champ. I watched but had no interest in boxing.

Then someone called the attention to me. Before I could protest, someone grabbed my little arms and put the heavy gloves on my hands. My opponent was hitting his gloves together, indicating he was ready to box. Someone did a count down and the number three was the last number I heard. The boy started hitting me so hard and fast, I couldn't think to move my arms. The men stopped the fight when they saw I couldn't box. I was thankful, but I didn't cry.

Most of us boys worked the fields for extra money. We picked cabbage, okra, beans, sweet potatoes, mustard greens and tomatoes. I didn't like picking okra because the leaves made me itch. But the okra pay was the best, 75 cents per bushel; the pay for beans was only 55 cents per bushel. If a bushel wasn't full, the farmer sent us back into the field to top it off (filling it above the rim). Not everyone was allowed to pick tomatoes, because those had to be handled gently.

The farmer would constantly yell out to the boys, "Handle the tomatoes like eggs!"

When he wasn't looking, we ate loads of tomatoes.

1967–1968 (Seventh Grade)

I was supposed to go to Dorseyville Junior High. But a letter was sent from the Iberville, Louisiana School Board stating I'd begin attending White Castle High School in September 1967. This was part of the state's initiative to integrate the schools by transporting Black students to an all-White school.

I don't recall volunteering to go to White Castle High, but I had been forging my mother's signature since fourth grade, so maybe I had signed paperwork without understanding it. My second thought was, *Maybe I was selected because Brother Pasqua tried to enroll me into the all-White Catholic school.* My parents didn't ask any questions; we just complied. I didn't know if any other Black students were selected to attend White Castle High.

On the first day of school, the school bus came to our house. I had always walked to school and school buses never came down our street. The big yellow bus turned around at the end of the dead-end street. The driver opened the door and I got on. No words were exchanged. The bus wasn't full, and all the White students sat toward the front. As the first Black student to board the bus, I walked to the back and took a seat. No one talked as we drove through Bayou Goula. When the driver arrived on the main street and picked up more Black students, I realized I wasn't the only Black student to attend White Castle High. We all sat quietly on the ride to White Castle High.

Upon entering the campus, we saw a cluster of Black students. We joined them and learned they were from Dorseyville

Junior High. There were 325 White students and 12 Black students in different grades—and one Black teacher, Mr. Leroy Washington, a science teacher. We all stood in a huddle. The White boys were bold. Occasionally, a group of them passed and yelled, "Niggers!" We ignored the name calling and continued to talk among ourselves.

White Castle High School encompassed grades 7 through 12. That first day was the start of a long, disruptive semester.

The main building was an old three-story brick building with stairs, wooden floors and four to six classrooms on each floor. Another single-level brick building housed the principal's office and eight classrooms. A gym, band room, woodshop classroom, and the cafeteria were in a separate building.

When the bell rang, we had to disseminate. I don't remember when, or how, we learned to get around. But at the sound of the bell, I started toward my class and joined many students heading up or down the stairs. Many of the White students laughed and talked with their friends as we made our way to class. Still in the crowd of students, I heard the word "nigger" yelled out.

In my first class, I sat in the first desk in the first row next to the door. I felt safe sitting near the door. As White boys passed my desk, they'd mumble "nigger," and some bumped my desk as if by accident. As the teacher went through roll call, the name calling continued; the teacher ignored it.

I believe the White students were as curious about us as we were about them. But as we integrated into the school, some of the White boys' curiosity turned to hate, disrespect and meanness. The White girls didn't display this same level of hatred.

Most of the White students didn't want Black students at their school. I assume some of the Black students would rather have not been there, either. The daily pressure of being teased, harassed and called "monkey," "stupid" and "nigger" grew tiresome. We received no support from the White teachers, who didn't want us at their school, either. This was my introduction to racial discrimination.

My previous association with White people was limited. I had held odd jobs working for White families. Charles "Chuckie" Landry, Jr. lived in Bayou Goula and his father was a sugarcane farmer. Chuckie worked in the fields with his father and drove the pickup truck that carried the field workers. I saw Chuckie at Bayou Goula Catholic Church, where he was an altar boy; he attended White Castle Catholic School. We were the same age and had been friends for years. Most Black people in Bayou Goula knew Chuckie, and he had the utmost respect for Black people. Brother Pasqua was my catechism teacher and I never viewed him as White. He was always visiting Black families' homes and he liked everyone—and everyone liked him. These were the only two White people I had personally known. I assumed other White people I met would have these same characteristics. Sadly, the White students (mostly boys) I met at that time were mean spirited.

Seventh grade was divided into two classes. A Class and B Class. I was assigned to B Class. We used the same textbooks and had the same teachers as A Class. The only difference was A Class material was taught at an aggressive pace. B Class was always a week or two behind.

My first weeks at White Castle High weren't for academics. I was just focused on surviving and navigating through the confusion as to why I was so disliked by the White boys. Most teachers had no control over their classrooms. The White boys would complain daily and blurt out, "Why is this nigger in this classroom?" The teacher ignored them. It was like the White boys didn't know the South was going through changes. I didn't know how to explain my presence, because I knew little about the Louisiana State integration policies.

As a Black student at White Castle High, my only friend was another Black student. Even the teachers avoided interacting with me as much as possible. When forced, teacher communication was limited to classroom assignments. No one wanted to touch me or sit close to me. I heard comments that I was unclean or had some sort of disease. When a White boy walked past me, he'd hold his nose as though he smelled a bad odor.

If I raised my hand to answer a question, the teacher pretended not to see it. Seldom was I called on to answer a question. Even when my answer was right, the White boys ridiculed me.

While I sat at my desk, the White boys behind me enjoyed throwing balls of paper at me. When I turned around, everyone pretended not to have seen anything. I couldn't complain to the teachers because they ignored what was happening. At the end of class, loads of paper balls lay on the floor around my desk. Still not one teacher said anything.

My classmates were primarily of Italian and French descent. One French boy especially hated Black people. He was always the leader of the harassment, encouraging the others to harass me, as well. He'd say, "Nigger, how much money are you paid to attend this White school?" I ignored him because no matter what answer I gave, it always led to further harassment.

I'd never heard of the Ku Klux Klan (KKK) until I attended White Castle High. The White boys told me of the bad things the KKK would do to me if I continued attending their school. They'd ask if I wanted to join the KKK. They'd even offer to bring me an application and invite me to the KKK's next scheduled meeting.

I was 12, the same age as the White boys in my class. I wondered how they'd learned to be so mean and hateful at such a young age. The awful things they said had never crossed my mind. Years later, I found my answer: Those White boys weren't any smarter than me; their parents fed them hateful information. I never shared my experiences at White Castle High with my parents, and they'd never have encouraged me to be mean and hateful toward anyone.

I was called nigger so many times a day, the word didn't bother me. Plus, I never considered myself a nigger. Therefore, nigger didn't apply to me. The White boys would ask me to show them my hands. Without thinking, I fell into their trap by complying. They'd all burst into laughter and talk about the inside of my hands being the lightest part of my body.

Seventh Grade

When moving from one class to another, I was always the last person walking to class, and I avoided getting too close to a White student, otherwise I was called names and harassed.

My American History teacher was a middle-aged woman. When we learned about the transport of Negro slaves to America, she would call upon a student to read aloud from the book. Every time someone said the word, "Negro," the White boys would burst into laughter. A White boy once whispered to me, asking if I had known the slaves referenced in the book. The follow up question was to ask if they were my cousins, then the observation, "They were some ugly people, too." The teacher ignored their insults. I just absorbed the pain. I could never focus on learning when I was in the classroom; I was in survival mode.

The good part of the daily drama was the White girls; they

were nice and never insulted me. When the White boys harassed me, the White girls came to my rescue, insisting they stop. Even though the White girls gave a good effort, the White boys continued their daily torment. They never hit me; it was just unrelenting daily verbal abuse.

Raymond Shaheen became my guardian angel. Raymond was in all my classes. Whenever I was bullied, he would position himself between the bully and me. The other White boys would slap him, push him against the wall, push him to the floor, and make him cry. He'd get up off the floor and get into their face and say, "Hit me again!" Then they'd call Raymond a nigger lover. No matter what the White boys did, Raymond defended me. I felt sorry for him. He was taking all the beatings for me. Raymond and I became the best of friends.

Each boy was told a jock strap was required to participate in physical education. When the coach mentioned the jock strap, I had no idea what one looked like. Because I was mostly ignored, I didn't want to ask what a jock strap was and have everyone laugh at me. So, I went along for days as if I knew what it was. Then one day, the coach asked the boys to raise their hand if they weren't wearing one. As we stood in formation, the coach walked around and pulled the back of each boy's shorts, checking for a jock strap.

He asked why I lied about having one. I said I thought it was the same as jockey shorts. He explained what a jock strap was and why I needed one to play sports. He told me to tell my parents to buy me one.

On my way home, I thought hard about how to explain it to my mother. I was embarrassed to even have the conversation with her. I assumed she wouldn't know what one was, and I didn't feel I knew enough about them to describe it to her, but I couldn't go to gym class without one.

When I arrived home, I blurted out to my mother that the coach said I needed a jock strap.

She replied with a nonchalant, "Okay."

I was shocked, first, because she didn't say she didn't have the money for a jock strap and secondly, she knew what I was talking about. I was glad I didn't have to explain anything. The next day, I had my first jock strap.

During gym class, one of our exercises was to climb the rope attached to the gym ceiling. One student held the end of the rope to keep it from swaying as another student climbed, touched the ceiling, and came back down. Of the White boys, maybe three made it to the top. The others climbed halfway up and turned red in the face. Due to a lack of upper-arm strength, they terminated the climb. As the only Black boy in the class, I was also the last boy to climb. As Raymond held the rope, I jumped on it and, not missing a beat, propelled myself to the top. I touched the ceiling and was back on the gym floor in record time. The coach was forced to congratulate me. I realized I was better than all the other boys in that regard—and that realization felt great.

One day, I went into the locker room and the only boy there was the French boy who hated Black people. I walked to my locker, waiting for him to say something. In the classroom, he harassed me constantly. I wouldn't start a fight, but if he raised a hand to hit me, I was capable of hurting him badly. He was red in the face, sweating and shaking. He was a bully around his friends, but without his posse, he was a coward. After that locker-room interaction, he never found himself alone with me again.

I tried to avoid going to the bathroom at recess. The White boys would crowd into the bathroom to smoke cigarettes. If I went in there, each boy I walked past would insult me.

Even though I experienced daily verbal abuse, there was never any physical body contact. I was confident that one on one, I could beat most of the White boys in the class. Li'l Sister told me, if they ganged up on me, focus on one boy. When the fight was over, that one would have my marks all over him, and he would never forget me. Fortunately, I never had to implement my plan.

My band teacher, Mr. Zito, a kind, middle-aged Italian

man, made me feel welcome when I was in the band room, and he assisted me as much as he could.

Before joining the band, a student had to have an instrument, or be willing to buy one. We were given a catalog of musical instruments. Parents selected from the catalog the instrument they'd buy for their child. I wanted to be in the band, but I knew money was scarce and the chances of my parents buying an instrument weren't good. The starting price was $40, and they went up from there. I decided not to show the catalog to my mother because it'd be an automatic no.

While my father was eating supper, I shared the catalog with him. When he got to the page with the trumpet, he said he thought I should get it, since it had three valves and it'd be easier for me to play. I didn't disagree with his reasoning. I was ecstatic he'd even suggested I could get one. It might have been the cheapest instrument in the catalog. If I had a choice, I'd have selected the saxophone, but I wasn't about to push my luck. I told my father I'd gladly play trumpet. I completed the order form, and the next day, I brought it and the money to Mr. Zito. Within a week, I had my new trumpet.

When I boarded the school bus, I carried my schoolbooks in one hand and my trumpet in the other. As soon as I started walking down the aisle, the White bus driver would shift the gears to make me stagger. White students sat in the aisle seats to prevent my sitting with them. Once I got to my seat, I'd see the driver smirking in his rearview mirror.

One wintry morning, the bus windows were fogged. I looked at one window and a White student had written "KKK" and drawn a swastika symbol into the fog on the window.

I'd learned to read music in elementary school. Mr. Zito taught me how to blow into the trumpet to obtain specific notes. Every day for an hour, I went to the band room, and he gave me private lessons. When he was satisfied with my playing, Mr. Zito gave me a new lesson.

My music lessons included learning flats and sharps. I

never had to be told to practice, and I practiced often. Learning to blow the trumpet was easy. I sometimes tried playing along to songs on the radio.

I found the band room to be my safe space. I could go there and not be harassed or be called "nigger." Raymond was learning to play clarinet. Whenever we didn't have to be in a class, we'd go to the band room and practice, even during recess.

One day, Raymond insisted I let him play my trumpet. I was shocked that a White boy wanted to blow into the mouthpiece of a Black boy's trumpet. I gave it to him and he tried, but he couldn't get it to make a sound. Then he insisted I try his clarinet. That day our friendship was sealed.

I wondered why we had been placed in an environment where we were unwanted. However, I believed being selected to go to an all-White school during those times made me a stronger person. I learned a lot about myself—and even more about other people.

This harassment and mistreatment had gone on for a month or more. Then one night, a little past midnight, while most people in Bayou Goula were home asleep, we all awakened to a fire. The Bayou Goula old school building—an old wooden structure that had stood in the community for years—was burning. My parents had attended school there as children. Now it was on fire.

Almost everyone in Bayou Goula went out into the night to watch the burning building. Ladies wore their nightgowns, with rollers in their hair. Men were partially dressed, some in trousers and T-shirts, others bare chested. I went down to the fire with my father.

The nearest fire department was in White Castle. By the time the fire truck arrived, the building had burned to the ground. The firemen sprayed water to ensure the fire didn't reignite.

The next night, again past midnight, we awakened to another burning building. This time, a vacant house near the river road was set ablaze. People were out in their nightwear, the same as the previous night. Everyone was nervous about this second midnight fire.

When the fire truck arrived, the house was engulfed. The firemen used their equipment to fight the fire. There were no fire hydrants, so when the truck ran out of water, the firemen had to leave the burning house to go to the Mississippi River to refill it with water.

Once the firemen left to refill the truck, the locals stood watching as the house burned, and the scorching heat warmed the night air. The local men did what they could to put out the fire with buckets of well water as everyone waited for the return of the fire truck. Minutes later, the fire truck returned and soon the fire was out. Everyone walked home in disturbing silence.

Since the fires occurred late at night, it was rumored they'd been started by the KKK. No one could ever prove it, and no one was caught. Then the old post office was set on fire in the middle of the night. Whoever started the fires succeeded in instilling fear in the community.

Many people were afraid to go to sleep, fearing their houses would be next to burn. I don't remember how it was started, but everyone in Bayou Goula was told to pin a black cloth above the entrance of their home. Also, people were told to leave their porch lights on at night. Pinning a black cloth above the door was supposed to prevent someone from burning the home. All the houses in Bayou Goula had this black cloth hanging at their door; it was as if the whole community was mourning a death.

I don't remember how it was communicated, but all 12 Black students were told not to go to school because it was unsafe. The White bus driver didn't come to my house. I didn't know what was happening, but on the news, I saw demonstrations throughout the South, including northern Louisiana. Policemen were unleashing dogs and turning water hoses on demonstrators. We never encountered those things in Bayou Goula.

However, a local demonstration was held. Some adults

recruited kids to walk picket lines. I joined the demonstration and was given a sign. We picketed the two White-owned stores in Bayou Goula. We marched in front of the stores, holding our signs, and sang "We Shall Overcome" and "Ain't Gonna Let Nobody Turn Me Around."

Weeks later, with compromises made, an agreement was struck. We were told to go back to school. The White bus driver came to pick me up. Upon arriving at White Castle High, I noticed the name calling was toned down. I was still hassled, but not as much. My class participation improved. I fell behind in my lessons due to my absence during the demonstrations. There were no make-up exams, and the teachers didn't help me get up to speed with anything I had missed. They continued teaching, and it was my responsibility to catch up.

Months later, local demonstrations calmed down. But demonstrations in other parts of the South intensified. I was walking into the gym one April morning when a White boy I didn't know yelled out, "Hey, nigger, your leader is dead; what are you going to do now?"

I had no idea what he was talking about. I didn't realize I had a leader. That was the day I learned of Dr. Martin Luther King, Jr., what a great man he was, and that he'd been assassinated. As I read about Dr. King's life work, I learned of another admirable leader, Frederick Douglass.

My seventh-grade year wasn't smooth sailing. I had many challenges to overcome, including desegregation and demonstrations. I had to study extra hard to stay focused. In retrospect, I feel honored to be a pioneer in social change. My parents never knew the issues I faced daily because I never came home crying or complaining. All they knew was that I was attending an all-White school and they were proud of my being enrolled there. If I had told them the problems I was encountering, they would have withdrawn me, and I didn't want that. So, I stayed the course and, at the end of the school year, advanced to eighth grade.

During the summer, I had a chance to re-energize. My

friends and I enjoyed fishing in the Mississippi River. We walked across the levee with homemade bamboo fishing poles and red worms in a tin can to fish.

We didn't have access to a public library. During the summer, a bookmobile came to Bayou Goula. The driver parked under a pecan tree and kids queued up, walked through the bookmobile, and selected a few books to check out. I was always looking for books about the Navy.

After selling bread and doughnuts, the bread man would park at the end of the street under a pecan tree and nap for 30 minutes. He was a White man in a Black neighborhood, and no one ever harassed him. During the riots and demonstrations, he came down the street as usual. While he was napping under the pecan tree, some Black teenagers mugged him. They beat him, stole his money, and took all the goods from the truck. It was the last day the bread man came through Bayou Goula.

On weekends, while we worked on the houses, my father played his latest 45-rpm record on the high-fi stereo. It was Dr. Martin Luther King, Jr.'s "I Have a Dream" speech. As we worked, he would play it repeatedly. I had heard the speech so many times, I could recite it verbatim.

Because I'd worked on so many houses with my father, he bought me a new bike. Maroon with silver fenders and a banana seat, it had high handlebars, a wide-track rear tire and a thin red stripe on both tires. It always looked new because I washed it almost daily. My mother didn't let me bring it into the house at night, so Abraham let me keep it in his corn shed.

Whenever I went into the shed to retrieve my bicycle, I heard rats scrambling around in the corn. They never bothered me. But one day when I went inside, I felt a rat run up my pant leg. I dropped the bike and ran out into the yard, screaming and jumping up and down. I could feel the rat attached to my leg, so I pulled off my pants. Tee Nachie heard my yelling and came to my rescue. The rat was still holding on tightly to my thigh as I jumped around in my jockey shorts, screaming. Tee Nachie grabbed the rat and threw it to the ground. Laughing uncontrollably, she said I'd scared the rat, and it was probably in shock. I never went back in the corn shed again and instead left my bicycle on our patio overnight.

Caring for and feeding the rabbits and hog were still my job. Due to the multiplication of the rabbits, we'd all had our fill of rabbits for meals, so our rabbit raising ended. I wasn't disappointed. But I still had to go into the field morning and night to cut grass for the hog. I wanted this hog out of my life, but we couldn't kill it because it was still too skinny. Its growth was likely stunted because I fed it grass and little else.

The State Fair came to Donaldsonville annually. With my pecan money, I was off to the fair. Most kids looked forward to the various rides, but I spent my money on footlong hot dogs. I'd order a footlong and walk around the fair, looking at the attractions. Later, I'd ordered a second footlong. Before leaving the fair, I'd eaten three footlongs and not gone on any rides.

Men in the community recruited boys for a newly founded Bayou Goula Little League team. All the local boys were invited to try out. I couldn't play baseball, but I joined the tryout because my friends were baseball players. During the tryout, I didn't catch one ball thrown to me. Those boys threw the ball hard, and when they threw it to me, I would duck rather than try to catch it. I was put in center field, where I hoped the ball wouldn't be hit to me. If it came my way, I let it hit the ground. Then I'd pick it up and throw it to the appropriate base. When I was up to bat, I didn't hit one ball. By the time I swung the bat, the ball was already in the catcher's mitt.

At the end of the tryout, I wasn't assigned a position. I asked the coach what position I'd play. He said he'd assign my position later. I sat on the bench and watched the other boys play and felt fine about that, because I was afraid of the ball.

Because the coach told me he'd assign my position later, I figured I was a part of the team. I attended practices and did my job of keeping the bench warm. Finally, team T-shirts arrived. All the boys were thrilled to receive their T-shirts and immediately put them on.

After the T-shirts were distributed, I asked the coach where mine was. He said I wasn't on the team. The other boys looked at me like they'd already known I wouldn't get a T-shirt. The coach called the boys into a huddle to discuss a game plan, and I walked off the field without a word to anyone.

As I walked home through the sugarcane field, I had a conversation with myself. I knew I wasn't a good baseball player. I'd allowed the coach to make me think otherwise. I re-evaluated my situation and decided music, not baseball, was my strength and interest. I thought further that those boys could play ball because it was their strength and interest. But none of them could read music or blow a trumpet as well as me. That made me feel better. My rejection from the team taught me I should follow my own passions.

Brother Pasqua had been preparing several of us for the Sacrament of Confirmation. The ceremony was held at Our Lady of Prompt Succor Catholic Church. Because this was a night event, my mother drove me to the church. Emma Mae went to the confirmation ceremony, too.

Brother Pasqua told us the bishop would be present. None of us had ever seen a bishop, and I looked forward to meeting him. However, he left the church without ever saying a word to any of us. I was disappointed; I thought I'd have a chance to meet personally with him.

Because I didn't have a license, my father wouldn't let me drive the car alone. When I drove, it was usually to church on Sunday, or to visit relatives locally, and he was in the car.

One day, as we worked on our house, my father needed something from the store and didn't want to stop working. He gave me the keys and told me to go to the store. This was my first time to drive in the car alone. I left the house, driving as though he were in the passenger seat. I'd always been a good driver and always did the right thing.

On my return home, I got the urge to drive fast. Breaux Street was a narrow street and cars traveled in two directions. Normally, I drove 20 mph down our street. But I wanted to drive faster. I accelerated to 45 mph. As I approached two cars double parked on each side of the street, I knew I was going too fast to maneuver around both of them. In a blink of an eye, I'd cleared the parked cars. I gave thanks to God, because at the speed I was traveling, I knew I didn't steer the car through the narrow path. I learned my lesson. After that day, I never drove recklessly again.

Plute let me drive his car and his pickup truck, which was a stick shift. It was three gears, and the shift was attached to the steering wheel. The high-beam switch was a knob on the floor you pressed with your foot to switch from low beam to high beams. I'd often watched Plute shifting the gears on his truck. The day he allowed me to drive, I didn't tell him I'd never driven a standard. He assumed I could drive a stick because I drove other cars. I sat in the truck and shifted into first gear. With my foot on the clutch, I shifted into second and then third. I must have done it convincingly, because he never knew it was my first time.

One day Plute asked me to go with him to buy a car in Baton Rouge. On the lot, he saw a white 1963 Chevy Impala he liked. A salesman let us take it for a test drive. We got in and Plute drove off the lot.

After a few blocks, I asked him to stop so I could check the engine. I checked for oil leaks. I checked the headlights, low beam and high beams. I told him to turn on the signal lights, wipers and brake lights. I checked the horn, the spare and the jack. When we'd inspected everything I could think of, he asked how I knew to check these things. I said I just knew. It was a good car in good condition. When we got back to the dealer, Plute bargained for a lower price and drove his new car home.

Plute was a cheap man, but I enjoyed spending time with

him. It wasn't until he died in January 1994, at age 77, that I found out he never learned to read or write. But he could count money, and no one could cheat him out of a dollar.

1968–1969 (Eighth Grade)

In September 1968, the Iberville, Louisiana School Board directed the Black population at White Castle High be increased. More Black teachers and students from Dorseyville Junior High transferred to White Castle High. The Black to White student ratio still wasn't balanced, but each classroom now had four or five Black students. Also, several Black teachers were transferred to White Castle High. We were still harassed, but not to the level of the prior year.

Raymond and I were still good friends. And both diligent musicians. Because we'd shown initiative, this school semester we were assigned to play in the marching band and concert band. I was assigned as a third-chair trumpet player.

In August, I went to band practice. We practiced formations on the football field. At home games, we'd perform at half time. My mother drove me to practice, but I had to hitchhike home. When the band went on a road trip, my friend, Gus Jackson, father gave me a ride.

The day I was issued my White Castle High School band uniform, I was proud. The uniform included a black two-piece suit with "White Castle High School" embroidered in white on the upper left pocket. The white leather vest had WCHS in maroon old-English lettering on the front, and a maroon bulldog face on the back. The hat was white and black with a white feather on top.

Raymond and I practiced every chance we got. If we were in class and had completed our work, he would go to the teacher's desk to ask if we could go to the band room. The teacher would excuse us without ever looking at me. Once I asked to be excused to go to the band room and was denied. I never asked again and relied on Raymond asking for both of us.

In the band room, I'd wander around and play with various instruments. I practiced chords on the piano. And I'd beat the drums until Mr. Zito told me to practice my trumpet.

I still had the same bus driver, who was as unfriendly as the year before. He still shifted gears to make me stagger as I walked down the aisle with my trumpet and books.

One of the new students at White Castle High in 1968 was Fredrick Jackson. The first day we met, Fred and I bonded. We called each other "partners." We were enrolled in almost all the same classes. He had a brilliant mind for math and was a natural logical thinker.

We had to write a paper about someone we admired, explaining why we admired that person. I thought of all the people I knew. They were all good people, but their careers didn't match what I wanted when I thought of my future. I investigated our encyclopedias for ideas. I'd glanced through a few books when I stumbled upon a man who'd been an inventor. I don't recall his name or what he had invented. But I remember he'd invented several things. I identified with him and wanted to be an inventor like him.

Having identified my subject, I started writing my paper. The more I wrote, the more excited I became, thinking of the things I wanted to invent. I thought of the many patents I could generate. I became energized with the idea of being an inventor.

The next day, the teacher asked each student to stand and read their paper. One by one, they read, "I admire my mother because…" or "I admire my father because…" Some admired movie stars and professional athletes. Everyone had written about their admiration of a known person. As I listened, I felt good about my selection. No one wanted to be an inventor.

Finally, it was my turn. I stood and started by saying I wanted to be an inventor.

Before I could say another word, the teacher asked, "What?"

I repeated, "Inventor." The teacher told me to sit down. The whole class laughed. Because I didn't mention a recognizable name like the other students, I never had a chance to elaborate on the inventions and patents I wanted to create.

Across the street from the Little League field was a bar called the Tumble Inn. Since I'd been cut from the baseball team, I didn't care about watching baseball.

My cousin, Li'l Frank, was a musician whose band played at the bar. The owner kept a side door open for people going to the outside toilet. I'd stand there to watch the band. Periodically, an elderly man heading to the toilet would tell me to leave and go to the ball field, where the other children were. I ignored him because he was half drunk. Plus, I wasn't interested in what went on in the bar. My attention was on the band. I'd been watching Li'l Frank's drummer, who'd had more than his share of beer. Every time he missed a beat, Li'l Frank would give him a stern look. I knew my cousin wasn't happy with the drummer's playing, so I yelled out, "Let me play the drums."

Li'l Frank told me no.

But between every song, I continued pleading, "I want to play the drums."

When the drummer knocked his snare drum to the floor in the middle of a song, Li'l Frank insisted he take a break. He told me to take over, not even knowing if I could play.

After all my begging, I wasn't about to admit this was my first time playing drums, except that time in New Orleans and occasionally in the band room. I think Li'l Frank figured I couldn't do any worse than his drunk drummer.

I sat at the drums. I'd been watching his drummer, and in my mind, I knew I could play. It was my time to shine. Li'l Frank started playing a song and I joined in with the beat. He smiled at me as I played along. I was ready to play more, but after a second song, the drummer had sobered up a little and wanted to return.

As I left the stage, I felt great. I had surprised myself. That day I designated myself a drummer. All those nights when I went to bed with the radio on, I'd beat on my headboard and the walls with my hands. My mother would come in and tell me to stop beating on the wall and the bed, but I never did. I would just beat more softly. She had no idea I was teaching myself to play drums. And now I had proven to myself I could.

Friends at Dorseyville Junior High invited me to their basketball games. One night, my eyes zoomed in on a beautiful girl sitting in the bleachers with her family. I didn't know anything about her. But I knew I liked her and one day we'd meet. Every time I went to the basketball games, I'd look forward to seeing her. She was at every game. I sat across from her, oblivious to the action on the basketball court. I never introduced myself, but I eagerly awaited the next game.

Sometimes we went to Mass in White Castle. Occasionally I saw her there. I still didn't know her name, but I was pleased to know she was Catholic.

Growing up in Louisiana, I saw many "Colored" signs. Those posted signs were indicators for how people identified me and those who looked like me. I'd heard other people who looked like me call each other "nigger." They never used it in a negative context. My father was the first person to tell me I wasn't a nigger. He said I was a "Negro," which was how I referred to myself.

I stopped hearing people referring to me as Colored and Negro. Instead, now I was told I was "Black." Not only Black, but "Black and Proud." About this time, James Brown had a hit song, "Say it Loud, I Am Black and Proud." Black people started referring to each other as brother and sister. A regular handshake wasn't enough anymore. When greeting another Black person, we gave the dap (fist pounding and hand slapping). Or we offered the clenched-fist Black Power sign.

One day, I was in the car with Skin and his friend, headed to Baton Rouge. As we crossed the Mississippi River Bridge into Baton Rouge, a car drove past us. The boys in the other car gave us the Black Power sign. Skin's friend, who had never heard of Black Power, said, "Those boys are shaking their fists at us!"

Skin explained they weren't shaking their fists; rather, that was the "Black Power" sign.

In those days, everything around us was changing. Black males and females started wearing afros. Young Black boys walked around with afro picks in their back pockets.

1969–1970 (Ninth Grade)

Two weeks before the semester started, band members had to attend band practice twice a week. We had to rehearse marching routines and be ready to perform at half time during the first football game.

I had to hitchhike to school. Trumpet in hand, I walked to the river road. Practically everyone in Bayou Goula knew me, so I felt embarrassed hitchhiking, but I had no other choice. People who didn't want to stop pretended to adjust their rearview mirrors and not to see me. Finally, a car would stop. The driver always asked my reasons for going to White Castle. Since they were giving me a ride, I felt obliged to give an explanation. I said I was going to band practice. Once in White Castle, I still had to walk a half mile to the school, and I was never late.

During practice, I wasn't totally focused. I was thinking it'd be dark at the end of practice, and I hated hitchhiking in the dark. Standing on the road in the dark with my thumb out, I couldn't recognize oncoming cars because the headlights shone in my face. Fortunately, all the people who stopped were folks I knew. Again, I had to explain my reason for being in White Castle. Once we arrived in Bayou Goula, I was dropped off on the river road and had to walk at least another mile home in the dark.

Due to my embarrassment about hitchhiking, I often walked the five miles to White Castle. On the levee, I dodged grazing cows that sometimes chased me. Holding tight to my trumpet, I ran, trying to avoid stepping in cow manure.

In September 1969, the school board enforced integration.

White Castle High School was now the local high school for all students. Dorseyville Junior High was designated as the junior high school. Bayou Goula Elementary was the elementary school. Students and teachers were reassigned. White Castle High's ratio of Black to White students and teachers was realigned. But White families slowly migrated out of White Castle and their children transferred to a school of their choice.

Black school bus drivers now drove into White communities and vice versa. Before, Black school-bus drivers didn't drive door to door to pick up Black students. Black students who went to Dorseyville Junior High had to walk to specific locations in the community. The Black bus driver only drove door to door on rainy days. With the new busing arrangement, all students were bused door to door.

Because many Black students attended White Castle High, I was no longer harassed or called nigger. In fact, many of the White boys were now my friends.

I was getting to know many students from Dorseyville Junior High. I saw a female student and I really liked the way she walked. Because Fred was my best friend, I pointed her out to him. Fred told me she was his cousin and he introduced me to Lois Richard.

Most of my friends participated in school sports, but I was never interested in sports. We had football, basketball and track teams. The thought of having someone tackle and hit me wasn't appealing. I always knew I ran fast, but I didn't want to participate in track and field. My friends asked me to join them for basketball tryouts. I wasn't interested, but I gave it a try.

I found the game too complicated, with too many rules. I was told to stand in a specific spot or play a certain position. I just wanted to shoot the ball in the basket. However, I couldn't shoot, and I missed the basket almost all the time. I was cut from the team the first day.

At the beginning of the semester, Dorseyville Junior High band students joined our band. In the band room, all the students were preparing their instruments for practice. Looking across the room, to my surprise, I saw the girl I'd fantasized about at the Dorseyville basketball games. There she was, assembling her clarinet and talking to other clarinetists.

I was excited to see her, and it was even better to know she was in the band. As I pretended to focus on readying my trumpet, my heart pounded as I secretly admired her. I learned later her name was Patricia Clavier. I was in love with her.

Every day during band practice, I glanced at her as we played. One day, after learning I liked her, my friends took it upon themselves to tell her I was secretly in love with her. Patricia waited for me to approach her, but I never did. After weeks of no move from me, she wrote me a note, asking why I was denying I liked her. For some reason, I couldn't confess I was in love with her. She later found another boyfriend, and inside I was jealous, but we remained friendly.

Raymond and I continued to practice between classes. After football season, we played in the concert band. Because we were good players, Raymond was promoted to first-chair clarinet, and I was promoted to second-chair trumpet.

Because I had no interest in sports, I didn't want to participate in gym class. I did the normal stretching exercises and then the coach divided us into teams to play various games. I joined in the team games until I saw my friend, Lionel Gilbert, dressed in his gym clothes, sitting in the bleachers. He sang all the latest songs, so I started joining him in the bleachers. As he sang, I drummed on the bleachers and gave him a beat. The coach said we weren't participating.

Weeks later, Lionel stopped dressing in his gym clothes. He went directly to the bleachers. I dressed in my gym clothes and did the stretching exercises with the class. But when they divided into teams, I went to the bleachers to beat on the bleachers as Lionel sang. We were having fun as our classmates played games. The coach would tell us, "You're not participating."

That semester. I was stunned to receive a D in Physical Education. I'd never gotten below a C on my report card. I went to the coach and asked why I received a D. His response was "Lack of participation." That got my attention. I started participating and no longer sat with Lionel, who kept singing alone during gym class. The next semester I received an A in Physical Education.

Because of my participation, the coach saw I was a fast runner and asked me to try out for track and field, but I told him I wasn't interested.

I never warmed up to the hog. I still had to cut and haul grass from the field for it. When I went to the pen, it was like the hog knew me. I hated the thought of it knowing who I was because I didn't like the hog.

Our neighbors, the Brackens, had several sons, who taught me to play unorganized sports. We played touch football and softball, using sticks as a bat. Sometimes, if we didn't have a softball, we wrapped socks together for a ball. Our bases were cardboard, one piece for home plate, another for first base. We played in the street and paused for oncoming cars. We also played touch football in the street. I couldn't catch, but if the ball was passed to me, I could run it.

We played softball for hours. We had no strict rules. Hitting the ball into a beehive and seeing someone get stung was common. More than once I had a swollen eye from bee stings.

The Brackens had a hand pump in the yard. In the summer, the Mississippi River would rise, causing water to pour out. It looked clear as it flowed, but the water would turn a brownish/reddish color once it settled. After playing softball, we'd go to the pump and let the flowing water run over our heads to cool us. We drank the cool water until our stomachs ached. Then we lay on the grass to rest before starting another game.

We made our own kites, bows and arrows, pop guns and slingshots. We carried our slingshots in our back pockets.

I frequently went to Li'l Sister's house. One day I saw two

kids I'd never seen before. They had come to visit. Li'l Sister introduced them to me as my half-sister and half-brother. She explained they were my father's children, Gloria and Marcus. When I left Li'l Sister's house, I didn't say anything to anyone about meeting them. But I wondered why I hadn't been told about these kids. My father usually told me everything. But he didn't tell me about Gloria and Marcus, and I never knew where they lived, and as a child I never saw them again.

The Years 1970–1979

1970–1971 (Tenth Grade)

The band reported to school in August to practice marching formations. I wasn't allowed to drive alone or beyond Bayou Goula. My parents wouldn't drive me to practice, so my only option had been to hitchhike.

But now I had a second option. A senior in the band lived in Bayou Goula and had his license. His father let him drive to practice. He offered to drive me. I didn't know riding to and from practice could be so exciting. He turned into our driveway so fast, gravel and dust went flying. I jumped in and away we went. The river road parallels the Mississippi River and it curves from Bayou Goula to White Castle. Every curve we encountered, the tires squealed, and I was tossed from one side of the car to the other. I think he enjoyed scaring me. When we arrived, my heart was still beating double time.

I did well as second-chair trumpet player. I'd have preferred playing first chair, but the girl assigned to first chair was the best trumpet player in the band. She blew high notes effortlessly. Raymond advanced to first-chair clarinet. Still good friends, we canceled our study hall and used that extra hour practicing in the band room.

My favorite subjects were history, business, science, and band. I learned how to write a check, balance a checkbook, plus other aspects of business, including typing. I learned to type on an Underwood typewriter and became an excellent typist, without looking at the keyboard. I foresaw additional business studies in my future.

I'd seen my English teacher, Mr. Valenziano, many times at Mass. We had had no interaction until I was in his class. Now that I was his student, he felt as if he knew me, and vice versa. He was always fair and constantly encouraged me to work harder for better grades. He knew I put forth just enough effort to get passing grades. I'd often fancy joining the Navy and traveling the world.

Years after I graduated, when I was visiting family, Mr. V. invited me to dinner at an Italian restaurant in Baton Rouge. During dinner, he told me that at the beginning of integration, White teachers had strongly disapproved of our attending White Castle High. He apologized for the cruel treatment we'd endured. I assured him I carried no animosity in my heart.

I enrolled in driver education. Because I'd been driving since I was a youngster, I paid no attention to the lectures; I just wanted to drive. Finally, the day came. The teacher took two students at a time. I was taken to drive with a student who'd never driven. The teacher watched him closely and told him everything to do. When it was my turn, the teacher had confidence and trust in my driving.

During gym class, we were required to run sprints and the coach would time us. When he recorded my time, he said I was running as fast as the students on the track team. He encouraged me to join the team and I told him, once again, I wasn't interested.

Daily, my father came in from work and sat at the table to eat his supper. I'd join him there as he ate. We engaged in small talk, and he'd always ask about the hog. I still didn't like that thing, but I gave him a good hog report.

In the middle of one conversation, he casually asked if I'd like to have a motorcycle.

I'd never considered owning a motorcycle, but I said "Yes!" although I'd never ridden one. We continued talking and he said nothing more about it, so I gave it no further thought.

In Louisiana, driver's licenses were issued at age 15. I was 15, but I didn't ask my parents for a license because I didn't think they'd let me drive their cars. To my surprise, my father told me one day we should go and get my driver's license. We reported to the Department of Motor Vehicles and the examiner gave me the written test. I failed because I hadn't studied. They gave me a study guide and told me to come back in two weeks.

When we returned, I took the exam and passed with a perfect score. Then a police officer took me out for a road test. I drove my father's 1965 Volkswagen Bug. I had no doubt in my mind I'd pass the road test because I'd been driving since I was a child. The police officer sat in the passenger seat and I waited for his command. As I drove, he gave me commands when to turn. I used my turn signals properly and came to a complete stop at the stop signs. Each time I completed his requested command, he made a notation on his tablet. I wasn't concerned; I knew I wasn't making any errors. When we returned, he said I had executed all the driving moves flawlessly. I had my photo taken and they issued my license. Now that I had my license, I assumed I'd do more driving than the usual Sunday-morning trip to Mass and occasionally to the store. But my parents had other plans.

One afternoon after school, Skin came to get me to go to Baton Rouge. We drove through Plaquemine and saw my father's car parked at the motorcycle dealership, but we continued to Baton Rouge. On our return, my father's Volkswagen was still there. We stopped, and as we got out of the car, my father said he'd been waiting for me. He pointed to a brand-new shiny red 1970 Honda CL-100 and said, "That's yours."

I thought I was dreaming. I didn't know how to ride a motorcycle. I was in shock. My father talked with the salesman and introduced me as his son, asking the salesman to give me instructions for operating the motorcycle. As the salesman demonstrated shifting gears, the brakes, and other things, I was floating on a cloud, but my mind absorbed everything he said. The salesman told me to get on and ride around the parking lot, to get a feel for it. I took to it like a duck to water. It seemed to come naturally to me. I was shifting gears and riding as if I'd been riding a motorcycle all my life.

My father completed the paperwork. He told me to drive the Volkswagen home and he'd follow me on the motorcycle. As I drove, I constantly looked in the rearview mirror, I couldn't believe I had a motorcycle.

At home, my father told me to ride the motorcycle to the dead-end of the street. He wanted me to feel comfortable riding before going into traffic. I rode it up and down the street late into the night. I had to be told to come in and park the motorcycle. That night, I couldn't sleep. I was still thinking everything was a dream. I couldn't wait for the next day to ride it again. I still fed the hog I hated. Then it became clear to me. My parents had bought me a motorcycle because they weren't planning to let me drive their cars.

I rode my motorcycle to school and to nearby towns. I never had a curfew. But weekdays, I parked it at sunset and walked through the sugarcane field to sit with the local boys, talking. I was always back home before 9:00 p.m. on weeknights and never stayed out past midnight on weekends.

My father's Aunt Laura lived in Galveston, Texas. When we were young, my parents went to Galveston for their summer vacation. Audrey Mae, Josie and I stayed at Ma Flo's house. My parents brought us gifts and toys when they returned. We were happy for the toys because that was the closest we thought we'd ever get to Texas.

Now, my father had a white 1959 Ford Fairlane nine-passenger station wagon. That summer, the whole family, including Tee Nachie and Li'l Sister, traveled to Galveston. Abraham didn't go, so he agreed to feed the hog. I secretly hoped it would run wild and when I returned, it'd never be found.

This was our first long family road trip. I'd never traveled outside Louisiana. The furthest I'd gone before was New Orleans. Friday evening, I came in from school, changed the oil and washed the station wagon. I packed the car and mounted suitcases in the luggage rack. I even decided where everyone would sit. The rear seat faced out the rear window. Josie, Bobbie and I sat facing the rear. Li'l Sister and Tee Nachie sat in the middle seats, along with my baby sister, Judy, and the ice chest. Sam sat in front with my parents.

My father did all the driving. Li'l Sister brought fried chicken sandwiches and pound cake to eat on the road. The ice chest was full of sodas. We only stopped for gasoline and to use the bathroom. As we traveled, Josie, Bobbie and I counted all the bridges we passed. Later, my father corrected us and said we'd been counting overpasses, not bridges. Even though he explained the difference between the two, we continued counting overpasses as bridges.

In the early morning hours, we arrived in Galveston. As we drove down the seawall, we saw people swimming and surfing in the Gulf of Mexico. Laura and Robert came out to greet us. Laura loved to kiss, and she greeted everyone with a hug and kiss.

I couldn't escape the kisses. After her kiss, my jaw was wet. As people were getting out of the station wagon, I climbed on top to unstrap the suitcases. I brought them inside and immediately noticed Laura had a tiny house. No one told me she lived in a three-room shotgun house. I started to wonder where all these people would sleep, but Laura had it all figured out. She and Robert slept in their bed, the only one in the house. My parents slept on the sofa-bed. Li'l Sister slept in the recliner chair. Tee Nachie and the rest of us slept on the floor. Laura had nice clean bedding spread out on the floor in both rooms. And each morning, she cooked a Southern breakfast of grits, eggs, sausage, bacon, and toast for everyone. At dinner, she barbecued chicken and ribs, served with potato salad, peas and sliced bread. The kids drank all the sodas we wanted because the ice chest was always full.

Robert kept everyone giggling. He was full of life and a

natural comedian. He drank gin daily and carried a half-pint bottle in his back pocket. After a few sips, he'd take the party and laugher to a higher level. We never had a dull moment in his presence. Laura said on the weekends, Robert drank as though no more gin was being made.

Laura took us to the beach to swim in the Gulf of Mexico. We weren't good swimmers, but we had fun splashing in the water and riding waves. The adults sat on the beach, watching and taking photos of us in the water.

Having lived in Louisiana all my life, I had only known two kinds of people: White people and Black people. In Galveston, I saw people I had never seen before. I asked Laura who they were, and she said they were Mexicans from Mexico.

1971–1972 (Eleventh Grade)

I started the first semester doing mediocre work. I took all the required classes, but I didn't challenge myself. I did just enough work to get passing grades.

Only interested in band and business administration classes, I enrolled in Typing II and typed above 60 words per minute with no mistakes.

Again, the coach asked me to try out for track and field, and again I turned him down. My father told me, there was no benefit to running around a track field.

I no longer had to beg anyone for rides or hitchhike to summer band practice. I strapped my trumpet case to my motorcycle seat and away I went. It felt good not to have to rely on anyone.

Mr. Zito asked if I wanted to play the tuba. I felt privileged to be chosen. He recognized my talent and wanted to train me on a new instrument. It wasn't often a student got to play more than one instrument per semester.

He explained the tuba scale, how to read notes and correct fingering for the tuba, which was similar to trumpet fingering. I didn't fully comprehend the translation of notes from trumpet to tuba, but I had no problem playing the tuba. Sometimes, I didn't know which note to play, but I had a good ear and knew the songs we played. I faked reading the notes and Mr. Zito never complained.

When we were on the football field playing and marching in formation, I played all my music by ear. When I marched, I stepped high. I made sharp turns as I swung my tuba. Our signature formation was the school acronym, "WCHS."

I couldn't bring the tuba home to practice because it was a school instrument. Besides, it was too big to carry on my motorcycle. But I brought the mouthpiece home. I'd walk around the house, blowing into it. My favorite songs we played were the *Mission: Impossible* theme (I carried a strong bassline on this song) and the theme from *Hawaii Five-O*.

Again, Raymond and I cancelled study hall and used the hour to practice in the band room.

After football season, I returned to playing the trumpet as second chair for concert season. At graduation, we played "Pomp and Circumstance" repeatedly as the seniors marched across the stage to receive their diplomas. As I played, I couldn't help thinking this was my last time playing for graduation and that I'd march across the stage the following year.

On Saturdays, I still enjoyed watching *American Bandstand* on TV. Now a new dance show, *Soul Train*, featured all Black dancers. I'd watch it to learn the latest dance moves. I'd never been to a concert, so the closest I'd get to my favorite artists was seeing them perform on *Soul Train*. I was always overjoyed when Stevie Wonder or Al Green appeared on the show. They were, and still are, my favorite singers.

My cousin, Taylor, and I often went to teen dances at a community center in White Castle. The girls stood on one side of the dimly lit room, the boys on the other. Most of the lighting came from the doors' red exit signs. Whenever someone opened a door to the restrooms, more light filtered into the room. When the music began, boys would stroll across the room to ask a girl to dance. If a boy was dancing with a girl and another boy wanted to dance with her, he could cut in. A non-dancing boy tapped the dancing boy's shoulder. When that happened, you stopped and walked away; the other boy would dance with the girl. It was a more civilized time and I never saw any fighting or reluctance to stop dancing.

Some of my friends smoked marijuana. Bowing to peer pressure, I tried smoking with them, to prove I was cool and to satisfy my curiosity. I quickly learned I didn't like the paranoid effect pot had on me, so I stopped smoking, but continued hanging out with those friends.

My cousin, Herman "Pee Wee" Jones, invited me to join their four-piece band as a trumpet player. We practiced several songs for an upcoming birthday party. After our only gig, we disbanded due to a lack of interest by most of the players.

Mr. James, a schoolteacher at Dorseyville Junior High, formed a band; all its members were high school students. I had never heard them play, but I'd been told they were really good.

One Sunday afternoon, his band was playing at a local bar. As they set up, I wandered over and introduced myself. I told him I was a student at White Castle High and played trumpet in the band. I asked to join his band. He said he'd keep me in mind if he needed another trumpet player.

When they started playing, I was blown away. Their first song was Booker T. and the MGs' "Melting Pot." They played to perfection, every note and every beat right on time. The organist and guitar players were superb. It was the first time I'd seen a band with two drummers. They had really good horn players, too.

My uncles sang in a gospel group. Every Sunday morning, the Masonic Kings sang live on a local radio station, KEVL in White Castle. After attending morning Mass, I'd ride my motorcycle to the station and pretend to be there to assist my uncles in hauling their equipment. But honestly, I was using them to gain access to the radio station. After my uncles left, I'd go back inside to watch the DJ, Richard Ellis. He didn't know me, but he'd seen me come in with my uncles. When I said I wanted to watch him work, he invited me into the studio. I sat quietly in the studio and mentally took notes of his every move as he talked into the microphone and cued the music.

When the phone rang, he answered it and took requests. I enjoyed every minute I spent in the studio. I recorded everything he was doing in my mind. The cuing of records, timing the ends of songs and knowing exactly when to speak. At home, I used my portable recorder to practice what I'd seen Richard Ellis do. I told myself one day I'd perform on the radio. In my mind I was a DJ, and I couldn't let go of that dream. Even when my uncles didn't have to sing, I went to the studio and Richard Ellis let me sit and watch, but I could never touch any of the equipment.

One day I was riding my motorcycle during rush hour in Plaquemine. Traffic was slow when I noticed three girls on the sidewalk. They smiled and waved. Their pace was almost faster than the traffic, so I started flirting with them. I'd rev the engine and smile back. I was paying more attention to them than the road. Suddenly traffic stopped. I wasn't going fast, but when my front wheel hit the rear bumper of the car ahead of me, I was thrown over the handlebars and landed on the palms of my hands. I looked back at my motorcycle on the pavement. It was still running so I jumped up and inspected it for any damage. Meanwhile, traffic behind me had stopped and the car's owner was out of his vehicle, asking if I was okay. He realized there was no damage to his car and got back in as I pushed my motorcycle to the side of the street to let traffic flow. By now, the girls were laughing hysterically. I was embarrassed and ignored their laughter. I re-entered traffic with my attention on the road.

As my junior year came to an end and the summer months approached. I wondered what to do for the summer. Without telling anyone, I wrote to Laura, asking to come to Galveston. I told her I wanted to find a summer job.

Laura gave me her approval.

When my father found out, he was concerned I'd be a burden. He called Laura and they discussed my spending the summer there. He decided he would drive me there and, at the end of the summer, when she and Robert drove to Louisiana on vacation, I'd return with them.

Li'l Sister heard I was going to Galveston. She sent me to

the post office for an application for a Social Security number and helped me to complete it and within a few weeks, I had my Social Security card.

I could hardly wait for the last day of school and the day we'd leave for Galveston. My father had told me I'd do the driving. This would be the longest and farthest I'd ever driven. He told me to follow signs for Interstate 10 West and he napped in the passenger seat. He'd volunteered to take over the driving any time, but I wasn't about to relinquish the driver seat. I was having the time of my life.

Laura worked as a maid. Her boss owned a hotel and restaurant on Sea Wall Boulevard. Laura had spoken with him, and he agreed to give me a summer job. I'd work on the hotel grounds, assisting the maintenance man. My first day, I was introduced to a nice, middle-aged man. He didn't know who had hired me, he only knew I'd be his assistant. He gave me a tour of the workspace and explained my duties, such as washing hotel room windows, replacing burned-out light bulbs, touch-up painting, and upkeep of the lawn plants and hedges. It was my first real job, other than working on houses with my father, and I was eager to get started.

I did every job he assigned to me with no complaint. But my work as a maintenance assistant was short lived. I was washing windows and climbing up and down a ladder with a hose and bucket when Laura came to see what kind of work they had me doing. She saw me on the ladder and wasn't pleased. She went to the hotel owner's office and demanded he assign me another job, saying it was too hot for me to work in the sun. Plus, she said, climbing on a wet ladder was unsafe. She'd worked for him for years and they had a good relationship.

The owner came out and told me to come down off the ladder. It was my first time meeting him. He told the maintenance man I was being transferred to the Treasure Island Coffee Shop as a busboy.

Laura lived near Sea Wall Boulevard, so I walked to and

from her house to work. When I got home, I told her I'd been transferred and the next day I'd start work in the coffee shop. She told me she already knew. She explained she'd talked with the owner about my working in the heat. I was pleased she'd sought a new job for me. Working in the coffee shop was 100 percent better. Not only was it air conditioned, but the working environment was pleasant. I kept customers' glasses filled with ice water and when they finished eating, I bussed tables and brought the dishes to the dishwasher. At the end of my shift, I swept and mopped the dining room. Before going home, each waitress would give me a $1 tip for bussing their tables.

I saved the money I made and bought new clothing for school. Those days, the style was wearing matching-colored shirts and socks. I bought yellow, red and blue button-down collared shirts—all with matching socks. I bought black and blue trousers with cuffs high enough to show off the socks.

The manager, cooks and waitresses all approved of my work. At the end of the summer, I was told I could have a job there the next year.

Even though Robert drank a lot of gin, he never appeared drunk. My only complaint about him was he drove too slowly. Normally, the ride from Galveston to Bayou Goula was five hours. We left Galveston Friday evening with Robert driving 45 to 50 miles an hour on the freeway. I sat in the front. Laura sat in the back. Robert kept his bottle of gin in the trunk. Randomly, he'd stop on the highway, go to the trunk, take a sip, slam the trunk, and get back in the car. Laura was used to his driving, but I'd only ridden around Galveston with him. I knew he'd make frequent stops for a sip, but I had no idea he'd do the same on a long trip. I lost count of how many times he stopped. Laura slept on the backseat. I begged Robert to let me drive, but he always refused.

All night, we endured Robert's random highway gin stops. As the sun rose, and we were still en route to Louisiana. Thirty minutes from Bayou Goula, Robert was about to stop the car again. I said we were almost home, and we could make it without stopping. This was the only time he listened to me. The moment we pulled into the driveway (late morning), he went to the trunk for a sip of gin. Then he started with the jokes, and everyone laughed. Laura and I were dead tired, and we just wanted to go to sleep.

While I was away, my father and Abraham cared for the hog. I believed feeding the hog was too time consuming for them, so my father said it was time to kill it. Even though the hog wasn't big and fat like Plute's hogs, that news was music to my ears. I'd longed for the day to hear it was time to kill that hog. We took it to a slaughterhouse. Because the hog wasn't fat, we received little meat. Most of its parts weren't edible, but I didn't care, I was just happy to have the animal out of my life. However, the pecan trees continued shedding leaves, and tree branches continued to fall into the yard. I still had to mow the lawn, wash the cars and change the oil, plus do carpentry work with my father. These jobs, I preferred. The thought of not feeding a hog every day made me happy.

During the summer, Ma Flo had taken sick. After she was released from the hospital, she moved in with us. Once she recovered, she moved back home. Later, she developed a blood clot and a sore ankle that wouldn't heal. In September 1972, Ma Flo passed away.

Uncle Joe came home for her funeral. He wore his Navy uniform (crackerjack dress-blue jumper). When I saw him in uniform, it confirmed my decision to join the Navy after graduation.

1972–1973 (Twelfth Grade)

As a senior, the White students' relationship with Black students was far better than when I started at White Castle High. Some of my White friends called me their "Soul Brother #1." They didn't know what it meant. They heard other Black students say it, and I think the White boys thought it made them sound cool.

As a senior, I re-evaluated my life. I thought seriously about what I wanted to do after high school. My first conclusion was that my studies had been marginal. Though I felt the public education system was lacking, I carried most of the blame. I knew I had a good brain. But through the years, I didn't apply myself, and no one outside the classroom ever tracked my grades. I was the reason for my slacking off. Somewhere along the line, I stopped learning the concepts of a lesson. I succumbed to a bad habit of memorizing just enough to pass tests. And I wanted to be cool and not carry books to and from school every day. When I had to study, I carried sheets of paper in my back pocket. I always earned passing grades, but I wasn't doing my best work.

During my self-evaluation, I recognized my strong interest in music. I was a good trumpet player, a self-taught elementary-level organist and, in my mind, a disc jockey—though I'd never had the opportunity to perform. I couldn't immediately make a living in either of my musical interests. I decided with 100 percent certainty I wanted to join the Navy. I didn't know what I'd do in the Navy, but I wanted to be in the Navy. Now that I'd discussed my future plans with myself, I felt satisfied with my decision and was confident this was my next step.

But I still had to graduate from high school. I set two goals. I'd not made the honor roll since third grade, so my first goal was to make the honor roll by my final semester. My second goal was to join the track team. The coach had asked me since freshman year to join the team and each year, I'd declined.

I enrolled in all the required classes. I went to the gym and told the track coach I wanted to join the team. He didn't ask why I'd changed my mind; he simply said I was on the team. He'd seen my athletic abilities during gym class. I thought he'd assign me to a running event, but he had other plans for me.

The coach took me to the track field and introduced me to a jump pit, where students were practicing jumping into the sandbox. I had never seen this sandbox on the field. He explained the rules of jumping and told me he wanted me to compete in two jumping events: long jump and triple jump. I had never heard of either. As I watched students jump into the sandbox, I was confident I could do the jumps. But rather than letting me try, the coach led me back to the gym. In his office he had several tapes of professional jumpers performing long jumps and triple jumps. He told me to study the tapes, then he went back to the field. I knew I should do as he said, but I was thinking of my other goal: to make the honor roll. So, for two days I sat in his office and did my homework.

Finally, he told me I should have learned something from studying the tapes and he wanted me to try jumping. He brought me to the field and taught me how to mark a jump start position. I start running for the sandbox for my first jump. I hit the board perfectly, leapt and landed in the sandbox. When he measured my distance, he jumped and cheered. My first long jump was 19 feet. I'd just shattered the school's long jump record of 18 feet. As everyone cheered me on, it didn't register what I'd just done. The jump I completed was effortless and the coach was saying he believed I could jump further. He was sure the tapes had a big effect. I never told him I didn't watch them.

After successfully completing the long jump, he assisted

me in marking a triple jump start position. I started running for my first jump. I hit the first board with a hop and a skip and leapt into the sandbox.

The coach measured and yelled out, "Thirty-nine feet!"

The school triple jump record was 35 feet. My first day on the field, I'd broken both records and found my niche. But I still didn't quite understand what it all meant.

At the end of practice, the coach issued me a grey track uniform with maroon stripes. I'd never owned a jogging suit. The coach had yet another surprise for me. He assigned me as anchor for the mile relay.

At our first meet, I placed first in the long jump and took second place for the triple jump and the mile relay. I was awarded a trophy and ribbons. No one in my family knew I was on the team. It wasn't until I started bringing more trophies and ribbons home that they became aware. I'd tapped into a skill I didn't know I had, and it felt good. When I was passed the baton for the relay, I always felt it was my obligation to win, even if the previous runner didn't run his lap in record time.

I enrolled in woodshop class, because I thought I'd be able to do interesting carpentry work. Before entering the workshop, we had to read about carpentry tools. Because I'd done carpentry work since I was a youngster, I already knew the tools—and how to use them. This part of the class bored me, so my attention span was nonexistent. Because I was bored, I sat in the back of the class with Lionel Gilbert. As the other students read out aloud from the workbook, Lionel would say something funny to make me laugh. If he wasn't cracking me up, he was singing. So, I'd beat on the desk, adding rhythm.

Finally, the teacher had enough of our disturbing the class and sent us to the principal's office. I'd never been sent to the principal's office for misbehavior. Still singing and laughing, Lionel tried to convince me not to go to the principal's office. But I said we had to, so he followed me.

Busy with other school business, the principal asked why

we were there. When I told him, we were sent out to the track field to run a mile. Then he yelled for us to get out of his office.

As we headed to the track, Lionel insisted he wouldn't run in the hot sun. I tried to convince him, but he told me to go ahead and run, and he'd sit in the bleachers and watch. Every time I finished a lap, he'd laugh at me. I ran four laps and we reported back to the principal, who told us to go back to class. When we returned to the classroom, Lionel continued singing. I was quiet as a mouse. Misbehaving in the classroom wasn't in my repertoire. Lionel passed away in June 2021. He was a true friend.

The same day I was punished by the principal, we had a track meet, during which I broke another school long jump record. The next day, the principal asked if I thought my punishment had helped me break the record. We smiled and I knew that was his way of saying he was proud of me.

One day, after I completed my warmup runs and practice jumps, the coach sent me into the gym to study the professional jumper tapes. I noticed someone had left an almost-new pair of white Converse All-Stars high-top sneakers in the bleachers. In those days, All-Stars were very popular and expensive. They were my exact size. I'd never had a pair of expensive sneakers. I wore cheap ones to school. I thought hard about those sneakers. I'd never in my life stolen anything, but I really wanted them. I knew I'd be stealing, but in the moment, I felt weak. I couldn't control myself. I wrapped the sneakers in my towel and shoved them into my locker. When it was time to go home, I left the gym with the sneakers tightly wrapped inside my towel. I kept them hidden at home and didn't tell anyone. Not even my parents knew I had them. I couldn't wear them to school because I was afraid their owner would see them. I was uncomfortable with myself the whole time I held on to those sneakers. I knew in my heart I had no right to them. I promised myself I'd pay for those stolen sneakers.

While I served in the Navy, receiving a steady income,

every Sunday when I deposited money into the collection basket, I said a prayer for forgiveness for stealing the sneakers. Years later as an adult, during a conversation with my father, I told him about my stealing the sneakers from the gym. He told me I was forgiven, because as a man I'd confessed to my father. Stealing the sneakers had bothered me for a long, long time, but I felt my father had given me the ultimate forgivingness.

I was branded the best long jumper and triple jumper at White Castle High. I always finished in first, second, or third place in track meets at other district schools. At this point, my long jump had increased to 20 feet and my triple jump to 41 feet. Near the end of the season, we had only two more track meets: the district and state. I qualified for both, but still had not grasped my achievements in track and field. I was taking everything in stride.

District Track Meet

After winning at the district meet, the coach said the Louisiana State track meet would be at Louisiana State University. I'd represent White Castle High School in the long jump and triple jump events. He knew I'd face my toughest competitors at the state meet. His only request was that I do my best. I still didn't realize what a milestone this was, but I was thankful for the opportunities and achievements along the way.

I approached the State track meet at LSU as a regular meet. But, at the state competitions, my competitors made me jump farther. My best long jump was 21 feet 4½ inches; my best triple jump effort was 43 feet 6 inches. I finished in fifth place for both events.

It was my first time being defeated. I'd failed to work hard to improve my jumping abilities. Maybe I should have studied the tapes the coach encouraged me to watch. I went into the bleachers at LSU stadium and sat alone near the top. I flashed back to my early days on the track team and my accomplishments along the way. As I looked over the field, I saw other participants still competing. I wanted to go back out for one more jump. But it was too late, because it was all over.

Then I had another thought: I was one of the first Blacks to integrate White Castle High and a few short years later, I competed in the Louisiana State track meet. Before integration, Whites and Blacks didn't compete together in Iberville Parish. Plus, if integration had not occurred, I wouldn't be at LSU at all. I'd competed in an arena I couldn't even enter years earlier. This gave me a feeling of accomplishment. I didn't blame anyone else for my not winning. I blamed myself. Had I known earlier that track and field might have qualified me for a scholarship at a university, or possibly even an opportunity to participate in the Olympics, I'd have started freshman year. At the end of the track season, a bulletin board featuring all the school athletics was posted in the main hallway. My photo was there; printed underneath were my best long jump and triple jump records. That year, I was the number-one long jumper in Iberville Parish. My classmates dubbed me "Jumpin' Joe Walker."

Normally, after marching band season, Mr. Zito would transfer me back to trumpet. That year, he requested I play the tuba during concert season. Still the best of friends, Raymond and I practiced together on our own time.

One day near the end of the semester, the seniors were called into the gymnasium. When we were seated, the principal introduced a retired Naval officer. An old man with white hair in a dress uniform, who appeared to be in failing health, approached the microphone and talked about his Navy career. I don't remember anything exciting he had to say. His presentation didn't sway one student to join the Navy. I was sure I could've sold the Navy better than he had. Despite my assessment of his presentation, I still planned to join the Navy.

When I told my mother the cost for my class ring, she told me she didn't have $35. I knew I had to beg and nag at her until she gave it to me. She waited until the due date and then gave me the money.

I still wear that ring. Once I had it appraised; the jeweler told me the ring is now worth over $300.

Most of the White boys who bullied me in seventh grade didn't graduate. Most of them quit school or their families moved out of town.

When my final grades were tallied, I achieved my goal: I was an honor roll student in my last semester. I received no special recognition or award, but I didn't strive to make the honor roll for accolades. I did it to prove to myself I could do it if I applied myself.

From grades 1 through 12, I may have missed a total of three school days due to a cold. (My absence during the Civil Rights movement was justifiable.)

The night of my graduation, my mother and Emma Mae went. Emma Mae had attended all my school functions and church ceremonies. She was now supporting my last ceremony in Louisiana. In September 2015, Emma Mae passed away.

During the ceremony, I thought of all the things I wanted to do. I didn't share those plans with anyone. I couldn't stop thinking about how badly I wanted to join the Navy. I visualized myself in a Navy uniform and traveling the world. As diplomas were awarded, I returned my attention to the ceremony. I wanted to be alert when my name was called. Our names were always called alphabetically, so I was always last.

When my name was called, I walked to the stage, received my diploma and shook the principal's hand.

After the ceremony, we came home. Li'l Sister gave me $10, and Auntie Poncie and Tee Nachie each gave me $5. I didn't believe anyone was required to give me anything for finishing high school. But I was appreciative of the $20 I received. Someone took a photo of me in my cap and gown. I didn't know of any graduation parties, so I walked through the sugarcane field to sit in the parking lot of the Bonanza Bar with the other local boys.

The last week of school was half-day sessions. We took finals and were dismissed. I saw little of my friends, and never said a proper goodbye to anyone. Two weeks after graduation, I was gone.

Many local teenage boys worked in the sugarcane field on the weekends. It was the only available job for Black teenagers. My mother nagged me about getting a job in the sugarcane field. This was the last job I wanted to do, but I needed and wanted money, so I decided I'd work in the sugarcane field for a weekend.

I was hired to plant sugarcane. When the truck arrived at 5:00 a.m. several fieldworkers were already in it. Most of them were my cousins. They were already dirty, since they had on their work clothes from the previous day. When the farmer arrived in the field, the tractor drivers started their tractors and the planters positioned themselves between the rows. As we began work, the sun started to rise. I was in a row with my uncle. We pulled sugarcane from the same cart. At first, I kept pace, dropping the sugarcane in the rows. Because the tractor never stopped moving, I got behind and my uncle filled in the gaps I left. Soon, my arms were tired and the sun was *hot*. Planting sugarcane was hard labor.

At noon, everyone sat under a pecan tree to eat their bologna sandwiches and drink a soda. Soon, it was time to start planting again. When we left the field at 4:00 p.m., everyone was dusty and dirty. It was the dirtiest I'd ever been. I was tempted to not return. But I had to get paid. Next morning, I was still tired from the first day. I managed to survive the second day, and when the farmer said it was quitting time, he handed out the checks. I'd earned my pay. I was paid $21 for working the weekend. As I accepted my check, I knew I was never going back into the sugarcane field.

With my hard-earned money, I bought a silk shirt and gray bell-bottoms with a two-inch cuff. Because I worked hard to buy them, I kept those trousers as a reminder of the hard manual labor I did. Today, I still have the 28-inch waist trousers in my closet.

My red Honda CL-100 had served me well. Though I kept it clean and looking new, it began to succumb to its high mileage. The fastest it would go was 20 mph. Another major problem was the spark plug engine threads were stripped. My father decided to trade it in for a new one. We towed it to the dealer. I rode it in tow, making sure I didn't bump into my father's car whenever he stopped. I disconnected the rope, parked, and went to look at new motorcycles. We wanted a Honda CB-350. My father started negotiating. Once they agreed on a selling price, my father told the salesman we were trading in our CL-100, pointing to the clean shiny Honda in the lot. The salesman didn't bother to go and start the engine. We closed the deal, completed the paperwork and left. My father rode the new Honda home and I drove the Volkswagen.

When I left Louisiana, my father rode the motorcycle. Sam inherited the maroon bicycle I hadn't ridden for years.

Galveston, Texas
June–August 1973

We packed the car for our family trip to Galveston. Normally, I traveled light and packed my clothing into the same suitcase as everyone else. But on this trip, because I wasn't returning to Louisiana, I needed a separate suitcase. In the corn shed, I found an old, faded, fragile suitcase. I cleaned off the cobwebs and packed my clothing in it.

Laura had secured my job at the Treasure Island Coffee Shop. At the end of summer, I'd visit Audrey Mae and Uncle Joe in San Diego, with a long-term goal of joining the Navy.

Monday morning, I reported to work. Most of the people I met the previous summer were there. I was assigned the 7:00 a.m. to 3:00 p.m. day shift. I worked seven days a week and earned $65 a week. Plus, the three waitresses each gave me a $1 tip daily for bussing their tables.

With my first paycheck, I bought an AM/FM transistor radio. I missed going to sleep at night listening to the radio. I carried it with me to the beach. At night, I plugged in the earphone and fell asleep listening to it. I tuned in to a station out of Houston that played soul music. As I listened, I practiced being a DJ.

I never complained when I was told to work a different shift. When I worked the day shift, I walked to work. When I was transferred to nights, from 3:00 p.m. to 11:00 p.m., Laura didn't want me walking home in the dark; she picked me up. A cook got off work the same time, so Laura drove her home, too.

The first night Laura came to get us, I jumped into the

front passenger seat. Laura told me to get out and open the door for the girl, even though she was already in the backseat. We both exited the car, and I opened the door for her. Then I closed the door and got in the front seat. At the girl's house, Laura made me get out and open the door. Every night that Laura came to get us, I opened and closed the door for the girl. At the restaurant, she told everyone my aunt made me do that for her. They all said I was a chivalrous man.

I was sometimes assigned to work overnights, from 11:00 p.m. to 7:00 a.m. After working all night, when I walked home at 7:15 a.m. Saturday, I wanted to sleep. But Robert would shake me and whisper, "Wake up, let's go for a ride."

We'd go to folks' houses and he'd entertain them by telling jokes. Soon, he'd reach into his back pocket and bring out the pint-sized bottle of gin. Raising the bottle into the air, he'd say, "Hello Hilda" as he took a sip. Never missing a beat, he'd throw in another joke and everyone would laugh. Eventually, we ended up at the liquor store, where he'd buy another pint. Then we'd head home, and he'd fall asleep. Only then could I get in a few hours' sleep before going back to work. I never complained because he was fun to be with.

I knew going into the Navy I should know how to swim, but I was afraid of the water. To conquer my fear, I enrolled in a swimming class at the Galveston YMCA. The first day, I learned various swimming techniques, including how to float. I did well at the shallow end.

For my final test, I had to jump into the deep end. I climbed onto the diving board. It was flexible and bounced as I stood on it. As I collected my thoughts, the instructor reminded me to dive feet first.

When I hit the water, I went straight to the bottom. Looking up, I almost freaked out. But I remained calm, pushed up with my feet and sprang to the surface. I'd conquered my worst fear. I swam to the shallow end, then returned to the diving board and completed several more jumps.

I walked to the YMCA daily to swim. One day, a car pulled up beside me. The driver was a middle-aged White man. He asked where I was going, and I replied to the YMCA. He asked if I wanted a ride and I told him no.

Instead of driving away, he drove at a slow pace, following me. I started running and he accelerated. I detoured into an alley to lose him. When he was out of sight, I ran back to Laura's house. She was sitting on the porch with her neighbor. I was breathing hard, so she asked what happened. I told her of the man in the car and she told me to go in the house to rest. I also walked to Sacred Heart Church for Mass, but was never bothered again.

When I left the coffee shop, I told everyone I was going to California and planned to join the Navy. They wished me well; some cried because they knew they wouldn't see me again. The people I worked with at the coffee shop were like family.

At a men's store in Galveston, I bought a two-piece suit, a white shirt and a striped necktie. The fragile suitcase I'd retrieved from the shed was falling apart. I reinforced it with glue and tape. I bought psychedelic flower wallpaper and pasted it on the outside to give it a newer look. As the locks didn't work, I wrapped rope around the outside to keep it securely closed.

I said goodbye to Robert and told him how much I'd miss him. His eyes were almost teary. Laura drove me to the Galveston Greyhound bus station. I bought a one-way ticket to San Diego and checked my psychedelic-flower wallpaper suitcase. Laura had made me fried chicken sandwiches and told me to buy a soda when I was ready to eat. We said our goodbyes and hugged. She told me to call her once I arrived in San Diego. When the announcer made the boarding call, I got on, carrying my radio in one hand and the brown paper bag with my sandwiches in the other. I had $120 cash, all my savings. Laura told me to put it in my wallet and keep the wallet in my front pocket. It was my first time traveling alone. I was on my way to California with everything I owned.

I had no idea the ride from Texas to California would take

days. The bus stopped in almost every little town along the way. At each stop, we could get off to use the bathroom. Some folks got off the bus. Others got on. I didn't befriend anyone. I plugged in the earphone on my radio to keep me company. When the signal was clear, I listened to music. I just took naps; I wanted to be awake and see the things and places I'd never seen before. As I looked out the window, the signs were all about Texas. I'd been traveling for days, and we were still in Texas. I thought we'd never get out of Texas.

Finally, the driver announced we were entering New Mexico. I was thrilled to hear this. I saw mountains for the first time and thought the scenery was beautiful.

Once we left Texas, all I saw was desert. When we stopped in Arizona, the sun was bright, and I immediately felt heat. Something was different about the heat. It was a heat I'd never felt. A thermometer read 115 degrees. If I were in Louisiana with a temperature of 115 degrees, I'd faint. I didn't know why I was able to tolerate this heat without fainting.

After three days of riding the bus, the driver said we'd reached the San Diego city limits. It was sunset and I saw city lights in the distance and houses dotting the mountains. It was a beautiful sight.

San Diego, California
August 1973–September 1973

I was relieved to get off the bus. I retrieved my suitcase and walked to a pay phone. Audrey Mae's phone rang and rang. I called my cousin, Geraldine, and told her I was at the bus station. She said Audrey Mae worked the night shift but that she and her husband, Smitty, would pick me up.

. When Geraldine left Louisiana, she was single, but was now married. We greeted each other and she introduced me to Smitty. I took a liking to him immediately. They brought me to their apartment, and when Audrey Mae got off work at midnight, she came to get me.

The next morning, I called Laura to say I'd arrived. I thanked her for everything she'd done for me. Outside, the air wasn't hot like the air in Arizona. It was cool and refreshing. It felt like outside air conditioning. Audrey Mae explained to me that San Diego was a dry climate, with no mosquitoes and it seldom rained. I was in love with San Diego, and I'd only stepped outside Audrey Mae's front door.

Audrey Mae told me she was going to look for a new apartment. She didn't have a car and took the bus to work. We found a large one-bedroom apartment in National City. She borrowed a friend's car and I helped her move in that day. I noticed St. Rita's Catholic Church was nearby and that became the church I went to for Mass.

When Audrey Mae signed her lease, the manager asked about my status. She said I was visiting and was joining the Navy. He said I could stay as a guest for just two weeks.

I called Uncle Joe to tell him I was in San Diego. He told me he'd bring me to his house to see his wife, Faye, and my cousins, Pam, Tanya and Ricky. He joined the Navy the year I was born, and he was still serving. He had a four-piece band that played at all the Naval bases in San Diego. After I had met the family, he invited me to go to the club with him.

Uncle Joe sang and played organ. I helped him set up. He introduced me to the other band members and said I was free to wander around the club, but not to go outside the bar. Because I was non-military, he had to sponsor me to be in the club.

It was my first time seeing Uncle Joe perform. He was really good. I was surprised when a lady asked me to dance; after that first dance, I was ready to party.

I learned 21 was the minimum age to enter clubs in San Diego. But the minimum age was 18 on base. Any night Uncle Joe played, I went, too. He introduced me to many people and let me play tambourine with the band. "Love Train" was one of their signature songs.

When Uncle Joe didn't have to play, he gave me the keys to his car and I learned my way around San Diego. His Volkswagen had a military sticker, so I could drive onto any of the several military bases in the city. But I couldn't get into the Enlisted Men's (EM) Club, as I didn't have a military ID. So, I would stand outside and when a serviceman walked by, I'd ask him to sponsor me. Once inside, I was on my own. All the EM clubs in San Diego were party clubs, crowded with civilians. Having the time of my life, I longed to join the Navy, just to have my ID card and get into the EM clubs.

I was still in love with radio. San Diego had one good station. At night I'd listen to it and practice being a DJ. I made a comparison of the California radio DJs, but I preferred the Southern DJs.

I began relaxing my hair, to be like Uncle Joe. To be cool, I carried a shoulder bag and wore my sunglasses at night when I went to the EM clubs.

Behind Uncle Joe's house was a large hill, where the dirt slid down into the yard. He asked me to help him build a retaining wall. We graded the ground, then built a concrete foundation and a four-foot block retaining wall. He was impressed with the finished wall. He told me he didn't have a clue as to what I was doing. But he was good at repairing cars, which I hated. Whenever he worked on his cars, I stood back and watched, and tried to avoid getting any grease on me.

From the day I arrived in California, I felt I'd been set free. There were no public places I couldn't enter. I tested all the places, too. It didn't matter if I was the only Black person in the place. I entered classic restaurants, churches, upscale hotels and resorts. If I was at a hotel where a wedding reception was going on, I crashed it. The only public places I didn't enter were those with a minimum age of 21.

I went to my first live concert. The Watt STAX concert was held at the Coliseum in Los Angeles. Smitty and Geraldine invited Audrey Mae and me to go. We left early to avoid the traffic. When we arrived, we couldn't find a place to park., then we saw vacant parking meters on the street.

This was my first time seeing Richard Pryor live; he was the master of ceremonies. We were enjoying ourselves. Richard Pryor would tell jokes between performances. Suddenly, there was a big disruption. People started whispering about the Crips and the Bloods. I'd never heard of either of them. Teenage boys gathered on the field and started fighting.

Richard Pryor tried humor to calm the audience, but the Crips and Bloods had taken over. They were fighting and the crowd grew out of control. Yells and screams came from all sides. Due to the chaos, the next band was delayed. By that time, it was getting late, so we left.

We walked to where we thought we'd parked the car, but it wasn't there. As we stood on the street, trying to convince ourselves that was where we'd parked, we overheard other folks saying the same thing. After people had parked and gone inside, someone put up "no parking" signs. All the cars were towed. When we arrived at the tow yard, lots of other people from the concert were there. We had to pay to get the car back and we didn't get back to San Diego until 3:00 a.m.

Stationed at Naval Air Station Miramar, Uncle Joe invited me to go to work with him, to see the Navy up close and get some exposure to it. He was a chief aviation structural mechanic. In his workshop, I met sailors who worked for him and got to go on the flight line and see various aircraft. Back home, I'd only seen planes in the sky. I was now watching sailors work on them. They took me into the control tower, and I saw aircraft controllers communicate to pilots. Everything I'd seen excited me and I wanted even more to be a part of the Navy. My uncle's advice was to enlist in the Naval Aviation Program. That was some of the best advice I'd ever received.

Almost every night I was at the EM Club, where something was always going on. But now it was time to follow through with my plans to complete 20 years of military service.

Uncle Joe took me to the Navy recruiting office in National City. The recruiter escorted me into a private room, where I took the entrance exam. Uncle Joe waited for me. After the recruiter graded my test, he told me I didn't pass.

I was shocked and disappointed. My dream was to join the Navy, and I didn't have a backup plan.

The recruiter said he saw this all the time, people coming in unprepared. He recommended I study the ARCO Military Test Tutor book and retake the test.

We left his office and went to the library to check out the book he'd recommended. I set up a routine for myself and studied at least five hours daily.

Meanwhile, I learned about the Navy Band. Because I'd been a good trumpet player, I scheduled an audition. I didn't know the steep qualifications to become a member of the Navy Band. Sight reading was mandatory, plus it helped if you played more than one instrument professionally. I read music, but once I learned a song, I played by ear. At my audition, the instructor presented sheet music for songs I'd never heard. I fumbled my way through them. The Navy expected its musicians to be able to read any piece of music presented. I didn't pass the audition.

After studying the ARCO Military book every day, I felt ready to re-take the exam. When I walked in the door, the recruiter remembered me. I told him I was ready to re-take the test. Even though I felt confident, I said a quick prayer. When I completed the exam, I gave it to the recruiter and watched as he graded it. I passed. Quietly, I gave thanks to God. The day before, I'd gone to the weekday Mass. When I left the church, I saw a vision of myself in a Navy uniform. The recruiter said he'd call me in a few days to let me know when I'd start boot camp.

I walked back to Audrey Mae's apartment feeling good. I called Uncle Joe and told him I'd passed. Then I called Audrey Mae at work and told her the good news.

Two days later, the Navy recruiter called. "Walker, are you ready to go to boot camp?"

He told me to be at his office in two hours to ship out.

Hundreds of thoughts flowed through my mind as I prioritized things to do. I called Audrey Mae at work and told her I was leaving immediately. I left my remaining $80 for her. I called my parents and Uncle Joe and told them I was on my way to boot camp.

The recruiter told me not to bring anything. I left with only the clothes I was wearing, my wallet, the crucifix around my neck, and a toothbrush in my pocket.

Naval Training Center
San Diego, California
September 1973–November 1973

When I arrived at 4:30 p.m., the recruiter was waiting at the door. We discussed paperwork he'd prepared for me. He gave me transportation passes, a city-bus pass to the San Diego Greyhound station and a one-way ticket to Los Angeles. Holding tight to my large brown envelope of Navy paperwork, I left his office to wait for the city-bus.

On the bus ride to Los Angeles, I sat next to an elderly woman and told her I was joining the Navy. I was proud to say it. She congratulated me and assured me I'd enjoy the Navy life.

In Los Angeles, I followed the recruiter's directions to a hotel downtown, where a recruiter assigned me a room to share with another guy and gave me a ticket for dinner at the hotel restaurant. There, I met several other new recruits. Later, we played pool in the lobby until we were told to go to bed.

The next morning after breakfast, we boarded a Navy bus to a government building downtown, where an extensive physical examination process started. If you didn't pass the physical exam, you were sent home.

We were ushered into a large room with about 40 guys, ages 18 to 20. We lined up, 10 to a row. A commander entered the room and everyone was told to raise their right hand and repeat the oath of enlistment. As we were sworn in, I felt proud to be among my fellow recruits.

After our swearing in, the commander said, "Congratulations! You're in the Navy."

Then we followed the chief to the parking lot. Each of us was given a plastic bag and told to pick up cigarette butts.

Some guys complained, saying, "I didn't join the Navy to pick up cigarette butts."

But no one refused. I'd had years of experience picking up pecan limbs, so it didn't bother me.

After dinner, we were told to go to bed early because we'd be going to San Diego the next morning. We were awakened at 3:00 a.m. to board the Navy bus. The civilian driver didn't speak a word as he drove. Some guys were cursing or talking loudly, but most of us were trying to sleep. When we arrived, it was still dark.

When we stopped, a Marine boarded the bus, yelling at us to get off. He pushed guys as they exited and yelled for us to fall in at attention and stand on the white dot. Guys scrambled to find an available dot. Some guys stood at attention, but not on a white dot. They were told to get down and do push-ups. This got everyone's attention, and we wondered what was going on. Still the sun had not risen, and we were all in a state of confusion.

Everyone quickly learned the purpose of the white dots. We learned to shut up and stand at attention. The Marine was fully in charge.

"Who can sing?" he yelled out.

A few guys raised their hands, and the Marine was all in their faces. He started insulting them and telling them they wished they could sing. I saw those who said they could sing march away and disappeared into the dark.

"Who can march?" he yelled. I wasn't about to raise my hand after seeing those other guys march away into the dark. Those who raised their hands were also sent away. Later, I learned the guys who left were assigned to a choir and the military drill team.

The remainder of us were assigned to Company 304. The

Marine left, and a Navy chief was now in charge. He'd be our Company Commander (CC) for the rest of boot camp. He must have taken lessons from the Marine because he yelled as much as the Marine did. I quickly learned there wasn't a thing recruits could do to please the CC. No matter what you did, he'd still yell at you.

Soon we were marching everywhere. Some recruits were confused and didn't know their right from their left when making a turn. The CC would yell, "Not your left, the Navy left!"

We marched to a large building, where everyone was issued a sea bag. We marched through the building and at each of various stations, a piece of clothing was thrown to us to put into our sea bag. At the end of the queue, we had full sea bags, including skivvies, T-shirts, shoes, hats, dungarees, towels, soap, toothpaste, and everything else we'd need. I was disappointed when they issued us the Navy dress blue uniform. I didn't know they'd just implemented a new policy change for the enlisted uniform. Enlisted sailors were no longer issued the crackerjack sailor uniform and white sailor hat. Instead, we received a dark double-breasted jacket, white shirt and black necktie with a combination hat.

Finally, we exited. Everyone marched with a heavy sea bag full of clothing; we were expected to keep in step as we marched to the barrack, our home for the next eight weeks. Once there, we were still being yelled at. Some guys started to cry because they couldn't follow instructions, so they were given extra duty. We were told nothing we'd brought—including clothing we'd worn—could remain in our custody. Given boxes, we were told to pack everything and mail it home. I only had my clothing, wallet and crucifix. I'd worn a crucifix since I was 10. Now dog tags would replace my crucifix.

Going forward, we had nothing of our own. Everything was issued by the Navy. We had no personal identity. Everyone had the same haircut—bald. I had a mustache, but I'd never shaved. The Navy issued us shaving kits and insisted everyone shave daily. Today, I still use the shaving kit I was issued in boot camp. I've tried other shavers, but I prefer my Navy issue.

We woke every morning while it was still dark. Recruits who had a hard time waking up early and getting started had problems. Every morning, the CC inspected each recruit for facial hair, all buttons buttoned, shoestrings tied, ID card inserted into the coat pocket correctly, zippers zipped, and no lint in pockets, among other things. After two or three inspections, you'd think recruits would know exactly what the CC was looking for. Still, every day several recruits failed personal inspection and were assigned extra duty.

We were taught how to fold our clothing. Everything had to be folded a special way, with no margin for error. When done correctly, everything fit perfectly in a small compartment locker. Those having a difficult time learning how to fold clothes were given extra duty. If one item wasn't folded correctly, the CC threw everything on the floor. After inspection, it wasn't uncommon to see a locker thrown to the floor with everything inside tossed about the barrack. If a rack (bed) wasn't made up correctly, with the blanket folded and centered on the rack, the mattress was tossed to the floor. If this was done, the recruit had to start all over again. Some recruits cried when they didn't pass inspection. I was a quick learner, and I was good with details. The making of the rack was easy for me. I never failed inspection. Recruits often asked me to help them with folding their clothes and making up their rack. I assisted one recruit with preparation for inspection and he finally passed. That day he decided not to sleep in his rack again; he slept on the floor for fear of failing another inspection.

I'd been in Company 304 for a week when the CC told me to report to the Battalion Office. I thought I must have done something terribly wrong. *But what?* I'd passed every inspection. And daily I assisted and taught other recruits how to pass their inspections. I'd become popular in the company. The only thing I could think of was, perhaps, someone had reported me for helping recruits pass inspection.

I entered the Battalion Office, braced to be yelled at and belittled. Since I started boot camp, anyone who addressed a recruit yelled. Even if the recruit had done a good job, he was still yelled at. To my surprise, the chief warrant officer greeted me with a smile. He said I'd been selected, along with two other recruits, to work in the office as a battalion yeoman. My job was answering phones and typing paperwork when a recruit was processed out of the Navy. I assumed someone had checked my personnel record and learned I had excellent typing skills.

When there was no typing to be done, we had to study the Bluejacket Manual (Navy basic handbook). We also had to know the eleven General Orders on command—I knew them backward and forward. We spit shined our boots daily. Because of my work assignment, I was issued a dog tag with special privileges. I could walk outside the recruiting area during the day without permission. If a chief or officer saw me, I flashed the dog tag and they'd say, "Carry on." I could walk to the Navy Exchange because I had this special privilege. Other recruits couldn't go anywhere without marching with the company.

At the end of the day, I reported back to Company 304. I slept in the barrack with the other recruits. Everyone in Company 304 knew me, but I didn't train or march with them daily. However, I had to report to certain mandatory classes. These included scholastic testing, damage control, firefighting, first aid, weapons, Uniform Code of Military Justice (UCMJ) and swimming.

Everyone was ordered to dress in their swimming trunks and report to the Olympic-sized pool for the swimming class. The instructor said it didn't matter if we didn't know how to swim, but everyone had to get in the pool. He gave instructions regarding which swimming methods we'd need to complete to pass the test. Everyone was expected to swim the length of the pool, tread water and float. If a recruit couldn't perform these tests, he'd be held back an extra week in boot camp to learn how to swim. The instructor had a long pole in his hand. If a recruit who couldn't swim started sinking, the instructor would pull him to the side of the pool. He said if we panicked and started to climb up the pole, he'd let go.

One at a time, a recruit would jump into the pool and start the swim test. Some recruits who couldn't swim were afraid to jump in the water. The instructor pushed them in with his pole. Once they started sinking, some recruits panicked and tried to climb up the pole. He pulled them out with the pole, and they were sent to a swimming class. Swimming wasn't my strong point, but I'd learned the basics at the YMCA in Galveston. I positioned myself at the end of the queue. By the time I had to jump in, it was late in the day, and the instructor had been yelling at non-swimmers all day. I figured, being the last swimmer, he'd want to get it over with quickly. I jumped in like a pro.

I'd swum halfway around the pool when the instructor yelled to me, "Get out of the pool, you passed."

I got out and said, "Thank you, Jesus!" Had I continued, I'd have failed and would've been sent to swimming class and an extra week in boot camp.

I had to stand duty watch in the barrack, same as the others. We stood a 15-minute watch, which meant we wore a duty belt, carried a flashlight, and walked around inside the barrack while the other recruits slept.

All recruits were scheduled for a dental checkup. I'd never been to a dentist. I was fascinated with the dental chair and the instruments. When I had my exam, the dentist said I had strong teeth, but they hadn't grown in straight and I had cavities. He said when I checked in at my next duty station, the Navy would fill the cavities. He cleaned my teeth—it was my first time having them cleaned. I didn't know people had their teeth cleaned twice a year.

At Thanksgiving, selected local recruits were allowed to go home. Because I'd listed San Diego as my home address, I was granted permission to go home, and I could take three recruits with me. I invited my three best friends. They were from Texas and were in California for the first time. Uncle Joe couldn't believe I was able to leave before graduation, plus bring other recruits with me. We wore our dress-blue uniforms. Uncle Joe had never seen the new enlisted dress uniform and he said we looked sharp. I still would have preferred the sailor crackerjack uniform.

Faye cooked a large Thanksgiving dinner. After dinner, Uncle Joe gave me the keys to his car. I wanted to take my friends to the EM Club, but it didn't open until 7:00 p.m.—and we had to be back at 6:00 p.m., so we drove around San Diego to see some of the sights.

Finally, graduation day arrived. The recruits I'd met eight weeks earlier were no longer confused or misdirected recruits. We'd matured, bonded, and developed trusted friendships. We were part of something bigger than ourselves. We wore our Navy uniforms with pride.

I learned everything in boot camp the other recruits learned, except marching. Because I was a battalion yeoman, I hadn't done the daily marching and didn't know the maneuvers Company 304 had learned. On graduation day, they perform marching maneuvers on the field. As we prepared to go to the graduation field, I approached the CC to ask what I should do. He said I'd sit in the stands with the guests. Because I still had my special dog tag, I walked to the graduation field, where the civilians had assembled. I sat in the stands in my dress-blue uniform, waiting for the ceremony to start. Soon an announcement was made and the graduation companies marched across the field, performing sharp marching maneuvers. The civilians cheered and clapped. Finally, Company 304 appeared. I waved to my friends. I didn't feel bad about not marching. I'd have looked like Gomer Pyle, marching out of step.

After the ceremony, civilians ran onto the field, and I joined them. Recruits in Company 304 were hugging and congratulating each other. Some of my friends grabbed my hand and led me to meet their families and girlfriends. I got to meet people they'd talked about throughout our training. I had no family member present. After meeting many families, I walked to the Base Exchange with recruits who had no family in attendance.

The day after graduation, we boarded a Navy bus to a Navy park in San Diego for a picnic. Throughout boot camp, most of the recruits talked about how they longed for a beer. Finally, they had the opportunity to partake of one. We were served hot dogs, hamburgers, chips, sodas and all the beer we could drink. I drank soda and ate all the hot dogs and hamburgers I wanted. My friends had been drinking beer, and I was among the few sober recruits. My drunken friends decided I should drink, too, so they wrestled me to the ground and poured beer in my mouth. I didn't like the taste, but to get them to stop, I agreed to switch to drinking beer. Once I was walking around with a beer in my hand, they were satisfied. The rest of the day, I sipped the same beer. On the bus ride back, I was still sober, while most of the other recruits were smashed.

Most of my friends received orders to an "A" School. My scholastic test scores didn't qualify me for that. But, having chosen to pursue the Naval Aviation Program, I was assigned a two-week aviation apprenticeship class at the Naval Training Center.

Upon completing the class, I was qualified to work in the Navy aviation fleet. I was to report to Naval Air Station Fallon, Nevada, within 30 days. I had no idea where Fallon, Nevada, was. Uncle Joe had served there. I asked whether the base had an EM Club; he assured me it did and didn't elaborate on more. That's all I needed to know. I knew I'd enjoy my tour in Nevada.

Armed with my military ID card, I was at the EM Club every night. I'd even sponsor civilians waiting to go in. I remembered waiting for someone to sponsor me and paid it forward.

I was having the time of my life, until Uncle Joe asked if I was going to Louisiana before reporting to Fallon. He reminded me that everyone at home probably would like to see me in my Navy uniform.

Bayou Goula, Louisiana
December 1973

My sea bag was packed with my Navy and civilian clothing. Holding my one-way airline ticket to Baton Rouge and wearing my dress uniform (as an E-1, airman recruit, I had one emerald stripe), I made my way through the airport. Many civilians asked about the new uniform.

During my check-in, the agent asked if I wanted to sit in the smoking or non-smoking section. I didn't smoke, but I thought people who smoked were cool, so I sat in the smoking section.

I'd just completed my aviation apprenticeship, so I felt unafraid taking my first flight. As the pilot started the engines, I mentally reviewed lessons from my class, especially the launch requirements.

When my plane landed in Baton Rouge, my father met me. He commented on how nice I looked in my uniform. On the drive home, we chatted about the things I'd done since we last saw each other in Galveston.

We stopped at Li'l Sister's house, so she, Riley and Bobbie could see me in my uniform. At home, I was greeted by my mother, Josie, Judy, and Sam. In the few months I had been gone, they had grown an inch taller. In my mind, they were still the babies whose diapers I'd changed.

The next day I went to visit relatives and friends. We sat and talked for hours. Everyone offered to feed me. California's drinking age was 21, but in Louisiana it was 18, so I went to a bar to see Li'l Frank. On his break, we talked, and I told him I'd joined the Navy. I told him about Uncle Joe's band. Uncle Joe tried to encourage Li'l Frank to come to California, but he didn't want to leave Louisiana. Li'l Frank is now deceased, but he was always my Black Elvis Presley.

Sunday morning, I wore my dress blues to Mass. Most people there were surprised to learn I had joined the Navy. The Blacks still sat in the pews on the right-hand side of the church.

New Year's Eve night, I was with my friends at the Bonanza Bar. In prior years, I knelt to pray at the stroke of the New Year. Around 11:30 p.m., I slipped out, unnoticed. I went home and, as the clock struck midnight, I was on my knees. I prayed and thanked God for another new year. When I went back to the bar, no one ever knew I had left.

After two weeks in Louisiana, I was ready to go to Fallon. I wanted to make sure I arrived prior to my report date. I said my goodbyes and my father drove me to the airport, where I bought a one-way ticket to Reno.

Naval Air Station Fallon, Nevada
Public Affairs Office,
Special Services and Maintenance
January 1974–January 1976

The pilot announced we were minutes from landing. It was a night landing, and as I looked out the window, the city lights flickered. In the terminal, I saw slot machines for the first time in my life. People were depositing coins. Lights flashed, bells rang. I took a nickel from my pocket and deposited it in one of the machines. As I pulled the handle, a security guard asked to see my ID. I proudly flashed my Navy ID card. He said I had to be 21 to gamble. I glanced into the slot machine's tray, thinking I might have won money, but nothing was there, so I walked away and went to retrieve my sea bag.

I'd never seen snow and was excited to see the white flakes falling to the ground. Although it was cold, I couldn't help grabbing some of it and making my first snowball. It must have been snowing for some time because there was a lot of snow on the sidewalk.

At the bus station, I saw more slot machines. With no security guard in sight, I deposited a few coins in the machine, but I didn't win anything. That satisfied my interest. I felt no need to put more money into a machine that didn't pay out.

As the largely empty bus departed Reno, I saw fewer city lights and soon there were none. As we rode through snow-covered mountains, I recalled the good times I'd had in San Diego.

We had been riding for little more than an hour when we arrived in a town with few lights and one flashing yellow caution light. It was downtown Fallon. I could easily run a 100-yard dash through downtown. It was that small.

We stopped at a casino. I went inside, feeling like I had entered the Wild West era. Real cowboys wore cowboy boots and hats. I even heard country and western music playing. I saw more slot machines, but had no interest in playing. I hoped the base EM Club would be as good as the ones in San Diego.

I went to the pay phone and dialed the number for Naval Air Station (NAS) Fallon. As I waited for the duty driver, I saw people gambling. Many were playing cards and some played a game that involved throwing dice.

As we left downtown Fallon, the driver took a country road with no streetlights. I saw some lights far off in the distance and assumed it was the Navy base. I asked if there was an EM Club on base and he replied there was, but didn't elaborate.

As we entered the base, it didn't look like the bases I had visited in San Diego. It looked deserted. The driver took me to the administration building to check in.

Everyone was away for the weekend and I was told to report back Monday morning. In the new barrack, which was within walking distance, I saw a few sailors in the lobby watching TV. They introduced themselves and welcomed me aboard. Normally, two sailors were assigned to a room, but I was assigned to a room alone.

I started unpacking. The sailors in the lobby invited me to watch TV, but I didn't feel like being sociable. I sat in my room, thinking I had been sent to the end of the earth. Everything was spooky quiet. Plus, it was cold and snowing. I told myself the Navy should have assigned me to a base in San Diego since there were so many of them. It was Saturday night. If I were in San Diego, I would be at the EM Club. Instead, I was in a lonely room on a Navy base in Fallon, Nevada.

The next day, after Mass, I walked to the chow hall and met other sailors. One had just come from boot camp; he was in Company 303 and had seen me in Company 304. I wasn't surprised he recognized me; my special privilege dog tag had allowed me to walk by many companies standing at attention. He was from Texas. We became good friends. Another guy in boot camp with us had also been sent to Fallon. As we sat, eating and chatting, the sailors filled me in. Mostly civilians worked here. NAS Fallon was a remote base and provided support to fleet squadrons. Everything they said made me wish I was in San Diego. After lunch, we walked to the base EM Club. I saw one car in the parking lot. When we went inside, I was heartbroken. The only person there was the bartender. I had naïvely thought every Navy EM Club would be like the ones in San Diego. Now I understood why Uncle Joe didn't say much about Fallon. He didn't want me to be disappointed before my arrival. The sailors were excited to play pool, which was the main thing to do. There was no live band, no queue of people to come inside and dance. Oh, how I missed the San Diego EM Clubs.

Monday morning, I reported to the administration office to complete my check-in process. I was paraded through the office so everyone could see the new enlisted uniform. I received many compliments on my smart uniform. I even heard comments that I looked like a model sailor. I was assigned to the Public Affairs Office (PAO).

Two attractive women worked there. A tall, shapely blonde ensign, about 25, managed the department. A lovely second-class petty officer was about 21. Aware of my boot camp training and protocols, all my replies were, "Yes, ma'am," as they tried to get me to relax.

I was briefed on the duties of PAO. On a larger naval base, the PAO controlled the base broadcasting communication (radio and TV). When I heard "radio," they had my full attention. I knew this was where I wanted to work. As they continued the briefing,

I was told smaller bases didn't operate broadcasting facilities. Instead, at NAS Fallon, the PAO published the base weekly newspaper. I would be trained to assist with that.

Carrying a portable tape recorder and camera, I interviewed sailors on base. When I returned to the office, the second-class petty officer helped me write stories. She taught me how to search local papers for interesting articles. Every Thursday, we went to the print shop downtown, where we manually cut and pasted the articles. Once the formatting was completed, we printed the paper. I would distribute them throughout the base on Friday morning. Monday, we started the process all over again.

All sailors received an annual written evaluation. The highest mark was 4.0. My first enlisted evaluation was all 4.0s. Because I was always sharp, patriotic and proud to serve, everyone on base started calling me "4.0 Joe." They also referred to me as a "Lifer" because I planned to complete 20 years of service. Most sailors wanted to complete their enlistment and go back to their hometown.

As months passed, I continued to think NAS Fallon was the worst duty station. Being under 21 years old, there wasn't much I could do there. I told the chief I wanted to be transferred to San Diego. He told me I could transfer to a ship in San Diego, so I filled out a request chit. I wanted to be in San Diego just to go to the EM clubs. After work, I told some of the senior sailors I had submitted a request chit to be transferred to a Navy ship. They had served on many Navy ships and began telling me about the working and living conditions. Nothing they said sounded good. I reminded myself I was bunked in a new barrack building, in a private room. Their advice was, "The worst shore duty is better than the best sea duty." The next day, I told the chief I'd changed my mind. As he tore up my chit, he said I had made the right decision.

I was getting antsy in PAO. I wanted a different job. If the PAO had a radio station, I would have been more interested in working there. But publishing a weekly newspaper was no longer interesting. I expressed my job dissatisfaction and was told about an opening in Special Services. I had no idea what Special Services did, but I accepted.

Special Services managed all the recreational activities on base, including the bowling alley, theater, gymnasium, hobby shop and pool. My assignment was in the gym. The chief brought me to meet my new supervisor, an E-6, petty officer first class. He gave me a tour and explained the routines for maintaining the facility. Camping gear and ski equipment were kept in the gym, so sailors came there to check them out. I figured working there would be fun and easy. I could work out, play racquetball or lift weights all day and not have to wear a uniform or stand duty watch.

Later that day, a new hire arrived: another recruit who had gone to boot camp with me. We had both advanced to E-2, airman apprentice. Each morning, we cleaned the basketball court, and scrubbed and cleaned the showers before the gym opened at 7:30 a.m. We issued sporting gear, camping gear and whatever else was requested. In between, we played basketball and racquetball with the customers. During baseball season, we maintained the baseball field and the golf driving range. We secured the gym at 4:00 p.m.; a civilian worked the night shift until 11:00 p.m. When I left work, I would go to the chow hall for dinner, then I returned to the gym, where the sailors went after work to play basketball. Sometimes, I would assist the night shift with closing.

I'd only been in Special Services about two months when the first-class petty officer got his transfer orders. When I asked who our new gym supervisor would be, he said he and the chief felt confident I could manage the facility. Just like that, I became the supervisor. I'd never supervised or managed others, but I wasn't about to let them down.

My first week as supervisor, I went to the chief to report the gym was ready for inspection each morning after we finished cleaning. He inspected all our workspaces. After a few inspections, he said he didn't need to do inspections. He said, "I trust you."

Beginning that day, I performed daily inspections, managed, and reported money collected from sports-gear rentals. I made decisions regarding staff work schedules and duties.

I'd watched the sailors who came in to play basketball. They played well and with passion. I suggested to the chief we form a base basketball team. He said he would support whatever I wanted.

I discussed the idea with the sailors, who were onboard. A nearby junior college had a basketball team, so I made calls and scheduled a game.

The NAS Fallon basketball team played the Quincy Junior College basketball team. We lost, but we all had fun. It got the sailors away from the base and exposed them to a civilian community. On our return, we stopped at McDonald's; the chief had given me money to buy the team burgers, fries and drinks.

Because I successfully managed the daily operations of the gym, I was assigned to manage the base theater. Only one movie showed each night. During the summer months, teenage military dependents ran the projector and sold tickets and concessions.

I was also given responsibility for making the Navy money exchange. Each day the Shore Patrol escorted me to the Fallon bank with funds collected from the theater, bowling alley, gym, discount tickets and all other Special Services activities. I completed my transaction while the patrols stood guard at the bank entrance with machine guns.

I advanced to E-3, airman, and the chief wrote me a special evaluation. I received 4.0s across the board. His writeup stated, "As an airman, Airman Walker is assigned the duties and responsibilities of a senior petty officer."

Airman Walker

When the chief told me I had been awarded Sailor of the Quarter, I was shocked. I received a plaque, a 72-hour liberty, and dinner for two at the Fallon Nugget.

My division officer recommended me for the Navy Broadened Opportunity for Officer Selection and Training (BOOST) Program. It was designed to help junior sailors become officers. He made arrangements for me to go to Naval Station Treasure Island, California, to begin testing.

I was transported to California on a Navy aircraft. I was assigned a room and told to get a good night's sleep as my testing would start early the next morning.

The testing process was explained to me. There would be several parts: history, math, science, mechanical and English; the testing would take all day. Each exam section was timed. Some of the math problems were difficult and the history questions had never been a part of my education. I didn't pass. I knew I was capable, but I wasn't a scholar.

When I returned to base, my division officer encouraged me to enroll at the community college in Fallon. I took a math class at night. Prior to taking the BOOST exam, I was satisfied just being in the Navy. Now I looked through a different set of lenses and expected more from myself. My division officer planted a seed, and now it was my responsibility to nurture it. I began visualizing myself as an officer. I would tell myself, "Lieutenant Walker sounds better than Airman or Petty Officer Walker." I knew it wouldn't be easy, but I was ready to do whatever it took to obtain a Navy commission. I believed in myself, and I had faith.

NAS Fallon was a training base, and after a race riot aboard the USS Kitty Hawk, the Navy implemented required race-relations training for everyone. The E-6, first-class petty officer in charge, asked how long I had been working in Special Services among other questions. He insisted I was being denied advancement because of my race.

I disagreed, said I enjoyed my job in Special Services, and would someday like to work in aviation maintenance. He asked me to sign a document indicating I had been counseled. I signed it without reading it entirely.

The next day, my chief called me into his office. I didn't know why he was upset, because we had a perfect working relationship. He trusted me to manage the gym and I trusted him.

"Walker, I've honestly respected all your wishes and

supported whatever you wanted to do," he said. "So I don't understand why you would report that I'm denying you advancement. Why didn't you come and talk to me if you weren't happy in Special Services?"

He explained he had received a discrepancy report from the E-6, first-class petty officer of race relationship, indicating he had denied my advancement. This was false, but I had signed the document without reading it. I tried my best to explain the situation, but I don't think I convinced him.

We discussed my future career plans. I told him I enjoyed working in Special Services, and he said I had been quite valuable there. Then he said if I wanted to transfer to aircraft maintenance, he would support me.

I was an E-3, airman, and had completed the Petty Officer Leadership Course. I was waiting to take the E-4, petty officer third class exam. We agreed I should transfer to maintenance where I could work in aviation maintenance. I would get hands-on experience before my transfer date. We parted on good terms.

NAS Fallon had one UH-1N helicopter. It was used for search-and-rescue operations. Also, transient aircraft flew into NAS Fallon for refueling.

After reviewing the various aviation ratings, I decided to strike for Aviation Maintenance Administrator (AZ). Out of all my Navy testing, I scored highest in clerical. Plus, I had learned additional organizational skills. An AZ maintained the aircraft logbooks and performed various trend analysis, administrative and managerial duties. An E-6, first-class petty officer (AZ1) was assigned as my mentor. He wasn't overly eager to train me, but he answered my questions, and his assistance prepared me for the E-4, petty officer third class exam, which I passed.

Still the junior sailor in the shop, I had to make coffee and perform field day.

I learned plane captain duties and procedures for aircraft launch and recovery. I enjoyed driving the tow tractor and, when moving aircraft in and out of the hangar, I was assigned as a wing walker. I assisted with washing and refueling the aircraft.

One night when I was on duty, we received a call of an incoming aircraft. As it was my first time performing as a plane captain at night, I reviewed in my mind everything I had learned. I was assigned to direct the aircraft in, using the night wands while the senior petty officer chocked the wheels.

During weekend duty at the hangar, we drove the duty truck to the chow hall at lunchtime. Rather than drive around the base to the chow hall, we took a shorter route by driving across the runway (which was legal).

Because Fallon was a remote base, aircraft seldom landed. One day, I was in the truck alone. The procedure for crossing the runway was to drive to the crossing point of the runway and stop, then radio the tower to request permission to cross. I stopped, picked up the microphone and, in my DJ voice, said, "Fallon 41 (the truck) permission to cross Fallon 25 (the runway) on the parallel."

If there was no traffic coming, the tower would respond, "Fallon 41, permission granted."

This day, there was no incoming aircraft within my sight. The tower responded, "Fallon 41, hold."

I had never been told to hold. I didn't hear the word "hold." Instead, I automatically drove across the runway.

The radio started blasting, "Fallon 41, what are you doing? I told you to hold! Report to the tower immediately!"

When I arrived, the duty officer chewed me out, saying I could have killed someone including myself. All I could do was stand at attention. That day, I developed better listening skills.

Every Sunday, I walked to the base chapel. My friends would stand outside the barrack lobby, smoking cigarettes and talking about what they would be doing if they were home. Someone would yell out, "Joe, you don't have to go to Mass this morning. Your mother's not here, and we won't tell on you."

My mother had done her job of raising me and instilling the steadfast values I now carried. I was going to Mass for me. I later became involved in church ministry and volunteered as an usher. I always felt God enabled me to get out of bed each morning for work. The least I could do was rise on Sunday morning for Mass.

On my birthday, my mother sent me a birthday card with $10 inside. I told her she shouldn't send money to me because I was now working. The next year, she mailed me a birthday cake. I kept it in my locker. Morning and night, I dug into it with my fingers and scooped out a hunk. Within two days, I had eaten the whole cake by myself. A good homemade cake has always been my weakness.

I received a call that my grandfather, Riley, had passed. I wanted to go home for the funeral, but I didn't have the money. I was still a low-ranking airman with no savings. A sailor told me to call the American Red Cross and explain I had a death in my family and they would buy me an airline ticket. I had never heard of the American Red Cross, but I made the call, told them my situation and in a few hours, I had a round-trip airline ticket. I was very thankful, and over the years, I have made annual donations to the organization, and now that I am retired, I plan to donate my time.

My Navy pay was $300 a month. I lived on base and ate three meals a day in the chow hall. The Navy deducted money for these expenses. I had $50 deposited in my savings account, leaving $160 a month for spending money. On payday, we went to the Navy Exchange and cashed our checks.

A sailor from Washington would drive home once a month and he invited me to go with him one weekend. We left the base on a Friday afternoon and traveled all night. Early Saturday morning, with the sun rising, I saw open land and mountains, unlike the city I expected. When we arrived, the family was sitting near a campfire, eating breakfast. He didn't tell me he lived on an Indian reservation. We joined everyone at the campfire. Later we went fishing in the nearby stream and washed in it. They lived in tents and at nightfall, I was given a sleeping bag and slept on the ground. Early Sunday morning, we left the reservation and drove back to the base.

I'd been enjoying my private room in the barrack, but I was finally assigned a roommate. He was from Pasadena and had just married his high school sweetheart before enlisting. She lived with his parents. Once or twice a month, we went to Southern California. He drove a 1965 Mustang, and early Friday afternoon, we would leave Fallon. When we arrived, he trusted me with his car. I'd go to San Diego, and Saturday night I would be at the EM Club. I knew many people there, and I was always meeting new people. Sunday at noon, I'd drive back to Pasadena, and we would get back to the base near midnight.

By now, I had saved $900 for a car. I wanted a Volkswagen! My father had one and they were almost maintenance free and really reliable.

One Friday after work, I took a bus to Reno. There, I walked and passed several car dealers, until I came upon Hal's Chevrolet. I saw a forest-green 1969 Volkswagen I liked, but I pretended to ignore it.

When the salesman approached, I purposely asked about other cars on the lot and eventually worked my way back to the VW. Its body and interior looked perfect, but I saw an oil leak where it was parked. The salesman insisted I take it for a test drive. Afterward, I expressed concern about the car's lack of power and the oil leak.

The salesman said I could take it for the weekend and return it Monday. That was a tempting offer, as I didn't have transportation. He said I wouldn't be committed to buying it. With no money exchanged, no commitments and no signatures, I drove back to Fallon. On the freeway, it didn't go over 45 mph. Although I was in love with the car, I couldn't ignore its lack of power.

When I sought my buddies' approval, everyone suggested I not buy it, but I ignored their advice because I really wanted the car.

Monday morning, I took it to a local repair shop. The mechanic who inspected the car said it was nice, but the engine needed an $80 overhaul. I thanked him and drove back to Reno.

I told the salesman I couldn't afford $1,200. Plus, I reiterated my concerns about the oil leak and lack of power. We haggled. His best offer was $1,000. Taking out my cash, I said I would pay $900.

We completed the paperwork and I drove back to Fallon, where the mechanic overhauled the engine. I kept that Volkswagen for 12 years and clocked over 350,000 miles. And I never had a car payment or a major repair.

I would drive to Reno on weekends. Billy Jack's was the number-one disco club in town. After midnight, the bouncers stopped checking IDs. Lit only by disco lights, the club was shoulder to shoulder with people. I danced until closing. Back on base, all the sailors wanted to hear about my weekend.

Most sailors stationed at Fallon were afraid to leave the base. They ordered all their clothes from catalogs. They bought platform shoes, dog-collar silk shirts and bell-bottoms, which they wore in the lobby on weekends to watch TV.

I ordered from the catalog, too—but not for sitting around and watching TV. When I dressed to go to the disco club, I wore sunglasses, and a fake gold chain with a Capricorn symbol completed my ensembles.

On weekends, with my 8-track tape player blasting, I went to Reno, Sacramento or San Diego—but mostly to Sacramento.

While I worked in Special Services, I was responsible for checking out ski equipment. When folks returned the equipment, I would ask about their trips. Everything they told me sounded like fun, and I wanted to give it a try.

My friend, Robert, also had an interest in skiing. We were two Southern boys who had never seen snow until our arrival in Fallon. We had never skied, but we were ready to give it a try.

We packed my car with ski equipment we figured was the right size and dressed in clothing we thought would keep us warm. We arrived at the ski lodge on the north shore of Lake Tahoe, agreeing we would first just watch what other people were doing. We quickly realized we weren't properly dressed. Shivering, but still determined to try skiing, we bought lift tickets and attached them to our jackets, as we saw other people doing. We watched them snap on their boots and ski down the mountain. It looked easy and we were sure we could do it. We walked back to the car for our ski equipment. People were putting on ski boots at their cars, which posed our first challenge. Our feet were cold because we weren't wearing proper socks. We struggled to get the boots on, and once they were on, we couldn't bend down to buckle them. I had to snap Robert's boots, and he snapped mine. By then, we were tired from the exertion of putting on our boots and trembling from the cold.

People walked like Frankenstein in their boots. We did the same because we couldn't bend. Trying to carry skis and poles, plus walking in ski boots, proved to be tricky. When we dropped a pole or ski, we couldn't pick them up. People passing felt sorry for us and would pick up our equipment.

We finally made it to the lift, where we saw people strapping on skis. We watched people slip their boots into skis and ski away. They were queuing up for the chair lift, which never stopped. It looked easy and we thought we were ready for the next phase.

We tried slipping our boots into the skis. After several attempts, we managed to get them attached. After repeatedly falling to the ground, our clothing was soaked, and we were shivering. Our ski poles were bent because we'd used them so many times getting up from the ground. We'd fallen so many times, we decided to stand in one place to rest. We'd tried to play it cool, like we knew what we were doing. By this time, being cool was no longer a priority, and we were satisfied just to be standing upright.

Once we could stand for 30 seconds without falling, we felt ready to tackle the chair lift. We had watched people maneuver into the queue and were sure we were ready to follow suit. As we dragged ourselves to the chair lift, we fell and accidentally knocked other people to the ground. We were like two drunk men, holding on to each other. When it was our turn to get on the chair lift, we missed the chair because we were on the ground. The lift operator had to press the emergency stop. He helped us off the ground and onto the lift. Finally, we were in the lift, cruising up the mountain. We looked at the beautiful snow on the mountains and labeled ourselves skiers. We watched skiers gliding down the mountain and convinced ourselves we could do the same. When we reached the top, the lift operator yelled for us to stand. We didn't know what to expect and, rather than ski away from the lift, we fell to the ground and he had to press the emergency button to keep the chair from hitting us. That's when we discovered we had taken the advanced ski lift to the top of the mountain.

We took some time to enjoy the gorgeous view before making our way down the mountain. Each time we tried to stand, we toppled over. We'd fallen so many times, we were no longer cold. We were numb. About halfway down, we could finally stay upright, without immediately falling. But we didn't know how to slow down or stop. Near the bottom of the mountain, I lost control. My skis spun around so I was skiing backward. Fully out of control, when my skis spun around, I was skiing forward, then backward again. People in the lift line were staring at me, and I'm positive they were thinking I was trying to be a hot dog skier.

I careened into the people standing in the queue and plowed them down one by one. They couldn't move out of my way fast enough. The entire lift line was now on the ground. All I could say was, "I'm sorry," as I was being helped up from the ground.

Not to be outdone, Robert similarly wiped out the second lift queue.

We moved to the beginner chair lift. At the end of the day, we were able to at least stand on our skis, and we had the most fun in the snow that any two Southern boys could enjoy. We had loads of stories to tell the other sailors when we got back on base. I tried skiing again; the more I skied, the more I enjoyed it. Although I never took lessons, I'm now a good downhill skier and enjoy it each winter.

I'd never met a real cowboy until I was in Fallon. A sailor from Oklahoma, while off duty, wore cowboy boots, hat and a scarf tied around his neck. He chewed tobacco, drove a pickup truck and listened to country music. He invited me to a rodeo, and I witnessed bull wrestling and roping of cows and bulls. He also played country music on his guitar. He was an authentic Black cowboy, and we became good friends.

I was often meeting new people. Because I wore my high-school ring, people would ask the name of my school. When I told them the school was White Castle High, their response was, "They named your school after a hamburger!" I was the only person in Fallon who'd never heard of White Castle hamburgers.

One summer evening I was driving to Reno, and I had my car radio tuned to a local station. As I listened to the DJ, I knew he couldn't have a large audience in the desert. After he gave the call letters, I stopped at a phone booth and found the station's address in the phone book. I drove there and, as I approached the building, I saw a red light flashing on its roof.

I knocked on the door and the DJ opened it. He said he was on the air and to be quiet until he finished talking.

I told him I'd tuned in on my way to Reno and decided to visit. I lied and said I'd hosted a radio show before joining the Navy. While I'd never hosted a radio show, I'd spent hours observing every move Richard Ellis made at KEVL in White Castle. I'd convinced myself I was a DJ. Having no reason to question my story, the DJ said he'd introduce me and I could cue up the next song. It was just the two of us in the studio, and only I knew it was my first time on the air.

After he announced my name and said I was a guest, he gave me my cue.

I went into my DJ voice and spoke clearly into the microphone before playing the next song. At that moment, I branded myself as a disc jockey. I stayed until the end of his shift, and he invited me to come back again. This is how I began radio broadcasting.

I had never had a toothache, but the dentist at boot camp had told me the Navy would fix my cavities at my next duty station. I called the base dental office and scheduled an appointment. The dentist took x-rays and I asked about braces. He filled my cavities and told me the Navy covered preventive care, but not cosmetic work. He referred me to an orthodontist in Reno.

I scheduled an appointment. When he looked in my mouth, he said I needed a lot of work. To help me with financing, he wrote to the Navy and told them I was his patient. He requested the Navy do x-rays, extractions and anything else that would save me money. But NAS Fallon wasn't equipped to do all the work I needed, including surgery to remove impacted teeth. The Navy flew me to Naval Hospital Oakland, California, to have the work completed under general anesthesia.

My orthodontist installed wire braces at my next appointment, and I returned monthly to have them adjusted.

Leaving Naval Air Station Fallon, Nevada

I'd spent my entire tour in Nevada as a minor. The night before my 21st birthday, I drove to Reno. At the stroke of midnight, I was in the casino at a penny slot machine. A security officer came over and asked to see my ID.

I gladly pulled out my military ID card and gave it to him. He told me I barely made it.

I continued gambling until I was out of pennies. After that night, I no longer had an interest in gambling.

I was transferred to a squadron, VXE-6, Point Mugu, California. I had no idea where it was and knew nothing about the squadron's mission. Other sailors said I would be going to the South Pole. As an E-4, aviation maintenance administrator (AZ3), I knew little about the AZ rating. I worried whether I would be qualified to work in the squadron.

I recalled how badly I wanted to leave Fallon when I arrived, but I found myself not wanting to go. I had made many friends and knew where to have fun. Life was good in Nevada. I had arrived with one sea bag. When I finished packing, my VW was stuffed with military and civilian clothing (bell-bottoms, platform shoes, leisure suits and dog-collar silk shirts), a hi-fi stereo, albums and personal photos.

I said my goodbyes and drove away with Stevie Wonder blaring on my 8-track player. The front seat contained all my favorite 8-tracks: Earth, Wind and Fire, Al Green and Johnnie Taylor. Anytime I went on long drives, I would practice my DJ patter. Music always made me happy. I told myself my new duty station would be as good as NAS Fallon.

Naval Air Station Point Mugu, California
Antarctic Development Squadron Six (VXE-6)
Maintenance Control and Maintenance Admin
February 1976–October 1976

When I arrived at Point Mugu, most of the squadron personnel were still at the South Pole. They deployed every year in October and returned in February. The first thing I noticed was the barracks here were older. Plus, I had a roommate. I unpacked and got settled. In those days, the barracks had cigarette and beer machines. My roommate would walk down the hall to the machines to get a beer and a pack of cigarettes. Then he'd lie in his rack, drink beer and smoke. I spent the least amount of time possible in the room with him.

The sailor who did my check-in had a radio on. We started talking about music; he said he was a DJ at the Point Mugu and Port Hueneme EM clubs. I told him I was a DJ and he invited me to come by the club some night.

Petty Officer First-Class J. D. Whitaker was a yeoman who worked in the administration office. He knew all the Navy policies and instructions. He encouraged me to complete Navy courses other than those required for my rating. Working those courses would help with my advancement.

As a junior petty officer, I was assigned the line watch once or twice a week. Given a duty belt and flashlight, I had to guard the aircraft parked on the flight line. Walking the flight line at 3:00 a.m., I'd sing to myself to stay awake.

The squadron had four C-130 Hercules aircraft and four

UH-1N Twin Huey helicopters. I was assigned to work in Maintenance Control. I adapted quickly, and the maintenance chief came to rely heavily on me. Also working there were two junior aviation maintenance administrators (AZs). I enjoyed working in Maintenance Control. Then someone investigated my record and learned I was a good typist. After two weeks, I was reassigned to Maintenance Admin. There were two Senior AZ1s in Maintenance Admin; I was the junior AZ3. Admin was overloaded with typing documents, letters and evaluations. I was exactly what they needed because the AZ1s couldn't type fast. They were one-finger pickers. I completed tasks quickly and error free. Being in the office with senior AZs, I thought I'd get decent on-the-job training, but they weren't keen on sharing information. They wanted me for my typing skills only.

I was authorized to attend a five-day Maintenance Admin class at Naval Air Station Point Mugu. Ten of us, officers and enlisted, took the class. I sat next to a commander and we developed a friendship. During breaks, we talked about our jobs; he shared how he'd received his commission and suggested I should pursue becoming a Naval officer. I told him I'd taken the BOOST test while at NAS Fallon, so that was fresh on my mind. The last day of class he wished me well in my career. He gave me a handwritten note and walked away. I opened the note and saw he'd outlined a course of action for me. To become successful in the Navy: 1) Enroll in night classes, 2) Swap duty with sailors to attend class, 3) Study hard and learn the subject matter, 4) Set goals and visualize what you want to be doing within 10 years, 5) Surround yourself with smart people, and 6) Apply for the Navy Officer Program.

I kept that note for years. I followed his advice and was grateful he'd entered my life when he did. I never saw him again, but I learned people come into our lives when we least expect it, and we should be ready to accept what they have to share.

I was promoted to E-5, petty officer second class. As an

AZ2, I was qualified, and I was an asset in all my assigned maintenance departments.

My orthodontist in Reno transferred my records to an orthodontist in Oxnard. I continued monthly adjustments and the braces came off before the squadron deployed overseas. He told me to wear my retainer daily for four to six months. I was thrilled to have the braces off, but I didn't follow his instructions. I wore my retainer less than half the recommended time.

September 1976, the squadron prepared to deploy to Antarctica. It would be my first time outside the United States, and I was excited to be going overseas. Since childhood, I'd wanted to travel abroad. As I looked about the terminal, I saw sailors holding their wives' hands, kissing babies, and hugging, with tears in their eyes. I sat alone. No one was at the terminal to see me off. I'd said goodbye to my friends in Oxnard the day before. I was eager and ready to go. I'd brought my car to Uncle Joe to keep until my return. I'd put my civilian clothing, stereo, albums and everything else I owned in storage.

Once we were airborne, I wondered what I might be missing in Oxnard. Then I reminded myself to be open to this new journey. Most of these sailors had made this trip multiple times. The single sailors discussed liberty in Christchurch. One guy said he had telephoned his girlfriend there, and she'd be at the terminal to greet him. Another's girlfriend was throwing a welcome party at her house, and everyone was invited. I knew I would have a good time in Christchurch.

Christchurch, New Zealand
October 1976–January 1977

As we deplaned in Christchurch, many women in the terminal greeted sailors. Sailors who had arrived on an earlier flight returned to greet us, telling us what they'd done the night before and what would happen later that night. Christchurch was a layover for issuing foul-weather clothing and we didn't have to work while we were there. We were assigned rooms in a building near the airport. It wasn't a military base. Like everyone else, I went to the club. The locals knew we were passing through on our way to Antarctica.

Kiwi women were everywhere. Everything the sailors had said on the airplane was true. The women were very forward, and they'd come up to us and introduce themselves. They weren't there to rip anyone off; they just wanted to party.

At my first meal, I noticed their dairy products were superior to American dairy products. I couldn't get enough of the milk, cheese, and ice cream.

Our second night in Christchurch, we went to a disco party at a convention center with a huge dance floor. Many American sailors were there, and everyone was drinking, dancing and having a great time. I'd been listening to the Kiwi DJ talk as he played music and was itching to go on stage. I'd told some friends I was a DJ, and they encouraged me. I could no longer contain myself, so I went to the booth and introduced myself. I didn't have to say I was American, as he could tell from my accent. He reacted as if I was famous. I asked to introduce the next song. He agreed, and

I cued up Johnnie Taylor's "Disco Lady," the number-one song in New Zealand. The DJ booth was on a stage, about three feet above the dance floor. All night everyone had been listening to a Kiwi voice. At the first beat of the song, I introduced myself as "The Joe Walker, the water walker, the boss talker. A man that gives you nothing more or nothing less, but the very best. Romping and stomping with back-to-back, bumper-to-bumper sooooul music." I'd left the turntable and pranced across the stage, microphone in hand. At the different voice coming from the speaker, everyone on the dance floor paused to look at me. The more I rapped, the more everyone cheered and clapped. That put me in orbit. I was treated as a celebrity the remainder of the night.

After our stopover in Christchurch, it was time to go to the South Pole. We were issued foul-weather military clothing, including utility greens, a parka, boots, gloves and headgear.

We boarded the Air Force C-141 for an eight-hour flight. With everyone dressed in their foul-weather clothing, it was hard to identify anyone, unless you were face to face. Nobody talked; we all knew life would be different for the next four months.

Antarctica South Pole
McMurdo Station Helo Shop
October 1976–January 1977

VXE-6 mission was to support the National Science Foundation. Scientists from various universities deployed with us. Antarctica has six months of darkness and six months of daylight. We'd celebrate Halloween, Thanksgiving, Christmas and New Year's on that ice-covered continent.

We arrived at McMurdo and the sun was still coming up. All I could see was snow and ice.

As I exited the aircraft, my facial muscles instantly numbed and tightened. As I exhaled, I felt like I had a pack of boogers in my nose. I couldn't enunciate a word; my face was frozen. Sailors who had flown ahead were there to greet us. Everyone were dressed in foul-weather clothing, and I couldn't identify anyone. The sailors greeting us wore white, crusty ice beards. We huddled in a tow tractor trailer to be transported to the barracks. The wind was howling and I thought, *What did I get myself into?*

The barracks were almost covered with snow; but the inside was nice and warm. Due to 24-hour sunlight, the barracks had no windows. AZ2 Don Naylor was my roommate.

The squadron's AZ resources were assigned to the C-130 aircraft. In both of my assignments in California, my job performance was high-quality. The Helicopter Shop, UH-1N Twin Huey operated independently and was manned by a select crew. Complaints had been reported regarding the helo shop, regarding errors in their submission of maintenance reports. Everyone in the shop were mechanics and electricians, with limited admin knowledge.

KNEELING: ADAN Clyde Simpson, AD2 John Marshall, LT Boyd Brown, LCDR Michael Brinck, AT3 Garth VanDuesen, ADC Don Cupit, LT Randall Graham, AMS2 Benjamin Midyette, AMS2 Keith Cramer and AD2 Robert Nilson.
STANDING: LT Samuel Feola, LTJG Henry Lane, AMS2 James Walthall, LT Richard Sluys, LTJG Kenneth Kreper, AE1 Don Loper, AE3 Dennis Shatzel, AMH1 Leslie Dikes, AN James Hughey, AZ3 Joe Walker, Tom Daley (Bell Tech Rep) and LT Luther Wheat.
AIRBORNE: LT Andrejs Auskaps, AD3 Vince Huff, AD3 Michael Kuchenberg and AD2 Roderick Law.

Helo Crew at McMurdo Station

It was recommended an AZ be assigned there to manage the helo administration. I was told I was the ideal candidate and everyone believed in me. Still with many things I didn't know about the AZ rating, I took it as a challenge. No longer working directly with the other AZs, I worked directly with Maintenance Chief Cupit, who trusted me and assigned me to manage the Helo Maintenance Control. I learned loads about the job from Chief Cupit.

I scheduled all the helo daily, turn-around and phase inspections. I monitored all the helo maintenance admin work through job completion. Whenever I didn't have an answer for a question, I referenced the OPNAV 4790 Instruction. If I still didn't find my answers, I asked Chief Cupit for assistance, because he possessed exceptional knowledge of aviation maintenance. If neither of us could find an answer, he told me to call one of the squadron's senior AZs.

I rarely called them for assistance because they were reluctant to share their knowledge. Once I learned the answers to all my questions could be found in the OPNAV 4790 Instruction, I studied the manual daily and learned about aviation maintenance and the AZ rating. The Helo Shop maintenance reports were now error free.

Because I was never afraid of work, whenever the crew needed an extra hand moving the helo in and out the hangar, I was there to help.

Chief Cupit once told me, "Walker, I wish all my sailors were like you. My job would be much easier."

Because we had to conserve water, we were taught to take Navy showers. This meant, turn the shower on to get wet, soap down, and rinse. Sailors often left the shower with soap still in their hair.

On laundry day, we put all our dirty clothing into our laundry bag. Some sailors worked as mechanics and their clothing would be greasy and smelly with JP-5 fuel, but it did not matter. All the bags were thrown into a large washing machine and dryer. Clothing never left the laundry bag. Any white shirts and shorts were now green and looked dirtier than before washing. Sailors got their laundry bags back with their "clean" clothing wrinkled and smelly.

After seeing this process, I befriended the laundry supervisor, who let me come in after hours. I hand washed my clothes and used the laundry press to iron my uniform. I was one of the few sailors with a pressed and clean uniform every day.

AFAN McMurdo, Antarctica

Before we deployed, I learned about the American Forces Antarctic Network (AFAN) radio station in McMurdo, Antarctica. It operated 24/7 and, of course, I wanted a show. After I was settled in, I went to where the studio was located, introduced myself and offered my qualifications. I asked for a night slot. I wanted to be on the air when the sailors would be in the barracks reading, writing letters, playing cards and listening to the radio. I was given a four-hour nightly show from 6:00 to 10:00 p.m. I told all my buddies when I'd be on the radio. The first night, I found my opening song, "Always There" by Ronnie Laws. In my signature radio voice, I introduced myself: "This is AFAN McMurdo, and you're listening to The Joe Walker Show. My telephone line is open for dedications. Dial extension 5454 and submit your request now!" I'd play a commercial and give the weather report. Several listeners called in with requests; some just wanted to chat. The station maintained an excellent record library. I played nothing but soul music. When I was behind the mic, I was in my own world and felt comfortable on the air. When I left the studio, I resumed being my usual reserved self.

The next day at work, Chief Cupit told me he had listened to my show the night before and couldn't believe it was me.

My division officer said, "Petty Officer Walker, one would not have known it was you on the radio. In person, you're reserved and quiet, but on the radio, you're so alive!"

He was right. I came alive when I was on the air.

We held a Las Vegas night. The event raised funds for charitable organizations in the United States. This was also a night for sailors to have fun, with a buffet, drinks, and games. I rounded up a band to entertain the squadron. Don Naylor played bass guitar, and Larry Bumpus and J.D. Whitaker both sang. I played the drums.

I attended Mass at the on-station chapel weekly. At the Christmas Mass, I played the organ. Each day we had more daylight. By mid-December, the sun stayed in its 12 noon position for a day before slowly moving downward.

On New Year's Eve, sailors called in to the radio station to make requests. I announced their names on the air, then played their songs. In the barracks that night the wine and beer flowed freely. The guys drank Boone's Farm wine, feeling sorry for themselves because they weren't home with loved ones. Listening to my show and getting drunk was the order of the day.

After my show, when I walked to the barrack, everyone was drunk. Each sailor had a bottle of Boone's Farm wine in hand. Someone handed me a bottle and, because I was the only sober guy in the room, I joined the party. Soon, I was just as drunk as they were. It was the only time I ever got drunk. We all welcomed 1977 with hangovers.

Sometimes, I was authorized to go on day trips with the helo crew. They flew scientists from various universities in the U.S. around the South Pole, studying the climate, among other things. We'd pack lunches because we'd be gone the whole day. The scientists told us where they wanted to go, and we flew into huge ice caves where we could hear the helo's rotor echo. We landed inside the caves and the scientists would put samples of ice in plastic bags for lab testing and research. On one mission, we caught penguins and put them in the helo, for transport back to SeaWorld in San Diego. Everyone assigned to the Helo Shop was presented with an award letter from SeaWorld.

On one such trip in Antarctica, my division officer allowed me to fly the helo. He taught me how to control it with my feet and the throttle controls. I flew for at least 20 minutes before he took the controls back.

I also had a chance to go to the Ceremonial South Pole, the southernmost point on earth. It's surrounded by flags from various countries and I got to take photos standing there. We met some Russians there and went to their camp, where they insisted on giving us vodka.

Many first-time sailors to Antarctica were initiated or hazed. When a sailor least expected it, a group of sailors would charge him, strip him, and bury him in the snow naked. I never participated, nor did I watch. I didn't approve of hazing and it never happened to me during my tour there.

While on isolated duty at McMurdo, I thought back to my eighth grade paper about wanting to be an inventor, when I wasn't taken seriously. I recollected my thoughts of various inventions. My passion was always music, so my thoughts were always music related. I enjoyed singing. Then I thought about the many people who liked to sing but couldn't sing in tune. I thought I could create a musical platform for them to sing on stage into a dead microphone. Today, that concept is known as Karaoke. I had another thought of scouting the world for unknown raw talent, then grooming the person until he or she was ready to sign a recording contract. Today, my idea is *American Idol*.

We departed Antarctica in February when the sun was in the late-afternoon position. Some people remained on Antarctica during the winter months, when it was completely dark.

Departing McMurdo, we boarded the C-130 Hercules aircraft for the eight-hour flight to Christchurch. Once in flight, sailors found sleeping spaces. From my position in the back of the aircraft, tucked between two cargo boxes, I heard the aircraft commander announce a celebrity on board. He identified the star as McMurdo AFAN Radio DJ, Joe Walker. From the clapping and cheering, it was evident they'd enjoyed my show. I felt touched to be recognized by my shipmates in this manner.

We stayed in Christchurch for two or three days to rest and readjust. During this time, we returned our foul-weather clothing. It was good to be able to take a long, hot shower again. I wasn't eager to get home and, because of my superb job performance at McMurdo, Chief Cupit authorized me to stay in Christchurch longer. I went snow skiing in Auckland with the locals—and enjoyed the advanced runs.

Naval Air Station Point Mugu, California
Antarctic Development Squadron Six (VXE-6)
Maintenance Analysis
January 1977–August 1977

Upon returning to the U.S., everyone who had deployed to Antarctica for the first time earned the Antarctica Service Medal.

I had performed flawlessly in the Helo Shop, managing maintenance control. I had a brief working experience in Maintenance Admin before deployment but hadn't worked in Quality Assurance or Maintenance Analysis. I requested a transfer to Analysis because I wanted on-the-job training. The AZ1 in Maintenance Analysis was knowledgeable, experienced, and took a liking to me. He trained me on how to create and interpret all the aircraft Maintenance Data Reporting (MDR). When he was transferred, I managed Maintenance Analysis alone. I extracted the data from MDR reports and submitted Naval messages to the need-to-know organizations.

Having won Sailor of the Month, my photo was posted on the Squadron Award Board. I'd also been nominated for Sailor of the Quarter.

The squadron Sailor of the Quarter program was decided by a board that included Navy chiefs. The board had gone through the process of eliminating sailors until only two of us remained. Sailor of the Quarter would be determined by an interview. When it was my turn, I was seated at a table with three chiefs.

Chief Burns said, "Petty Officer Walker, this selection process has been very difficult for the board. You and the other sailor are 'squared-away sailors' and the oral interview with each of you will help us decide who wins Sailor of the Quarter."

Each chief asked about my Navy career goals. As I gave my answers, they took notes.

One chief asked, "Petty Officer Walker, in a situation when you have a sailor refusing to cooperate and follow commands, what would you say to him?"

I thought of the times my father and I did carpentry work on houses and I'd have preferred playing with friends. When I slacked on the job, he'd simply say, "Son, don't dislike me, get like me." I repeated this phrase to the board. They stopped taking notes and dropped their pens.

The Chief Petty Officer of the Command said their decision had been made. On the basis of that answer, I was named Sailor of the Quarter.

My military evaluation marks continued to be 4.0. I don't recall doing anything special; I just did my job and always sought to do each job better than the last one. Because I enjoyed being in the Navy, everything seemed effortless. I was constantly recognized as a standout sailor. I just had to be myself, and Navy life was great!

I was recommended for the Limited Duty Officer (LDO) Program. I met all requirements for the program, except I wasn't a petty officer first class. I was told that once I was advanced to petty officer first class, my name would be submitted for the LDO Program.

A lieutenant in the squadron was an electrical engineer and ham-radio operator and he knew Morse code. During our lunch hour, he started a radio broadcast class. The course he taught was Radio Fundamentals and I completed the requirements for a Third-Class Federal Communications Commission Operator's permit.

The petty officer I had met during check-in heard me on the air at McMurdo. He ran the disco at Port Hueneme EM Club and had a large following. He also ran the disco at the Point Mugu

EM Club, where attendance was half the size. He asked if I wanted to take over as DJ at Point Mugu. He introduced me to the club manager, and I ran the disco there on Thursday nights. I'd had fun spinning records at McMurdo, and now I was spinning records in the EM club and getting paid.

I enrolled in Oxnard Community College. I had no plans for a major, so I took an English class. I had run the disco at the Point Mugu EM Club for a month. I was having fun, but I wanted a larger audience. One night after my class, I went to Oxnard's number-one dance club, The Basement. It had a full house Wednesday through Sunday. I sat at the bar, ordered a Coke and observed everything going on in the club. The band was excellent; they played for 45 minutes and a DJ spun records for 15 minutes while the band took a break. I noted every mistake he made. He had difficulty keeping people on the dance floor once the band left the stage. The more I watched his performance, the more I knew I was a better DJ.

I learned the guy who served my Coke was the owner, so I got his attention. "I know where you can find a better DJ," I told him.

"Where?"

"You're looking at him."

He told me to come back the next day at noon to show him what I could do.

The next day, I drove to The Basement. The owner was there alone, stocking the bar. He gave me the keys to the DJ booth and told me to go do my thing. I started looking for lights and switches. I had never seen this setup before, and I wasn't about to ask for assistance. After about five minutes of fumbling around, familiarizing myself with the equipment, I was ready to go live. I cued up a disco song and introduced myself as if the club was filled with people.

The owner stopped stocking the bar and stared at me. I had his attention, and I switched to a new song with a seamless introduction. I played music and rapped for another five minutes.

I turned everything off and locked the DJ booth and returned to the bar with the keys. Before I said a word, the owner asked if I could start that night.

I didn't even ask about the pay; I was excited to be asked to work at the number-one club in Oxnard.

My first night, I introduced myself to the band. Everyone in the band dressed professionally and so did I. I had discussed a routine with them. They'd signal to me their last song. People were on the dance floor, and I wanted to keep them there. As the band faded out, I faded in a similar groove that kept the music going non-stop. Therefore, people never left the dance floor. I was dancing and bouncing around in the booth as much as the people on the dance floor. They saw how much fun I was having, so they stayed engaged. The more the people danced, the more drinks they bought, and that was good for business. Occasionally, the old DJ came into the club. I assumed he was trying to get his gig back. But that ship had sailed. When I got my first check, it was more than I expected. It felt good to be receiving a paycheck for something I enjoyed doing and would have done for free.

Oxnard is between Santa Barbara and Los Angeles. Out-of-towners occasionally stopped in the club. One night, the club was packed and the bouncer had people in line waiting to come in. The band was hotter than hot, and I was on my A game. I was spinning records, people were dancing, and in the DJ booth, I was dancing hard to keep the party live.

At the end of my set, I cued up a song the band played. I gradually faded the music and the band continued the groove. The people never stopped dancing. When I came down from the booth, I was sweating hard. A man approached me and gave me his business card. He said he was a music producer from Hollywood and asked me to come to work for him. He said he liked my style.

I told him I couldn't accept the offer because I was on active duty in the Navy. He said to call him when I was discharged. I continued DJing at The Basement until I was transferred.

Between Navy promotions and my second job as a DJ, I was making good money. I never forgot about the airline ticket the American Red Cross bought for me to attend my grandfather's funeral. I showed my appreciation by making annual contributions to the American Red Cross.

Chief Cupit encouraged me to get involved with off-duty activities on base. Extra things I involved myself in outside of the normal work routine were included in my Navy evaluations. Chief Cupit's sons were in the Boy Scouts. He was a volunteer for the Scouts and I became a volunteer, as well. I worked with the Boy Scouts of America for Pack 3248, Point Mugu, California.

Leaving Naval Air Station Point Mugu, California

I passed the Petty Officer First-Class exam but was not advanced due to needs of the Navy. I had completed two years of shore duty at NAS Fallon and almost two years at VXE-6. While my overseas deployment with the squadron was classified as sea duty, I was required to complete more.

I discussed my re-enlistment plans with Chief Cupit. He recommended I go visit my detailer at the Pentagon the next time the squadron flew to Washington, D.C. A detailer assigns rotation orders. I called my detailer, who agreed to meet with me.

Days later, I was aboard the C-130, bound for Washington, D.C. My detailer invited me to come to his office. He said he had reviewed my records and found them impressive. He said I could have any duty station in the world and asked where I wanted to go. At Point Mugu, several sailors encouraged me to go to the Philippines. Even Uncle Joe had recommended it. I had considered going back to New Zealand because I liked the country and the people, but I wanted somewhere different, so I replied I wanted to go to the Philippines.

He said, "Done!"

A week later, I received orders to report to Naval Air Station Cubi Point, Philippines. I re-enlisted for another four years and received a re-enlistment bonus.

I'd been customizing my Volkswagen. I had it painted lime green with thin gold pinstripes. I had the rear seat removed and light-green and gold shag carpet installed. The two front seats and inside door panels were re-upholstered white. It sported a removable sunroof, wide track tires and mag wheels. I added a cassette player with large speakers in the rear, non-baffled chrome exhaust pipes, and a rear-mounted whip antenna. Attached to the antenna was a scarf that whipped around in the wind as I drove.

Before leaving, I drove to San Diego for a day to visit Audrey Mae and Uncle Joe's family.

Bayou Goula, Louisiana
and
San Diego, California
August 1977

Once I left for the Philippines, I'd be overseas for 18 months. I decided to drive across country to Louisiana. Uncle Joe did a tune-up on my Volkswagen to ensure everything mechanical worked fine.

Driving alone, with the sound of my cassette playing soul music, I stopped only for gas. I cruised through Arizona and New Mexico. Driving through Texas took a whole day.

Once I was in Louisiana, the rest of my drive was easy. As I exited I-10 onto Louisiana Highway 1, I saw a school bus ahead. As I followed it, the kids on the school bus waved and I waved back. It was the Southern University school bus transporting college kids. Minutes later I drove into my parents' driveway and everyone came out to greet me. My father had never seen a customized VW like mine. I let him drive it during my stay. My mother cooked my favorite red beans and rice. Bobbie was attending Southern University. Josie was a senior in high school, but my biggest surprise was how Judy and Sam had grown. I had only known them as small kids and they were now young teenagers.

When I went to Lil Sister's house, she looked at me and said, "Boy! You look good enough to eat." As she hugged and kissed me, I thought that was the ultimate compliment from my grandmother.

At Sunday Mass, I saw Brother Pasqua. He told me he was always praying for me. I thanked him for his prayers. He was the most spiritual man I had ever known. Even though I was no longer living in Louisiana, I remained in contact with him, and I occasionally sent him religious mementos.

I visited with Lionel Gilbert, Fred Jackson, Leonard Bracken and Chuckie Landry.

Patricia Clavier and I remained friends. Every time I went to Louisiana, I visited her. Also, she was enrolled at Southern University.

When it was time for me to leave Louisiana, I said my goodbyes and headed west on I-10. I stopped in Galveston to visit Laura and Robert. I hadn't seen them in four years. Laura hugged and kissed me. Years earlier, she had dubbed me her "All-American Boy," and she still referred to me by that moniker.

On my way back, I toured the Johnson Space Center in Houston. Before I knew it, I was back in San Diego. I visited friends and, although I was over 21, I still went to the EM Club. I spent a few days in San Diego before leaving for the Philippines. Audrey Mae drove me to the airport.

The Navy had given me a commercial airline ticket to Manila. I'd been told about the many items I could buy in the Philippines at bargain prices, so I traveled light. My sea bag contained mostly military clothing.

On the long flight to the Philippines, I wondered whether I had made the right decision. Maybe I should have gone back to New Zealand. I knew my friends in VXE-6 were preparing for deployment to Christchurch. I thought about the fun I had had at AFAN radio, but concluded I was embarking on a new journey.

Joe Walker

Naval Air Station Cubi Point, Philippines
Maintenance Control/Maintenance Admin
September 1977–January 1979

When I landed in Manila, I was struck by people's resemblance to each other. I couldn't distinguish facial differences. My second observation was the speech. Tagalog was a language I had never heard before. Fortunately, in-flight I met two sailors traveling to NAS Cubi Point. One had been to the Philippines before, so we relied on him to negotiate our transportation to the base. It was late evening, and the weather was hot. We got on a bus with no air conditioning and more people than seats. They also had animals and chickens on the bus. We traveled for miles on a dusty partially paved road, making many stops along the way. Although no more available seats remained, people still managed to get on. When we finally arrived in Olongapo City, we transferred to an old World War II military jeep used as public transportation. They were called "jeepneys." People piled in; every space was taken.

The jeepney drove us to the base main gate. As we got off, kids tried to sell us gum, and girls asked if we wanted a date. Crowds of people filled the street; loud noises emanated from jeepneys, motorcycles and music blasting from every building.

We pushed our way through the crowd to the main gate. I had been warned to guard against pickpockets, so my wallet was secured in my front pocket. I wanted to get on base, away from the crowd of people. Once on base, I finally relaxed. Looking back through the chain-link fence, many Filipinos leaned against the fence asking for pesos. I thought, *What a zoo!*

There were two bases, Naval Station (NS) Subic Bay, where the Navy ships docked, and up on the hill was NAS Cubi Point, the Navy aviation community.

A Navy bus ran every 30 minutes from NS Subic Bay to NAS Cubi Point. After checking in, we were assigned barrack rooms. I got a private room. Although I found the room and almost-new building impressive, I learned later that most sailors lived in town because of the cheap cost of living.

The next day, I checked in at the maintenance department. They'd been expecting me. I was assigned to work in Maintenance Control, along with another second-class petty officer (AZ2). He was senior to me in rank and had been in the Navy longer. He knew more about the AZ rating, too. We worked well together, and he didn't hesitate to share his knowledge with me.

Most sailors were granted permission to move off base, but I preferred living on base and eating in the chow hall. After work I rode the bus from NAS Cubi to NS Subic, to the EM club and other on-base entertainment. I would look through the chain-link fence into the crowds on the street. I didn't feel safe venturing into the town of Olongapo. When everything closed at NS Subic, I'd board the bus back to NAS Cubi.

Few sailors went to NAS Cubi late at night. As I boarded the bus, I saw a guy smiling. I sat across from him and struck up a conversation. He'd recently arrived in the Philippines. We talked all the way to NAS Cubi Point. When the bus stopped and we got off, we went our separate ways.

The next morning, I reported to Maintenance Control for work. I was resolving aircraft discrepancy signoffs and preparing the aircraft logbook for launch. As I looked up from my desk, I saw the pilot reviewing the aircraft logbook, and he was the guy I'd met the night before. He wore the same friendly smile. I was surprised to see him in an officer's flight uniform, but proud to learn he was a Naval officer. Part of me felt as if I had been instantly promoted. He signed for the aircraft logbook and left for his flight. Whenever I saw him in or around the hangar, we'd have brief conversations.

Lieutenant Commander Chuck Neville and I later became good friends.

I worked in Maintenance Control along with the second-class petty officer for at least a month. Then it was announced the first-class petty officer who managed Maintenance Admin had received transfer orders. One of us would be transferred to Maintenance Admin. I was a junior second-class petty officer, so I assumed I would remain in Maintenance Control. To my surprise, I was selected as the Maintenance Admin supervisor.

My first day in Maintenance Admin, I learned I'd have to prove myself to keep my position. The first-class petty officer had less than a month before his transfer and he was determined to take all his Maintenance Admin knowledge with him. He told me daily routines for running the office, but he wouldn't share information on how to complete tasks. He didn't want to share his contacts in and out of the maintenance department for getting things done. Each day, I was assigned tasks to complete without guidance or assistance. When I asked for advice, he told me to look up the information in the instruction manuals.

A critical part of the admin job was to complete an accurate daily aircraft status report. Aboard NAS Cubi Point were three C-117s and two HH-46 Helo aircraft. The operations department used the status report to schedule daily flights and update other reporting commands. Also, management wanted to know the percentage of flyable and non-flyable aircraft daily. Gathering this data for a status report could be difficult without knowing the proper contacts. I did my best to complete the report. When I found all the possible data I could locate, I gave the aircraft status report to the first-class petty officer for review.

He looked at my report and said, "This is inaccurate data." He completed the report himself and wouldn't divulge his sources. Each day we went through the same drill. I submitted my aircraft status report, and he re-did everything, then submitted his version to the operations department.

I asked him to walk me through the process for completing

the report and his reply was always that he was busy and would do it later. Despite the humiliation I had to endure with him, I never allowed myself to get angry or lose control.

After working hours, when everyone had left the office, I stayed behind to review previously submitted aircraft status reports. Copies were kept on file for years, so I had reliable documents to learn from. I found notations on old reports indicating contact names, telephone numbers, etc. Armed with this information, I felt confident I could complete the status reports. The next day, I submitted my completed report to the first-class petty officer. He offered no feedback, just accepted the report, so I knew I was submitting an accurate report. Still, he didn't make my job any easier. If I made a mistake in other admin jobs, he never said what I did wrong, just pointed out errors. He was a poor supervisor, and I was pleased to see him leave.

The day of his departure, I assumed all responsibilities of the admin office and successfully networked with other maintenance departments. My relationship with those departments made me a successful admin supervisor.

As Maintenance Admin Supervisor, all maintenance correspondence went through me. In those days, the Navy paid everyone with paper checks. On payday, the disbursing office sent the checks to me, and I was the most popular guy in the department. I gave the checks to the work-center supervisors, but sailors would crowd my desk, asking for theirs. If any issues arose with anyone's pay, I had to resolve them. If a sailor's performance had been lacking and the maintenance chief wanted to punish him, the chief would request that sailor's check be given to him. A sailor never wanted to hear the chief held his check.

Working in admin alone, I had seen an increase in duties. The maintenance officer recognized this and told me I would receive help in the office. A new airman recruit, straight out of boot camp, started working for me. Born and raised in Manila, he joined the Navy in the Philippines and went to San Diego for boot camp. Upon his graduation, the Navy assigned him to NAS Cubi Point.

Despite his limited English, he was a hard worker and eager to learn. I taught him everything I knew about being an aviation maintenance administrator (AZ). I taught him to complete the aircraft status report, type Naval messages, evaluations, and numerous other administrative duties.

As a supervisor, I ensured he didn't suffer from a lack of training due to poor supervision. I remembered when I was an airman and the first-class petty officers that I worked for refused to share knowledge. Those petty officers I worked for wouldn't answer the telephone, even if they were sitting next to it when it rang. It was always my job to answer the phone and then pass calls to them. I was determined never to be that kind of supervisor. I ensured he knew as much as I did. I even answered the phone if I was nearby when it rang. But I no longer performed field day or made coffee. Those were the airman's job. I performed the office inspection after field day.

Because I trained this recruit, I ensured he was prepared and ready when it was time for him to take the advancement test. The first time he took the test, he was promoted to petty officer third class. He gave me all the credit for his promotion, and I was proud of him because he was an outstanding sailor.

I was assigned collateral duty as a career counselor for the maintenance department. I encouraged and enrolled several sailors in night school. Many had been told to wait until they were discharged from the military to activate their GI Bill, but I encouraged them to follow my lead and initiate their further education while on active duty. I also encouraged them to continue their studies once discharged from military service. Some took my advice; others didn't.

Periodically, the maintenance department scheduled flights to Baguio on the C-117 aircraft. Maintenance people were given priority for these trips. One Saturday morning, my buddies and I went on a Baguio trip. Prior to landing, we were told we would be on deck for three hours. To make use of our limited time, we went straight to town. To keep cool on the especially hot day, we stopped at several bars and had a San Miguel beer at each stop. I wasn't much of a drinker, but I drank to keep cool. We ate little and continued our ongoing drinking. We lost track of time and had minutes to get back to the aircraft prior to takeoff. We ran, arriving back at the aircraft just in time.

We'd been flying for an hour when I started feeling sick. The more I thought about being sick, the worse I felt. My friend, Red, was asleep next to me. I attempted to exit my seat, but in an instant, he was covered in vomit. Everyone ran toward the rear of the aircraft, holding their noses. It was hot on the C-117 and the stink was unbearable. All I could do was stand there, dripping vomit, offering apologies to everyone—especially Red. When we landed, everyone hurriedly deplaned. I was left to clean the entire aircraft.

At the annual National Prayer Breakfast ceremony in 1978, the base Commanding Officer, other high-ranking officers, enlisted, and civilians were present. That year, I was selected to read the opening prayer for the ceremony.

National Prayer Breakfast

As the Admin Supervisor, and based on my job performance, I was awarded Senior Sailor of the Quarter.

Naval Air Station Cubi Point/
Olongapo City, Philippines

Before leaving the U.S., I was told what to expect when I arrived in the Philippines. Nothing compared to what I actually saw. At the main gate at NS Subic was a polluted river everyone called "Shit River." As we walked across the bridge, small children would jump into the river, diving for the American coins that sailors threw in the river. They'd surface from the filthy water with coins in their mouths.

Across the bridge was Olongapo City, with bars lining both sides of the street. In between bars were tailor shops or restaurants. Every bar had music blasting; standing at the doors were Filipino girls in bikinis. They'd invite sailors in for a drink. The music included country, rock & roll, pop and soul. The Filipino bands had outstanding musicians.

Not to be outdone, the Blacks had carved out their own section of Olongapo City, called the Jungle. Only Black sailors were allowed in the Jungle; the Filipino girls wore afros and they looked and dressed like Black girls. Every night felt like a Saturday-night party in the Philippines. It took me a week to learn the party never ended, from early morning until late at night. I was seeing and experiencing things I had never dreamed possible.

Philippine President Ferdinand Marcos strictly enforced martial law. Everyone had to be off the street by midnight. From 11:30 to 11:55 p.m. people rushed to hail rides home. Some ran; others walked hurriedly to their destinations. After 12:01, the streets were quiet, with not a soul in sight. Everyone abided by martial law and got inside before curfew. Filipino policemen carried machine guns, and anyone caught on the street after curfew was shot, no questions asked. If a sailor had duty watch between midnight and 5:00 a.m., they stayed on base because the base had no curfew.

After a month in the barracks, I moved to Olongapo City to be among the locals. I found a nice apartment a few blocks from the base. Because of the warm climate, apartment buildings had no hot running water. When taking showers, water from the rooftop tank was warm enough. During monsoon season, buckets of rain fell. Soon afterward, everything was dry, as if it had never rained.

Many local Filipino houses were outdated, with several families often living in one house. Most had no running water, and few had electricity. Women hand washed clothing and spread them on their rusty corrugated tin roofs to dry. The electrical power wasn't stable and many nights, the power would go off. People automatically brought out candles and continued doing whatever they were doing.

It wasn't uncommon to be awakened at 5:00 a.m. to the sound of a man's voice yelling out every five seconds, "Balut, balut, balut."

A balut is a fertilized duck egg, boiled and eaten from the shell. A man walked through the streets carrying a bucket filled with balut for sale. I enjoyed Filipino food but couldn't stomach the taste of a balut—or even the smell of one.

The cost of living in the Philippines was cheap. All the young sailors living off base had live-in maids who would clean their apartments, wash, iron their uniforms, shine their shoes, shop at the market and do whatever else needed to be done, for little pay. I refused to hire a maid. I did my own cleaning, and I washed my clothes at the on-base laundromat. Almost every sailor married his maid.

The apartment building I lived in had four units: two on top and two on the bottom. Mine was on the top left. The other three units were occupied by American sailors and their girlfriends. At various times, each one of their units was broken into, and their stereos were stolen, along with other items. I lived alone, left early each morning, and came home late every night. My apartment was never broken into.

The most common ways of getting around were by jeepney or motorcycle with an attached sidecar called a trac. The motorcycle driver was called a trac-driver. Several Filipino trac-drivers lived across the street from me and sat on the corner daily. Whenever I left my apartment, two or three drivers would request I get in their trac. I'd decide which one to get in and away we went. They drove me wherever I wanted to go. When I got out, they never accepted my pesos. I never knew their names, so I called all of them "Boss" and they did the same. When I walked off base across the bridge, I never knew how they immediately sorted me out among the crowds, but I'd hear, "Hey, Boss! Hey, Boss!" I'd then spot them and get into one of the tracs.

Periodically, I would buy them a carton of cigarettes or a bottle of whiskey for driving me around. The only work they did was being trac-drivers. Plus, I would bring bags of candy for their children. I never asked them to monitor my apartment, but I believe they looked out for me.

The locals knew how to distinguish between a stationed sailor versus one from a ship. When I left base, it amazed me how the Filipinos seemed to know me. Stationed sailors weren't hassled as much as the sailors from the ship. Sailors from the ship were in port for a week or two, then back to sea. The locals took advantage of them and stole from them regularly.

One night I left base and detoured along a side street through an alley. As three kids ran past me in the dark, I felt one of them touch me. It felt like he had accidentally bumped me while running. They never stopped running once they'd passed me. By the time I realized what had happened, they were out of sight. I'd been wearing a wristwatch with a stretch band and it was gone. Those kids were masters at stealing watches.

I finally convinced myself the party life in Olongapo City could go on without me. I wanted to do something to promote my career, so I pursued further education. I met with an educational counselor at the base Overseas Learning Center, who explained the requirements for completing an Associate of Arts (AA) degree at Los Angeles City College (LACC). A review of my record indicated that I was awarded six college credits for completing boot camp, and three more for my math class in Fallon. An AA required 60 credits. With my nine credits, I was ready to get started.

After my first semester at LACC, I majored in business, taking accounting and other business-related courses. During lunch breaks or whenever the office workload was light, I studied. I spent my weekends at the base library, completing term papers or studying for exams. I took three or four classes a semester, attending classes four nights a week. Class started at 5:00 p.m. and let out between 9:00 and 10:00 p.m. My goal was to obtain my AA before departing the Philippines.

My biggest challenge was resisting the temptation of going to Olongapo City every night. Most nights on my way home after class, I met friends at the local bars. When I walked in with my shoulder bag of schoolbooks and gym clothing, I heard, "Here comes the schoolboy."

I knew they all admired me but lacked the discipline to go to school themselves. I'd join in their festivities until closing.

There were many good tailors and tailor shops in the Philippines. If you drew a design, a tailor could produce it. And the cost was nominal. I bought a dozen custom-made three-piece gabardine suits, five jumpsuits, dog-collar silk shirts and tailor-made platform shoes. All my pants were bell bottoms.

I wrote to my parents to get their measurements. I had custom tops made from matching silk. I also had matching jumpsuits made, with their initials embroidered on the collars.

Easter in the Philippines was nothing like I'd ever experienced. On Good Friday, a large group of people paraded in the street, singing and praying. In the front of the group, a Filipino man portraying Jesus walked shirtless, carrying a cross through the streets. Other men following him beat his bare back until he bled. The event lasted for hours.

Lieutenant Commander Chuck Neville had moved off base into an apartment in Olongapo City. One Saturday, he invited me to his apartment. There was a green logbook on his table that I inquired about. He explained he logged important life events and occurrences in it. Later that day, I bought a writing tablet; in it, I noted dates and times of my entries. My first entries included: complete my AA degree, pursue a BA degree, and buy a condo when I return to the States.

Chuck told me his future plans included joining the Naval Reserve.

I always planned to complete 20 or more active years in the Navy, but I never considered alternatives. After talking with Chuck, I considered pursuing a second career. I'd had a stellar Navy career; I was on track for completing my AA degree and considered transitioning to the civilian world.

One advantage of being stationed overseas was the reasonable prices of quality music equipment. The day I saw a floor model Yamaha organ with built-in rhythm machine, foot pedals and a double-deck keyboard in the Navy Exchange, I had to have it! I also bought a stereo system with turntable, amplifier, cassette player and large floor speakers, plus a reel-to-reel tape deck.

I bought (and still have) a new 1978 Honda Hawk motorcycle. On weekends, I'd ride it to other provinces. As I'd enter a village, locals would gather around me. Most had never seen a new motorcycle. And the Filipino kids had never seen a Black person. They'd rub my arms or touch my hand, wanting to feel my skin. Their mothers explained to me that the kids were curious about the texture of my skin.

In December 1978, I earned my Associate in Arts degree from Los Angeles City College.

Leaving Naval Air Station Cubi Point, Philippines

Because everything was so cheap overseas, I had saved the most money I'd ever saved.

In January 1979, I was due for rotation and my division officer asked me to submit a one-year extension in the Philippines. I needed to readjust to a normal life. The Philippines was like living in a fantasy world. I felt I was losing my core values and moral compass. Plus, I was having second thoughts about making the Navy a career. I wanted to do more. I needed to be in the United States to start networking. I accepted Navy orders to San Diego.

My orders stated I must report to Naval Air Station North Island, Fleet Logistics Support Squadron Three Zero (VRC-30). An E-6, senior petty officer first class, had been selected to be my replacement as admin supervisor. I was ready to allow him to manage the office, but when he saw how smoothly the office was run, he told me to continue business as usual. He'd report to the office each morning at 7:30 a.m. and disappear by 9:00 a.m. I didn't see him again until the following morning. Sometimes he'd call during the day to check in and asked if the division officer was looking for him. He knew I'd cover for him. Because he was senior to me, I didn't tell him what to do, nor did I want him in the office telling me what to do. He trusted me, and I gladly managed the office until I transferred. I assumed he had to work once I was transferred. Two junior AZs in the office worked for me. I'd trained them both, and they were good AZs. Upon my leaving, I gave the senior petty officer first class a detailed log of all the daily duties, contacts, and report due dates, all of which had been missing when I accepted that job.

I wrote to Audrey Mae to tell her when I'd arrive at Travis Air Force Base and asked her to meet me.

I terminated the lease on my apartment. I'd come to the Philippines with one sea bag. Now, the Navy was packing all my household goods to ship back Stateside.

As I flew back to California, I knew everything would be different, especially the cost of living. I thought about my new job, wondering what I would do, and what the working environment would be like. I'd decided to leave the party life behind to advance my career. It was a decision I'd live with.

Naval Air Station North Island, California
Fleet Logistics Support Squadron
Three Zero (VRC-30)
Maintenance Control / Maintenance Admin /
Logs and Records
January 1979–July 1981

As I checked in, I wondered why several of the busily working sailors had dissatisfied expressions on their faces. I soon learned why.

The squadron's C-2 aircraft had exceeded their service life. With many approvals, they were still in service, flying mail out to aircraft carriers. After every flight, the aircraft were brought into the hangar for maintenance. There was always one hangar queen (grounded aircraft whose parts could be cannibalized for use in other aircraft). With long working hours required to keep the aging aircraft flying, sailors were overworked and squadron morale was low. Also assigned to the squadron was one T-39 Sabreliner aircraft for the admiral's use.

As an E-5, petty officer second class (AZ2), I was assigned to work in Maintenance Control along with two junior AZs; we reported to the maintenance chief. I was an expert in Maintenance Control, so I immediately added value and provided supervision for the junior AZs.

Along with working a regular shift, everyone was required to stand duty watch once or twice a week. Because I was authorized to live off base, I never checked into the barracks. I remembered Audrey Mae's apartment in National City. I went to the same one hoping for a vacancy. The manager said apartment #7 was vacant; it was my sister's old apartment, so I signed a lease and moved in.

I had been working in Maintenance Control about a month before I was transferred to Aircraft Logs and Records. Throughout my Navy career, I had excelled in all areas of the AZ rating. But I'd never gotten to work in Logs and Records. That job required great attention to detail. Proper logbook entries were mandatory for aircraft inspections, high-time component replacement, kit modifications, etc. When the shop removed and replaced parts, the proper paperwork had to be submitted to ensure accurate logbooks. If an aircraft crashed, the first order of business was to retrieve and secure its logbooks, which were used to investigate root causes. If proper and timely entries weren't made, someone could face a harsh penalty.

The squadron E-6, petty officer first class (AZ1), worked in Logs and Records alone. He was an expert and knew everything about maintaining aircraft logbooks. At our first meeting, I confessed I was clueless about aircraft logs and records. The only thing I knew was what I'd read in OPNAV 4790 Instructions. He put me at ease by saying maintenance staff selected me to work there because they believed in me. He said he'd teach me everything I needed to know. I quickly came to admire him; he was an excellent mentor.

About six months later, he was scheduled for transfer. He reported to the maintenance department that I was ready to take over as the squadron resident logs and records expert.

I appreciated his confidence, but felt I was still in the learning phase. Nevertheless, after his transfer, in addition to being the expert, I became the squadron senior AZ2, supervising the AZs assigned to Maintenance Admin.

We didn't perform major maintenance on the T-39 aircraft. It was sent to Rockwell International in St Louis, Missouri, for rework. Every time the aircraft was sent to Rockwell, the logbooks accompanied it. The T-39 was returned to the squadron with required maintenance completed, but no entries or notations in the logbooks. When I addressed the issue with the maintenance officer, we learned the staff at Rockwell had no knowledge of Naval aircraft logbook entries. The people who worked on the aircraft were mechanics and electricians—the same people responsible for making entries into the aircraft logbooks.

Rockwell submitted a request to the Navy for an instructor to come to St Louis to teach their civilian employees about Navy aircraft logs and record entries. I was assigned this duty. Aircraft work was done in St Louis and the engine work was done in Perryville. I held a three-day aircraft logbook class in St Louis and a two-day engine logbook class in Perryville. Most of the men in the class were old enough to be my father. I saw airplanes go through the assembly line from start to finish. My tour of the city included The Gateway Arch. Upon my return, Rockwell called my commanding officer with high praise for my performance, expressing gratitude for educating their staff. I also got a letter of appreciation from Rockwell International.

The squadron was scheduled for an Inspector General (IG) Inspection. Staff members would come from Washington, D.C. to inspect every maintenance department. I drilled my sailors through all our check lists multiple times. Our aircraft logs and records weren't only documented correctly, all pages were neatly and properly categorized. The sailors completed the office field day, and I performed an inspection. The day the inspectors arrived, I ensured my sailors wore clean and pressed uniforms, shined shoes, and had a fresh pot of coffee brewing.

After the maintenance inspection, the IG team reported that the maintenance department passed with zero discrepancies. Because we'd passed the IG Inspection, the Maintenance Chief told me to take the day off. Instead, I secured my team, and I worked the remainder of the day.

I was working long hours, and I enjoyed it. But I still was thinking of not re-enlisting. I wanted to do more. I knew I had to complete my BA before my discharge. I went to the education department at NAS North Island to ask about after-hours studies.

University of La Verne's off-campus studies were conducted on base. After researching the university, I enrolled in the program. I attended classes four evenings a week. Class started at 5:00 p.m. and ended at 9:00 p.m. I studied during lunch.

On weekends, I was often at the library. I got my first library card at Chula Vista Library (we had no public libraries where I grew up). Nights and weekends, I used my office typewriter for completing class reports. When I had to stand duty watch, I remembered the advice a commander had once given me: "Swap duty to ensure you attend class." If I had an early watch (4:00 p.m. to 8:00 p.m.) I swapped with a sailor who had a midnight to 4:00 a.m. watch. I'd also swap weekday duty with sailors who had weekend duty.

In one of my business classes, I had to research and turn in a term paper on a business of my choice. I chose IBM. After submitting my paper, I predicted one day I'd work for "Big Blue."

Squadron morale wasn't improving, and sailors were working day and night to maintain the extended service life of the C-2 aircraft. Someone came up with an idea to establish a SWAT Team of experts from each work center, including a maintenance chief; each person had to know not only his rating, but have skills in another rating. This core team would be exempt from duty watch.

As this team was assembled, I was selected to manage maintenance control alongside the maintenance chief. With approval from the maintenance chief, I scheduled and prioritized the work center's workload and tracked completion of maintenance discrepancies. As an AZ, I also knew the aviation storekeeper's (AK) job. Therefore, I managed the supply department. When parts had to be ordered or transferred, I completed those tasks, including logbook entries. The SWAT Team reported to work at noon on Fridays. After receiving a pass down, the squadron day shift personnel secured for the day. SWAT Team worked until midnight and reported back to work at 5:00 a.m. Saturday morning. We worked all day Saturday and sometimes past midnight. We reported back to work at 5:00 a.m. Sunday morning. We ensured the airplanes were in an "up" status and ready to fly on Monday morning. Our off days were Monday through Thursday. It was perfect for me because I was attending school. The SWAT Team turned around the maintenance department readiness. Our weekend work efforts improved squadron morale and sailors had more time to spend with their families and friends.

Again, I was awarded Sailor of the Quarter.

San Diego, California

As I left Mass at St. Rita Church one Sunday morning, Father Joe asked me to volunteer as a scout master for the Boy Scouts. I'd worked with the Boy Scouts in Point Mugu, so I knew a little about scouting.

Once a month, we took the boys on overnight camping trips in the San Diego mountains. They set up the tents and cooked meals on an open fire. I enjoyed working with them, but after several months, I told Father Joe I wanted to resign. He said, "Good, because there's a shortage of catechism teachers."

I taught the seventh-grade catechism class every Saturday morning. I even volunteered to play the church organ at Sunday Mass when there was no choir.

I rarely had free time on weekends, but sometimes my brother-in-law, Charles Lott, and I would get together. One Saturday, we left my apartment to go to the store. Upon our return, a San Diego police officer was parked in the driveway. He told us to halt and stand next to my car. We asked what the problem was; he said a local grocery store had been robbed and we fit the robbers' description. We tried to convince him we had no knowledge of the robbery. As he talked with us, a call came through on his radio announcing the robbers had been caught. The police officer apologized. We accepted his apology with no animosity toward him.

I liked my apartment in National City, but before leaving the Philippines, I'd set a goal to buy a condo. I found a realtor, who identified my qualifying price range. I was disappointed to learn I didn't have much buying power. I couldn't afford to live in the areas I wanted to live. But I was determined, and I envisioned myself as a homeowner.

The interest rate at that time for a 30-year fixed loan was 14 percent. Even with my GI Bill, I needed more money for closing costs. The realtor suggested I consider buying a mobile home or call my parents for a loan. I refused both suggestions and found a part-time job cleaning office buildings at night. I also sold magazine subscriptions over the telephone. I ate beans and rice and took tuna or peanut butter and jelly sandwiches to work for lunch.

We finally found a condo complex in southeast San Diego. The building was excellent, but the location wasn't the most desirable area. I reminded myself, I was buying it as an investment property, and it would enable me to buy future real estate. My offer was accepted and I became the owner of a new two-bedroom, two-bath condo with a covered parking garage. I was one of the first five buyers in the new 20-unit complex.

My first night there, I gave thanks to God. I had decided not to re-enlist, so I'd no longer have a guaranteed monthly income for mortgage payments. But I had faith, and I knew I'd find a way to pay my bills.

The Years 1980–1989

Leaving Fleet Logistics Support Squadron
Three Zero (VRC-30)
San Diego, California

Nineteen eighty was the year of the Jheri Curl and I wasn't conforming to Navy-regulation haircut. On the weekend, I allowed my hair to hang below my ears. When I reported to the Navy, I wore my Navy ballcap all day to cover the length of my hair.

I was no longer a minor, compelled to go to the EM Clubs. I wanted to position myself for the civilian workforce. I socialized in Mission Valley, Mission Bay, and La Costa's sophisticated, upscale hotels. I surrounded myself with smarter and more successful people and met three guys (Dan, James, and Roy) who became close friends. They were ex-military and about eight years older. After being discharged, they worked various jobs before landing careers as a stockbroker, a university professor, and an attorney. They encouraged me to follow my dreams. We met weekly for happy hour, and they drank cabernet or merlot. Therefore, red wine became my drink of choice, too.

I'd seek out business opportunities everywhere I went. A guy at a bar gave me a sales pitch about his business, which he wanted me to join. I was excited to hear his presentation—until he mentioned Amway. I gracefully declined. Selling Amway products was not on my agenda.

By now I was ready for graduation. In May 1981, I proudly received my Bachelor of Science degree in business management from the University of La Verne. Charles Lott was there to cheer me on. Charles passed away in March 2021. I miss his friendship.

While still on active duty, I completed a resume, high-lighting my military experience, awards, and college degree. I kept a dated list of each resume mailed or delivered. Weeks later, I'd receive the standard rejection letters, and I mailed thank you letters to each.

My Navy enlistment expired in July 1981. I hesitated to tell Uncle Joe I wasn't re-enlisting because he saw me as a career sailor. The day I told him, I saw disappointment in his eyes. He didn't try to discourage me, just asked my plans. I told him I wanted to pursue a career in banking. Then later, I'd join the Naval Reserve.

My division officer and chief tried to convince me to re-enlist. I'd be recommended for the Limited Duty Officer (LDO) Program once I was promoted to petty officer first class. I'd passed the exam but hadn't been promoted due to the needs of the Navy. I respected and appreciated their support, but I respectfully told them I felt this was something I had to do for myself. I told them if my civilian career plans failed, I could always return to the Navy. But I had to satisfy my immediate career hunger. I liked being a sailor, and the opportunities had been beyond my expectations. In fact, *I was the Navy!* But I'd reached a point in my life where I wanted more.

Military to Civilian Transition
San Diego, California
June–July 1981

Everyone now knew I was leaving the Navy. I'd grown accustomed to receiving that paycheck every two weeks. The U.S. was at the beginning of heading into a recession. Unemployment topped ten percent, the economy was at a record low, and I had a mortgage. While it was overwhelming, I still felt it was something I had to do. My fear made me want to undertake the journey even more.

Because I had planned for this, I had saved 30 days of vacation. Rather than sell my vacation days back to the Navy, I requested to take them, and in June 1981, I started a serious job search.

I told myself: I was seeking security and thought a job would bring that security. As I thought more, I realized security was within me, and *I* was security. The economy would not determine whether I succeeded or failed. I was in control of my destiny; and with faith, I would prevail.

I stopped listening to the news, because everything I heard was doom and gloom. Instead, I reflected on where I'd come from. It had only been eight years since I came to San Diego with a broken suitcase covered with psychedelic wallpaper and $120 in my pocket. I'd developed military leadership skills and traveled overseas. I owned a home and a car. At 26 with a college degree, I refused to believe the recession could stop me from finding a job or in any way affect my goals. I assumed every business that opened its doors each morning was hiring.

Each morning, I awakened early, recited my prayers, and gave thanks to God. I went jogging and practiced playing the organ. I played an hour in the morning and an hour at night. If I needed extra income, I was prepared to play music.

After my morning run, I dressed as if I was going to work. I left home by 9:00 a.m., my briefcase filled with resumes. I visited business offices in the San Diego area. I noted mistakes I made on interviews and didn't repeat them at the next interview. One interviewer recommended I read the book, *What Color Is Your Parachute?*—which I found helpful. I didn't return home until after 4:00 p.m. Then I prepared for the next day by scheduling which businesses I'd target.

I got to know the bartenders at all the area's prestigious bars. They made good money, plus tips. If I had to do temporary odd jobs, I figured bartending would be a good part-time job, so I enrolled in bartender school. At the end of the two-week class, I had to take a written test and demonstrate I could make a certain number of drinks within a minute. I completed the course and received a mixologist certificate. However, I never had to use those skills.

I seriously considered moving to Northern California. I took a road trip to Sacramento for a few days and disseminated resumes along the way. I also sent my resume to Naval Air Station Alameda, Aircraft Depot Level Maintenance Facility for a procurement analyst position. With my Naval aviation experience, I was invited for an interview. Several people interviewed me. One man was a career civil servant who advised me to set a goal to earn a salary that matched my age. He said he was thirty years old, and his annual salary was $30,000. He wanted his salary to always match his age. I didn't say it, but I thought that was the dumbest way to set a goal for a salary increase. I didn't accept the job offer because the starting pay was less than my Navy salary.

I applied for a manager trainee position at Security Pacific

Bank. During the interview, I was told I'd receive training in various areas of the bank, such as mortgage, commercial lending, tellers' duties, and daily operations. I'd always had an interest in banking… until I heard the starting salary. I declined the job offer. However, being an international banker still interested me.

I interviewed for a sales representative job at Hallmark. The interviewer was an ex-Marine. Knowing I was Navy, we chatted about our military careers. Then he told me about the job. I would be assigned a territory and a company car. I'd go to stores to ensure cards were available for various holidays. Then he told me many, many people had applied for this position and I'd be among the final candidates. I left the job interview feeling good. But I didn't get it.

I had no more prospects for that day and recalled Audrey Mae was working for Computer Sciences Corporation (CSC) as a data-entry clerk. She had suggested I fill out an application.

I drove to CSC. I walked toward the two-building complex and didn't see a company name on either building. About this time, a man came out the side door of one building. I approached him and asked which building was CSC.

He gave me directions to the lobby. I thanked him and had begun to walk away when he said, "Excuse me, what business are you with?"

I told him I was being discharged from the Navy and was looking for a job.

Pointing at the building he had just exited, he said, "I'm the president of this company," and he handed me his card. He told me to ask the receptionist for an application and said he would call me in a couple days. I thanked him and we parted.

I filled out an application at CSC and attached my resume. Then I walked next door and told the receptionist I'd met the president in the parking lot, as I displayed his business card. She gave me an application, and I completed it and attached my resume.

A few days later, as I returned home from my morning jog,

the phone rang. The caller reminded me we had met in the parking lot a few days earlier and said he would like me to come in for an interview that day.

As I drove to the Systems Consultants office, I wondered what he'd ask me. I knew he had read my resume. He would know more about me than I knew about his company. Would I have the right answers to his questions? I realized I was causing myself confusion for no reason and told myself to just be myself and answer all his questions forthrightly.

I entered the lobby and told the receptionist I was there to see the president. She remembered me and asked me to have a seat.

Within minutes, he greeted me with a smile and a firm handshake and invited me into his office.

He said, "I don't know you; I don't know what you can or can't do. But I do know good people when I see them." The next words out of his mouth were, "I want you to work for me."

Not ready for this, I didn't know how to respond.

He mentioned a starting salary that was twenty percent more than I'd made after eight years of military service.

When I was finally able to speak, I asked, "What does the company do?"

He told me the company business was computer hardware and software. He explained how the company operated. The more he talked, the more I knew I didn't have a clue what he was talking about. My only exposure to computers was running aircraft maintenance data reports and analyzing the data. He continued talking about programming computers. It was like he was speaking a foreign language.

He said he wanted me to meet with the marketing manager, who escorted me into his office and briefed me on the company business. As he talked, he wrote and drew on the whiteboard. I was trying to comprehend what he was saying. But the more he talked, the less I understood. At the end of his presentation, he asked if I had any questions.

I said, "No, I don't have any questions." I was overwhelmed

because he was a high-tech guy. We left his office, and he led me back to the president's office.

The president invited me to meet with the production manager, who was sitting at his desk as if he had been waiting for us. He asked me about basic computer terminology, and I had no answers. Then he asked me, "Do you know the difference between a bit and a byte?"

I replied that I did not. In fact, all my replies to his technical questions were, "I do not know the answer."

But when we discussed generalities, I was confident and forthright with the answers I did know. After our talk, he escorted me back to the president's office.

When we were alone, the president said, "We're going to increase your starting salary offer by five percent."

I was now more confused. I had just undergone two interviews in which I believed I had not demonstrated my best talent. But the president was offering me a higher salary. It was clear they saw something in me I didn't recognize in myself. Still, I couldn't accept the offer because I felt overwhelmed.

The president said I should take a day to think about the offer and call him. He assured me I would be given on-the-job training. He also said I could attend night classes at the company's expense.

I left the office befuddled. I didn't know anything about computer hardware or software, and they still wanted to hire me. I'd gone through many job interviews that month. But none of them could compare to the interview I had just had. I went to Uncle Joe and told him what had transpired.

His answer was, "They see talent in you, and they know you'll be an asset for the company."

Those were comforting words.

When I went to bed, my mind still felt like it was exploding. I was trying to pinpoint how I would add value to the company. I wasn't technical, but I had valuable, transferrable skills. I identified my strengths as being reliable, trustworthy, not afraid of work and willing to learn. Before I fell asleep, I reminded myself

I had left the Navy because I wanted to be challenged. I was facing my first challenge.

The next morning, I woke up feeling confident and I gave thanks to God. As I jogged, I replayed all the challenges I had faced in the Navy, and what I'd learned on all my job interviews. I was told computers were the future and future jobs would be in that industry. When I returned home, I called the company and asked to be transferred to the president.

When he answered, he told me, "I'm glad you called. I have good news for you. We're going to increase your starting salary another five percent."

I was happy to hear about the salary increase. But I wasn't thinking about the salary. I was thinking about the job and what it entailed. With a rush of excitement, I told him I'd accept the job offer. Then I told the president I wasn't officially discharged from the Navy; I was on terminal leave and my official discharge date would be in two weeks.

He said I could start work after I was discharged and suggested I go into human resources to fill out employment paperwork. He said he also wanted to give me some books to read before my start date.

I thought about how I had been told the country was in a recession and unemployment was high. I was deeply grateful I had secured employment in challenging times in less than 30 days. I gave my thanks to God.

At the office, I completed the employment paperwork and left carrying thick books. At home, I glanced inside them. They were technical manuals and I concluded they weren't interesting reading. I had to re-read lines of text to understand what I had just read.

I had two weeks free, so I decided to take a road trip. I'd always wanted to drive up the Pacific Coast Highway. I headed north on I-5. When I could, I drove on Highway 1 and 101. I stopped along the way to enjoy the sights. It was a wonderful, relaxing drive and the scenery was breathtaking. I drove through

California, Oregon, and Washington, and into Vancouver, Canada. I had brought the technical manuals with me, but every time I tried to read them, I got through a few pages and then closed the book. I didn't comprehend what I was reading.

Back in San Diego, I finalized my official Navy checkout. Everyone at the Navy wished me well on my new job.

To welcome me to civilian life, Audrey Mae organized a party at her house. She'd invited about twenty-five people, mostly family and close friends. She served Southern-cooked gumbo, along with various appetizers. A large, decorated cake had "Welcome to Civilian Life" written in icing.

Northrop Grumman
San Diego, California
Computer Operator/Programmer/
Software Tester/Student
July 1981–July 1986

I joined Systems Consultants Incorporated in July 1981, and in 1982, the company name was changed to SYSCON Corporation. A few years later, Logicon acquired SYSCON. Shortly after this merger, Northrop Grumman acquired Logicon. Today, the company is Northrop Grumman.

My first day on the job, I was assigned a private office. I met with several staff members for a briefing. I tried my best to comprehend what they were saying, but it was as if they were speaking a foreign language. I didn't know which questions to ask, so I took notes and let the others do all the talking. Initially, I figured I was in the wrong business, and this wasn't the right job for me. Then I reminded myself everything was new because I'd never been exposed to this work environment. I told myself it was the right job for me, and I'd learn everything they wanted to teach me.

Working hours were 8:00 a.m. to 5:00 p.m. I was at my desk at 7:30 a.m. and often didn't leave the office until 6:00 p.m. I wore a suit and tie every day. My office door was always open. I sat at my desk reading the manuals. Other employees would sometimes stop and ask what I was reading.

I couldn't explain anything I'd read. My standard reply was, "I'm learning about computers."

At work, I only left my desk to use the bathroom. Sometimes folks invited me to lunch, but I only went on special occasions. Otherwise, I packed my lunch (tuna or peanut butter and jelly sandwiches) and ate at my desk. I was intent on learning my job, plus I was trying to build up my savings.

Late in the afternoon, my reading comprehension would decline. But I kept reading and a little sank into my brain. I brought the manuals home every night and read before bed.

After reading the manuals for at least a month, I wanted to do real work. But I still didn't know enough to contribute. Late one evening, after everyone went home, I went into the president's office.

"I've been reading those manuals and I still don't grasp or interpret everything I am reading," I admitted, feeling frustrated.

He told me, "Joe, you're doing fine. You're the perfect candidate for the job. We know you don't have any previous experience or knowledge of this business. You can be objective, plus bring new and fresh ideas to the workforce." Then he said, "Let's go to the pub and have a beer."

We walked across the alley to the pub. As we drank our beers, he said, "The company isn't making any money off you, but in future time the company will receive dividends. All you must do is continue studying the technical manuals." Then he suggested I enroll in a programming class at San Diego City College. He said the company would pay my tuition and assured me a career in computer science would ensure a bright future for me.

I felt uplifted after his pep talk. However, I still felt guilty when I received my paycheck. I was being paid handsomely, and all I was doing was reading technical manuals. I wanted to do something that made me feel I was earning my paycheck.

A few weeks later, I was transferred to the computer lab and given the job title of computer operator. I was excited but wasn't sure what to expect. I figured anything was better than reading technical manuals all day. My first time in the computer lab, I saw large mainframe computers with blinking lights, humming. I was dumbfounded at their size and capabilities. I was introduced to the lab computer operator, who was assigned as my mentor. He wasn't afraid to share his knowledge. As he briefed me, I hung on to his every word. I took notes for important things I had to remember. It surprised me that I'd begun to understand the terminology. Those days spent reading manuals were beginning to pay dividends. He taught me how to perform daily disk backup and restore procedures. I learned to perform maintenance on the production printers.

I enrolled in a Fortran class at San Diego City College. The first few weeks, the instructor held classroom lectures. It was like a light bulb went on in my head. Again, my reading of those technical manuals was beginning to pay dividends. While learning to program, I was encouraged to enroll in an algebra class. I spent many evening hours with one-on-one training at San Diego Adult Learning Center. Re-learning algebra concepts assisted me with logical thinking.

Once the class learned the concepts of computer programming, we moved into the computer lab to run our programs. The school had outdated computer systems. Students used keypunch machines to key in their codes. The coding was printed on a deck of keypunch cards, which were then fed into a reader for compiling the program. It wasn't uncommon for a student to drop a deck of keypunch cards on the floor. If the cards got out of order, the program wouldn't compile.

Because I worked in the computer lab, I compiled my programs at work, on our updated hardware. The programmers in the office were always willing to help me compile my programs, too. My manager allowed me to complete my homework on company time. When I completed the Fortran class, I took COBOL and RPG courses.

Sometimes, on Saturday morning I would go to the college to play racquetball. Then I'd go to the lab to assist students in compiling programs. Because I had compiled my program at work, I could tell students if they had the correct output.

As I progressed through my studies in school and on-the-job training, I often felt confused and sometimes lost my confidence. I'd question whether I had made the right career choice. Each time I had doubts, my answer was always the same: I was in the right place, on a steep learning curve at a rapid pace. With this answer, I was able to remain focused on learning.

Each day I learned something new. Being introduced to so many new things, I made a few mistakes along the way. Once, I accidentally purged needed files from a production disk. I spent hours in the lab after work, performing a disk restore. I wanted to ensure it was operational the next day for the programmers. That critical mistake was a lesson learned and fortunately, not repeated.

Many nights, we worked until midnight. One night, the contractors and subcontractors had a project meeting. Everyone was present except a Northrop Grumman representative. I was called in to represent my company. It was my first time being included in a meeting as the sole representative for the company. The next day, I presented my colleagues with meeting minutes, and I finally felt I was adding value.

Because we spent long hours working, the company rewarded us with tickets to a San Diego Chargers football game. To get out of the office and clear my head, rather than take a lunch break, I sometimes went out to play soccer with co-workers. I also participated in the company's 5K runs.

After three months, I received my evaluation. I felt I was still struggling to learn everything I was being taught. The write-up was all positive, just like my Navy evaluations. However, in the Navy I didn't receive special pay. I was told my next paycheck would reflect a salary increase.

A few weeks after that, I was told I would get a bonus check. I had never heard of anyone getting a bonus check. I was thankful for the raise; a bonus was more than I expected. Within three months, my salary was 40 percent higher than my military pay after eight years. The more I earned, the harder I wanted to work. I wanted to ensure I earned my pay.

The day I was hired, I was told if I remained at the company for a certain number of years, I would receive a pension. Later, the company pension plan was replaced with a 401k plan. After reading the guidelines, I enrolled in the 401k and religiously invested the maximum contribution annually.

My performance in the lab had been successful. I had gained working knowledge of computer hardware and completed computer programming classes at San Diego City College. My job title was changed to computer programmer, and I was transferred to the office with other software programmers.

Northrop Grumman had recently won a new contract with the federal government. Several new programmers had been hired, all of them seasoned programmers with years of experience. Because everyone was newly hired, the programmers were trying to stand out and prove they were the most valuable employee. Sharing of information was limited.

The new project required everyone to have a secret clearance. All the programmers submitted applications and within a few months, they'd all received their secret clearance, except me. They could go in and out of the classified lab, plus have access to secret material. Because I hadn't received my clearance, I was restricted from the lab and all secret material. Each day, I hoped I would get my secret clearance. I couldn't figure out what the holdup was.

One day, I was sitting at my desk reading project work. My telephone rang.

The voice at the other end of the telephone said, "This is the San Diego FBI. Can you please come downtown to the FBI office tomorrow morning?"

I couldn't figure out why the FBI wanted to see me. That whole night, I couldn't sleep. The next morning, I went straight to the FBI office.

The FBI agent took me into his office and asked me to be

seated. He said, "I've been working on your file for your secret clearance. I've traced your life from the day you were born. I cannot find any illegal or unlawful acts that you've been involved in. However, on your clearance application you wrote you smoked marijuana."

"Wait a minute! I can explain," I said. "When I was in the Navy, under peer pressure, I tried smoking marijuana once, to gain my friends' trust, and I never smoked again."

The agent said, "That's all I needed to know."

I left the office feeling relieved.

By the time I arrived in my office, my secret clearance had been granted. Sometimes being too honest can cause more problems.

The coding for the new project was Fortran. I had completed a Fortran class at city college. With additional on-the-job training, I learned to draw detailed flow charts before writing the code. Whenever my compilation was in an endless loop, I engaged an experienced programmer for help.

Approximately six months after being assigned to this project, the manager said the project was being cancelled. All the other programmers panicked, wondering if they would be laid off. Since we were no longer coding, they came in every day to update their resumes and network with other departments to secure new employment. I heard them on the phone with prospective employers. I didn't have enough experience to advertise myself as a programmer. Nor was I concerned about being fired.

I decided not to pursue an undergraduate degree in computer science. Instead, I enrolled in a master's program, attending class at night. Northrop Grumman paid my tuition. Each day I came in and worked on my homework.

The other programmers noticed I wasn't panicking about the project cancellation. I began hearing whispering. Some were curious as to how I got hired with no programming experience. One day, someone asked if I was a spy for the company.

I smiled and said nothing. I thought it would end, but someone then said I had been hired under Affirmative Action; therefore, I couldn't be laid off. I ignored the speculation and didn't try to explain my being there to anyone.

One day, the manager walked into my office and asked what I was working on. I told him I was working on my school homework.

He told me, "I have a special project for you."

My project was to perform a digital backup of needed files from an outdated computer and catalog the tapes. I really believed this was "make work" to keep me busy until I could be assigned to a new project. The other programmers weren't assigned to any special projects. They continued polishing their resumes as they sought new employment.

Days later, everyone knew a layoff was coming. Most of the programmers working on their resumes were the first to be let go. Three exceptionally good programmers were reassigned.

The manager called me into his office. The first words out of his mouth were, "You're not going to be fired." I was being assigned to a classified project offsite at a Navy base. It included surveillance software inside a bunker on the base. Because I had a secret clearance, I was qualified to work on the project.

I was assigned the 3:00 p.m. to midnight shift. The software coding was CMS2 and C++. I was also trained to write shell script commands. Plus, I'd developed skills as a computer operator. At the end of my shift, I did daily backups for the mainframe computers and transferred software programs to microfiche.

Every day, I sought out new opportunities to learn. The company had developed a digital utility meter reader used to read electric and water usage. The project needed extra volunteers. Employees worked their regular job and contributed to this project after hours and on weekends. Because I worked the night shift, I came in three hours early to work on the project. As needed, I came in on weekends. I couldn't add programming experience to the project, but I performed testing and wrote user manuals. This assignment taught me critical thinking. Nothing could be assumed; I had to write manuals with this thought in mind: Users are using a computer for the first time.

Because I worked nights, I sometimes went to noon Mass. One night, I had a dream about the Virgin Mary. In my dream, I was organizing a September birthday party for her. After Mass the next day, I went to the priest to discuss my dream. I asked him in which month the Virgin Mary was born.

He looked at me and said, "You don't have a wedding ring on your finger. Maybe you should consider becoming a priest. Allow me to bless you." He put his hand on my forehead and said a prayer. Then he said, "Young man, you should be having fun and not dreaming of the Virgin Mary."

That was the end of our conversation—and he never answered my question.

Each year I received a raise and a bonus check. I was grateful because the bonus check was unexpected. However, I learned later that other employees had received larger bonuses. For a split second, I became furious. Then I checked myself. I was beginning to get greedy rather than being thankful for what I had. It wasn't my concern what other people got. I had negotiated my salary and agreed to the salary I received. There'd always be people making more money than me, and people making less money than me. Plus, not everyone in the company received a bonus. I believed I was being treated fairly for my work contribution. With those thoughts, I felt satisfied and my greed was alleviated.

Sometimes, before going to the Navy lab, I would stop in the office to check my mail. On my way in, I glanced at the office bulletin board and saw a new job advertisement posted. The company had won a contract with the Air Force in Sacramento. The job was for an onsite hardware/software support manager. I read the job description but wasn't positive I could do the work. However, I'd always wanted to move to Sacramento, so I made a copy of the posting and put it in my briefcase.

I remembered being told, "Don't stay on one job too long. Learn as much as you can about a job and move on. Never cease the learning." This advice made me want to apply for this job. The more I read the posting, the more I convinced myself I wanted to apply.

A few days later, I went into the office, and the manager advertising the job had interviewed me when I first joined the company. We had a good relationship. We both drove VWs and would occasionally chat about our cars. I entered his office and said I was interested in the job posting in Sacramento.

"Joe, I know your qualifications," he told me. "I'm not going to interview you. If you want the job, it's yours."

We shook hands and he said I would have to be onsite within a month.

After leaving his office, I had second thoughts. I asked myself whether I could do the work. Again, I had to reflect on my work history to assure myself I was qualified for the job.

When I arrived at the lab, I told my manager I had accepted the Sacramento job, and she was supportive.

San Diego, California
July 1981–July 1986

One day, I was scanning the newspaper and noticed that the Holiday Inn cocktail lounge had an ad for a DJ. Rather than call or submit a resume, I drove there. The hotel manager and bar manager were in the process of auditioning, so I told them I wanted to apply.

When the auditioning DJ left the lounge, the manager called me into the booth. The two managers sat and waited for me to start. Fortunately, the board was simple to operate. I mounted two upbeat albums and slid into my DJ voice, introducing myself over the music. I ensured there was no dead air as I entertained them. After my audition, the manager asked for my number. He said there were other DJs to be auditioned before they could make a final decision.

A few days later, the bar manager called. He had selected two DJs. One for Wednesday and Thursday, the other for Friday and Saturday. He congratulated me and said I was selected for Friday and Saturday nights. He told me the starting pay and asked if I would accept the job.

I did.

The DJ hired to work Wednesday and Thursday nights wanted to work Fridays and Saturdays because those were the busiest nights. He quit after two nights, so the bar manager asked if I wanted to work two additional nights. I was now spinning records Wednesday through Saturday nights.

Wednesdays and Thursdays weren't busy. I was in the

master's program and attended night school, too. After class, I went to the lounge. While in the DJ booth, I cued up songs and people danced. I'd stoop down in the booth and do homework. Before the end of the song, I'd cue the next record. Then back to my homework and was back in the office the next morning.

San Diego Holiday Inn, D.J.

The Holiday Inn was busy on Fridays and Saturdays. A band would play for an hour, and I would play during their 30-minute break. I met many people; some were regulars. I had loads of energy. I'd be in the DJ booth, dancing and sweating as much as the people on the dance floor. People came to the booth and gave me tips and told me how much they enjoyed the music. I would refuse the money, but they'd insist I take it. Some would ask me to play for their weddings. One regular often came to the booth to request songs. He was always dressed professionally, in a suit and tie. He managed a trucking company. Once, while I was on my break, he invited me to snort cocaine with him. I said I didn't do drugs, and that was the end of our conversation.

Months later, when he came in, I noticed his personal hygiene and attire had declined. He had a body odor; his hair was uncombed. His suit was wrinkled and his shirt was dirty. I asked what was going on in his life.

He'd been fired from his job; he was living and sleeping in his van parked on the beach. I never saw him in the club again.

On the nights I played music, the hotel's marquee displayed "D.J. Joe Walker" in neon lights. I enjoyed playing disco music. I was having the time of my life. Plus, I was getting paid to do what I enjoyed.

Through the years, I continued to have a strong love for radio. *WKRP in Cincinnati* disc jockeys, Johnny Fever and Venus Fly Trap, were my paragons. I studied and listened to Paul Harvey religiously. I listened to Casey Kasem's *American Top 40* countdown and practiced how I would do a countdown differently. Wolfman Jack commanded a stage presence I wanted to duplicate. The two TV personalities I idolized were Don Cornelius and Dick Clark.

In one of my MBA classes, each student was assigned to create a business that made a profit. At the end of the semester, we had to present to the class our newly formed business, the business process, and how money was generated. I created a mobile discotheque, Musical Magic. I presented my business plan to the class and received an A for the semester.

A year later, I implemented that business plan, and Musical Magic was born. I got a business license from the City of San Diego, had business cards printed, built a portable DJ stand, and bought a Volkswagen bus, albums, turntables, a microphone, amplifier and speakers. Within three months, I had made a 100 percent return on my investment. I played music throughout Southern California. I was hired for Christmas parties, birthday parties, weddings and dinner cruises on the San Diego Bay.

Any weekend I didn't have to play music, I visited friends in Orange County. One weekend, we went to a Dodgers game.

I wasn't a baseball fan, but I enjoyed the socializing. We went to many concerts at the Irvine Amphitheatre. Friends introduced me to the Custom Shirt Shop, and I started wearing custom-made shirts. We ate at elegant restaurants and drank fine wine. Orange County became my second home.

I was living a good life. I had been profoundly blessed. I tried to motivate my nieces and nephew by rewarding them with $10 for every A on their report cards. Not one accepted the challenge. Not giving up, I wanted them to think about saving. I purchased U.S. savings bonds for them and helped them set up Roth IRAs. Still, they persisted in their lack of interest.

My Aunt Laura, in Galveston, always supported me. As a teenager, I'd stayed with her during the summer and she helped me find work. Because of her kindness, I promised myself I would repay her.

The farthest Laura had ever traveled was from Texas to Louisiana. Wanting to do something special for her, I invited her to come to San Diego. She was overjoyed. I sent her a round-trip airline ticket and met her at the airport. She talked non-stop about her first-ever flight.

She stayed with me for two weeks. I took her to the major San Diego tourist attractions and Tijuana, Mexico. On Sunday, Audrey Mae invited Laura to her church. Afterward, Audrey Mae and Josie cooked a Southern-style dinner.

When it was time for Laura to leave, I drove her to the airport. Before she boarded the airplane, she told me again, "You're my All-American Boy."

I did my best to live up to her great compliment.

A few years later, after Robert passed away, my father went to Galveston and assisted Laura with relocating to Louisiana. Not long after she was settled into her mother's home in Louisiana, my beloved Laura passed away.

Christmas was approaching. Uncle Joe planned to drive across country to Louisiana with his family for the holidays. He invited me to come along. I did most of the driving. My cousin

Pam sat in the passenger seat, and we talked endlessly as the others slept.

While in Louisiana, I visited friends from high school. I encouraged them to consider careers in the software industry. The business had been good to me. I was an advocate for computer software technology. Personal computers weren't as popular as they are today, but I encouraged them to start familiarizing themselves with computer usage.

On New Year's Day, I went skiing in the Big Bear mountains. The best skiing in Southern California is early morning. Afternoon, the snow starts to melt and becomes slushy. By 9:00 a.m., I was on the slopes. About noon, I packed up and drove back to San Diego. By early afternoon, I was jogging on the beach, listening to the roar of the ocean. In Southern California, you can hit the ski slopes in the morning and go to the beach that same afternoon.

One friend, an experienced hiker, invited me to go on a hiking trip with her. We drove to the Imperial County mountains and hiked several miles through the trails up the mountain. We carried our backpacks, sleeping bags, food and drinks. At the top, we sat and observed many shooting stars while drinking a bottle of wine. It was a beautiful sight.

I had lived in my condo for three years and it was time to sell. I'd bought it as an investment property. It had appreciated in value, and I wanted to take the profit and invest in a house. Within a month I had a buyer. I had started searching for a house but hadn't found one I liked. I had to move into an apartment. I closed escrow on the condo and turned a 30 percent profit.

My new apartment was in Mission Valley, on a hill, within walking distance of the San Diego Stadium. Whenever there was an event, I had a bird's eye view from my living room.

My search for a house in the San Diego area in my price range was exhausting. I looked at many homes, old and new. Price was always my determining factor. The older homes weren't well maintained, so I narrowed my search to new homes.

I easily qualified for a three-bedroom, two-bath, single-family home in a new subdivision in the Mira Mesa area. Still under construction, it would be completed within a week. I couldn't move in until escrow closed. But the builder let me move my second car (a 1973 Datsun 240Z) and household goods into the garage, since I'd terminated my lease at the apartment in Mission Valley. I didn't tell the builder, but I slept two nights in the garage on a mattress. I showered inside before the workers arrived.

I secured a 13 percent loan (the best available at the time) and moved all my things into the house. I was thankful to have bought my first house, and it felt good. My first night, I kept walking through the house, assuring myself it was real. Most of the neighbors were first-time homebuyers and everyone was friendly. We helped each other with lawn development and building good neighbor fences. Upon completion of a fence, we celebrated with a beer-and-wine party in the yard.

My manager regularly went on cruises. When she returned, she'd share her experience with the people in the office. The more I listened to her account of cruising, I wanted to experience cruising, too.

Years later, I went on my first Caribbean cruise. At each port, I went ashore and took in all the tourist spots. I even tried scuba diving. I enjoyed cruising so much, I started taking cruises once a year.

On a cruise through the Panama Canal, the ship docked at a Caribbean port. I was returning to the ship when I noticed a party boat blasting Caribbean music. The people on board were dancing and drinking, about to depart to a private island. I sauntered over and climbed aboard. I was given a cup of Jamaican rum punch. I started socializing and chatted with a middle-aged man. As the boat cruised to the island, I danced and had a refill of punch. Because the weather was hot, I'd taken off my T-shirt and my Saint Christopher medal around my neck was displayed.

When the party boat arrived on the private island, everyone got off and went swimming or snorkeling. While snorkeling, I noticed the middle-aged man from the party boat snorkeling, too. We started chatting again, and he asked, "Have you ever considered becoming a priest?"

I thought, *What have I said to this man for him to suggest I become a priest?*

I told him I'd considered it, but then I discovered girls. Besides, I preferred playing music.

Then I said, "I don't believe I have the qualities to become a priest."

He told me, "I'm a priest."

That stunned me.

"God knows we are not perfect; he just wants us to do the best we can," he told me. Then he added, "You would be an excellent priest."

On our return to the ship, he told me he wanted to give me a book to read. It was *Hungry for More of Jesus*. As I read through its pages, I easily related to everything that was written.

Naval Reserve
Fleet Logistics Support Squadron (VR-57)
Naval Air Station North Island, California
July 1982–June 1986

A year after being discharged from the Navy, I had established my civilian career. I was playing music part-time and enrolled in night school. I always had plans to join the Naval Reserve once I was settled in a civilian career. It was time for me to add that to my busy schedule.

I wanted to be assigned to VR-57. The squadron was stationed at North Island and provided Fleet logistics support throughout the world via C-9 aircraft. I didn't know anyone in the squadron, nor did I have any connections. I decided to drive over and introduce myself.

I introduced myself to the maintenance chief and said I was seeking a billet in the squadron. I gave him a summary of my active Navy career. We walked to the maintenance officer's office together to talk.

The maintenance officer looked up from his desk. "Hi Joe, how are you doing?"

"You two know each other?" the maintenance chief asked, startled.

We'd served together in VXE-6 and had deployed to Antarctica. I greeted him with a handshake and explained I'd been discharged from active duty and had begun a civilian career. Now ready to join the Naval Reserve, I hoped to be assigned to VR-57.

Without further questions, the maintenance officer said, "We'll find a billet for you." He told the maintenance chief about my performance at VXE-6, and I was immediately assigned a billet in the squadron.

As a petty officer second class, aviation maintenance administrator (AZ2), I was assigned to Maintenance Control. Drilling reservists reported to duty once a month. The drill weekends were Saturday and Sunday. I was still spinning at the Holiday Inn, too. Saturdays, after working in the Reserves, I went to evening Mass. Then I went to the Holiday Inn to run disco. Sunday morning, I was back at work in the Navy. We maintained a busy flight schedule. Due to the squadron mission, reservists could perform extra drills. If I didn't have class during the week or wasn't playing music, I reported to the Navy after leaving my civilian job. I would work until midnight and be back at my civilian job the next morning.

Due to my performance in the squadron, I was awarded Reservist Sailor of The Quarter.

Sometimes, on a drill weekend, the squadron held a two-mile fun run during lunch. At the time, I completed the two-mile run within 15 minutes, then played a game of racquetball.

Reservists are required to complete two weeks' active-duty training per year. As an AZ, I requested and was approved to perform my two weeks' active duty on a Western Pacific (West Pac) deployment. Because the squadron provided support around the world, our West Pac cruise was temporarily assigned to NAS Cubi Point, Philippines.

We landed at NAS Barbers Point, Hawaii, for refueling. We overnighted on Wake Island, near the International Date Line. Fewer than 200 people lived on Wake Island. I met a local guy with access to the island radio station. When I told him I worked as a DJ, he gave me a station tour. No one was broadcasting, so I got to go on the air. The next morning, we flew to NAS Cubi Point, Philippines. While there, I worked in Maintenance Control. We flew daily missions. Once the aircraft was launched, I was free to go to Olongapo City. It was my first time back since 1979, and I got to see old friends. Nothing had changed. Olongapo City was the same as when I was stationed there (i.e., every night was a Saturday-night party).

West Pac Deployment

During our overseas deployment, we flew to Naval Air Facility Atsugi, Japan for two days. We were granted liberty, but no one wanted to go to Tokyo, so I set out alone. I boarded the bullet train, feeling uneasy because all the signs were in Japanese. I communicated with the ticket agent to purchase my rail ticket to Tokyo. Before the train arrived at each station, the announcer would call out the name of the town, in Japanese. I'd been riding for a while and hadn't heard "Tokyo" so I figured I must have missed the announcer's call. I exited the train at the next station.

I walked to the terminal and was the only foreigner there. I approached a Japanese man for directions, but he didn't understand and just stared at me. I went to someone else and got the same response. I panicked. Of all the people in that station, not one spoke English. Plus, I saw no signs in English. I was in a small town between Atsugi and Tokyo. I went back downstairs to get on the next incoming train.

When the train arrived at the station, I got on and listened to the calls for each station. After three stops, I heard, "Tokyo" and felt relieved. In Tokyo, I saw many Americans. Signs were posted in Japanese and English, and I had no problem getting around.

I entered the public toilet, and to my surprise, I saw a squat toilet, with the bowl embedded in the floor. Because no part of the body touches it, the squat toilet is believed to be more sanitary.

I went to a restaurant. There were no spoons, forks, or knives. Only chopsticks. Despite never having used chopsticks, I managed to eat my dinner. Afterward, I paid my bill and left a tip on the table. I'd exited the restaurant when my waitress approached me, extending her hand with the money I'd left on the table. I tried to tell her the money was for her. She refused to accept it. When I returned to my hotel, I learned tipping was not customary in Japan.

After leaving Naval Air Facility Atsugi, we flew to South Korea. After refueling, we went into town. I found a tailor and had a custom ski jacket made, and a winter coat. I got a good deal on tennis shoes, too.

After our West Pac mission, we had a layover on Guam, then overnighted in Hawaii. The Navy base in Hawaii had no available rooms, so our crew was authorized to stay in town, at a hotel overlooking the beach. The next day, we returned to San Diego and I had completed my two weeks training.

Leaving San Diego

I went to Sacramento to go house hunting and searched newspaper ads for apartments. I didn't know where I wanted to live. But I knew I didn't want to live within Sacramento's city limits.

I called about various apartments. After viewing several, I hadn't found one to my liking. I had circled one ad for an apartment listed in Rocklin. I didn't know that location, so I called to inquire. Everything I heard sounded perfect. I drove there and immediately fell in love with the area. The complex was a new building in a rural area. I signed a lease on a two-bedroom, two-bath apartment. I left my car in the garage and flew back to San Diego.

I scheduled a date for the movers to pack my household goods. The only things I packed were my personal items. After my household goods were loaded into the moving van, I needed a place to stay for three days. The manager at the Holiday Inn gave me a room free of charge.

At St. Rita Church, I resigned my position as a catechism teacher and said my goodbyes to my fellow parishioners.

I hired a property manager for my property in Mira Mesa; the house was rented immediately.

Within days, I'd tied up loose ends at work and said goodbye to my family. With my VW packed, I left San Diego. Driving north on I-5, I wondered if I would be able to learn my new job. I immediately buried those negative thoughts and reflected on all my job responsibilities in the Navy and my years at Northrop Grumman. My thoughts assured me I'd be successful. I felt relaxed and focused on listening to my music as I drove toward Northern California.

Northrop Grumman
Sacramento, California
Computer Onsite Manager/
Hardware & Software Installation/Student
July 1986–December 1989

Northrop Grumman's contract with the U.S. Air Force required onsite work at McClellan Air Force Base in Sacramento. The Air Force had many aircraft technical manuals, and Northrop Grumman was tasked with converting them all into digital format. The long-term goal was for airmen to use computer laptops when performing aircraft maintenance, and hardcopy manuals would be obsolete. Also, digital aircraft technical manual updates could be completed instantaneously.

The project was named Automated Technical Order System (ATOS). Prior to leaving San Diego, I was given limited training, with substantial reading assignments. I had a steep learning curve and was ready for the challenge.

My first day on the job, I was introduced to the government employees. Everyone had been waiting for my arrival. They'd read all about ATOS, eager to start the project, and they were ready to do whatever I requested. With my limited experience and knowledge of the project, we gathered in a conference room to discuss our plan of action.

After our meeting, I was taken to a large empty room, which had been designated the ATOS laboratory room. My manager gave me a list of action items to execute immediately. The first was to get phone lines installed in the lab. I needed a telephone to call in workers, and I needed a dedicated number for people to contact me. While working to get dedicated phone lines installed, I employed workers to install a computer raised floor.

Once I had a dedicated line, incoming calls were non-stop. I was on the phone constantly, approving security clearances for contractors to come on base, and scheduling future work. While the computer raised floor was under construction, I scheduled the electrician to come in and install an uninterruptible power supply (UPS).

Once the electrician had run the cables and the UPS was operational, large freight trucks unloaded computer hardware on the dock. I'd never seen this quantity of hardware—mainframes, disk drives, tape drives, digital scanners, CAD workstations, printers and IBM PCs.

As the project's main contact, I coordinated and scheduled the various vendors' hardware installation dates. Each night, at home, I read the manuals to shorten my learning curve on the hardware and the project activities.

Software programmers from the main office in San Diego installed software and performed testing. We worked seven days a week, 14 to 16 hours a day and delivered the system on time. I was included in the system delivery package; I stayed onsite to manage the project. Before they left, the software programmers gave me a crash course on the system's hardware and software debugging techniques. Plus, I was responsible for training all the government employees to operate the various workstations. The operators merged text and graphics to create digital aircraft technical manuals.

Solving system problems seemed endless. With no specific assigned working hours, I was in the office from early morning until late evening. I upgraded software after normal working hours. Because I was responsible for all facets of the project, I worked hard—and I enjoyed the challenge.

Months later, I was comfortable with the daily operation of the project. I kept detailed notes and could resolve most hardware and software problems quickly.

After working onsite a few years, the system stabilized, and I performed periodic hardware and software upgrades. Government employees were trained to resolve most of their own problems. My job became less hectic.

Sacramento, California
July 1986–December 1989

I left home early each morning and didn't return until late at night. I was coming home after work around 9:00 p.m. I exited the freeway and in my rearview mirror, I saw a police car following me. He engaged his flashing lights. I pulled to the side of the road and waited for the officer to approach my car. He asked for my driver's license and registration. I presented both. After looking at my license, I'm sure he noted my San Diego address. He asked where I was going. I said I was going home, and I lived in Rocklin. He returned my license and registration and said, "Have a good night," and walked away.

At the time, I was the only Black living in Rocklin. I assumed my going and coming had been monitored. After this encounter, I was never stopped again.

After driving from San Diego to Rocklin, my 1969 VW Bug started failing. I'd logged over 350,000 miles. One evening, on my way home, I drove into a car dealer's lot. I took one look at the Suzuki Samurai and knew that was the car I wanted. After hours of haggling over price, I traded in my VW and drove away in a new, blue 1986 Samurai. The Volkswagen Bug had served me well.

My first two months in Northern California, I lived out of boxes. Working seven days a week, I didn't have time to unpack. The first weekend that I had free time, I organized my apartment. My cousin, Regina Hicks, lived in Sacramento. As I settled into the area, she invited me over for Sunday dinners and introduced me to her circle of friends.

I was impressed with the Rocklin area. Within a year, I wanted to buy a condo there. I found a realtor and identified a new three-bedroom, two-bath condo. The builder had defaulted and the bank held the note. I told my realtor to submit an offer for two and a half percent less than the asking price. He told me it would be a waste of time, and the bank wouldn't accept my offer. Instead of arguing, I hired a new realtor and asked him to submit my offer. The bank accepted.

I met with the realtor to make a good-faith deposit. I was taken aback when he told me about the closing costs.

The next day, on my way to the realtor's office, I checked my mail and found a Northrop Grumman's bonus check I hadn't anticipated. In February 1987, I closed escrow and moved into my new condo.

Whenever I went to Louisiana, I visited as many people as possible. At Bayou Goula Elementary School, Miss Wisher greeted me with a hug. She was now the principal, a well-deserved promotion. She had been a dedicated teacher most of her career. I'll be forever in her debt for her fostering my academic skills and my enthusiasm for learning. I'd also visit with my former teachers and principal at White Castle High School.

During the Thanksgiving and Christmas holidays, I volunteered with the Salvation Army. I assisted with feeding the poor and homeless. I worked in the kitchen and, after everyone was fed, I assisted with cleanup.

My barber, who played guitar, volunteered to play music at the Sacramento homeless shelter. When I told him I played keyboard, he invited me to join him. We played music during dinner.

Having lived in Rocklin a few years, I considered it home. While I liked my condo, I heard of a new development in Stanford Ranch and wanted to learn about it.

I don't live my life searching for situations to complain about. But I'm not naïve, and I'm well aware when I'm disrespected or not welcome. That said, it was a Saturday morning when I left home in shorts, a T-shirt and flip flops. I went into a real estate office in Rocklin to inquire about the new housing development. An elderly woman with silver hair sat at a desk.

I greeted her and asked, "Do you have any available information on the new development in Stanford Ranch?"

As she looked at me, she said, "The houses in Stanford Ranch are very expensive, and you cannot afford the price of those homes."

My immediate instinct was to tell her exactly what I could afford. Instead, I calmly replied, "You're probably right." I turned around and walked out.

Weeks later, in search of a local internet provider, I was told about a computer office in Rocklin. The gentleman I spoke with was very helpful. We immediately bonded, and I learned he was in the Air Force Reserve. I told him I was in the Naval Reserve. We talked about our military careers. Then he said, in his civilian life, he was a realtor and was the owner and manager of a real estate office in Rocklin. I replied that I had been in his real estate office. I related the encounter I'd had with the silver-haired woman. He apologized for her actions, thanked me for telling him about my experience in his office, and said I wasn't the first person to complain about her behavior.

Weeks later, when I returned to the office to meet with him, she was no longer there.

I sold my condo, at a tidy profit. The Stanford Ranch homes under construction were selling fast. Many people submitted deposits before construction even began. When I met with the subdivision salesman, the only house left was the model home. On a corner lot, it was being used as the sales office. He told me it would be torn down, and two houses would be built on the lot. I made an offer on one of the houses, signed paperwork and gave my deposit.

Weeks later, I went to check out the progress and was surprised to see only one house being built on the corner lot. The salesman explained that the builder had made an inaccurate calculation. Two houses on the lot wouldn't be possible. Only one house was being built and the price I was quoted would be honored.

My three-bedroom, two-bath home was completed on the extra-large lot. I had now purchased my fourth property. I moved in and met my new neighbors. Alberto Recendez lived directly across the street. We mowed our lawns weekly at the same time. Afterward, we'd socialize. We became friends and took many skiing trips to Lake Tahoe.

On my way home from work one day, I passed a car dealership. A Porsche 944 on the lot caught my eye, so I went in and asked to do a test drive. As I drove along the freeway, its speed and curve handling impressed me. I drove back to the dealership, where the salesman tried to get me to buy it. I told him I wasn't ready to make a purchase. I wanted to buy the car, but I needed a strategy.

The next day after work, I went back. As I drove in, a different salesman approached me. The salesman from the previous day didn't notice me. I said I was interested in buying the Porsche 944. He tried to encourage me to take it for a test drive. I told him I didn't want to. I indicated the price posted in the window, made an offer, and said if he accepted the offer, I'd buy it. He said he couldn't sell it at that price.

I said, "Maybe you should get someone who will accept my offer." He got the message: I was serious. He took me to his manager, who offered a discount of the list price; I held to my original offer. I had arrived at 5:00 p.m. It was now 11:00 p.m. and we were still haggling.

I said, "If I leave tonight without closing this deal, I won't come back. Do you want to sell this car at the price I offered?"

We finally came to an agreement. I received the price I wanted, plus extra for the sale of my Datsun 240Z. I drove home in the 1987 Porsche 944, a car I cherish and still drive today.

Naval Reserve
Fleet Logistics Support Squadron (VR-55)
Naval Air Station Alameda, California
July 1986–August 1989

Before leaving for Sacramento, my division officer assisted me in securing a billet with VR-55 in Alameda. VR-55 provided the same mission as VR-57, and the squadron flew C-9 aircraft.

The first month I was supposed to report to VR-55, I was still working seven days a week at my civilian job. I called the maintenance chief to explain my working conditions. He said I could report to drill the following month. He mentioned a Naval and Marine Corps Reserve Center in Sacramento. "Navy sailors drill at the reserve center, too," he said. "Until your civilian work situation is resolved, drill in Sacramento."

Although my civilian work situation was still hectic, I was able to report to the Sacramento Reserve Center. The first time I went there, they wondered why I was there. Because my specialty was Naval Aviation, I didn't relate to the mission at the reserve center. Therefore, I was free to wander the passageway and talk with people.

As I walked past the recruiter's office, he called me in to chat. I told him my situation and that I was temporarily drilling at the Sacramento Reserve Center.

As our conversation progressed, I told him I was waiting to be promoted to petty officer first class. My plans were to then apply for the Navy Limited Duty Officer Program.

He asked if I had a degree.

I told him I had a BS.

The Navy had opened a new officer program, Direct Commission Officer (DCO). Its main requirement is having a BS or higher. I was excited to learn about it. The recruiter gave me an application package with instructions for completion. It took a couple of weeks to complete because I had to supply professional reference letters, a full physical, and other detailed paperwork. Once I had it completed, the recruiter said I should hear back from the recruiting board within a month. The only person I told about the DCO Program was Uncle Joe.

A month later, I was free to attend regular drill weekends at VR-55. As a petty officer second class, aviation maintenance administrator (AZ2), I was assigned to work in maintenance control. The maintenance chief assigned me work-center supervisor, with two airmen reporting to me.

Two months later, I heard back from the DCO Recruiting Board. I hadn't been accepted. I called the recruiter to share the sad news. He said, not everyone is accepted in the DCO Program and suggested I complete my MBA and reapply.

Uncle Joe was disappointed, too, but encouraged me to keep trying.

On Thanksgiving weekend, the squadron operated with minimum manpower. Reservists were often asked to volunteer during this time so the active-duty sailors could be with their families. My civilian job closed over the Thanksgiving holidays. I was off from Thursday through Sunday, so I volunteered to come into the Navy and work over the holiday.

Because the squadron provided support worldwide, I was authorized to perform my active training overseas. I departed Alameda with the C-9 Aircraft Crew for our two-week assignment to Rota, Spain, and Sigonella, Italy.

In Sigonella, I assisted with the aircraft maintenance before securing. Granted two days' liberty, most of the flight crew (who'd flown there many times) wasn't interested in touring the area. One sailor familiar with the town invited me to attend High

Mass. Afterward, I wanted to go to Rome, but he wasn't interested, so I went alone.

It was my first time traveling in Italy, and I didn't speak Italian. At the train station, I successfully communicated that I wanted a one-way ticket to Rome.

I reclined in my seat to read a book. Soon the conductor walked down the aisle, punching tickets. He motioned for my ticket. He gave it back and said something in Italian. Then he spoke louder, waving his hands in the air. I was the only American on the train. The Italian passengers sat in silence. I didn't understand him, so I got up and walked to the next car.

He entered the coach where I now sat. As he came down the aisle, punching tickets, I braced myself. He motioned for my ticket, punched it, and gave it back. I was relieved not to hear him rant.

Finally, the train arrived in Rome. I wandered the streets, taking photos. I walked to Vatican City and the Coliseum. Later I wandered to the center of the city. It was early in the afternoon, and the store managers started closing their shops. It was *riposo* (siesta) time.

Once the stores reopened, I sat at a sidewalk café, drank a glass of wine and people watched. It appeared motorists made their own driving rules. I witnessed many fender benders. I met some Americans and shared with them my train-ride experience. They said I had bought a regular ticket and I was sitting in the wrong section. The conductor was telling me to move to the coach section, which I hadn't understood.

Onboard NAS Sigonella, I went into the Navy Exchange to buy officer ensign bars. I wasn't a commissioned officer, but I felt one day I would be an ensign. I wanted the bars to keep me focused on my goal. I bought the gold bars and carried them in my briefcase. Each day, I looked at them as my reminder of what I wanted to accomplish.

While in Sicily, I had a chance to see Mount Etna spewing lava and hot ashes into the air.

We departed Italy and flew to a base in France to deliver cargo. After unloading the aircraft, I went into the air terminal for a drink of water. I didn't see a drinking fountain. In a small cafeteria, a lady stood behind the counter. I walked over and asked for a glass of water.

She retrieved a glass from a cabinet, held it toward the light, and inspected it. Then she rinsed it under running water in the sink and held the glass up for inspection a second time. At last, she filled it with water and presented it to me with a smile.

I returned her smiled with thanks. As I walked back to the aircraft, I mused that I had never been served a glass of water with such detailed attention.

At Naval Station Rota, Spain, I met a chief whom I had served with in the Philippines. He invited me to his home for dinner, where I met his family.

Upon completing our mission, we overnighted in Bermuda. I rented a moped (scooter) and traveled the island. I went to a restaurant, ate, and socialized with locals. At night, the restaurant was converted into a disco party.

Due to my maintenance control contributions on drill weekends, I was named Reservist Sailor of the Quarter.

In June 1988, I earned my MBA from National University, with an emphasis in Marketing.

Now I was ready to reapply for the Navy's DCO Program.

I scheduled a physical, procured reference letters, and completed all the forms. Within a month, I had compiled the package and proofread it several times. I was now ready to deliver it to the recruiter. We reviewed my package together. He submitted it to the recruiting board in Washington, D.C., saying I should hear back within a month.

I called Uncle Joe and told him. He was confident I would be selected this time.

A month later, I hadn't heard anything. I thought maybe my package was lost in the mail. I called the recruiter for a status update. He said not receiving a letter was a good sign; it meant I was still being considered.

The recruiter tracked my submission. All DCO packages were scrutinized by various Navy departments. He'd update me each time my package cleared a department. Several weeks later, he called to say it had been in limbo and he couldn't track it. He assured me that as long as it was in their custody, I was still being considered.

One day he called to share a Naval message. Only four candidates would be selected for that year's DCO Program. While he could no longer track my package, he assured me I was still being considered and shouldn't feel discouraged.

A few days later, at work, my phone rang. It was the Navy Recruiter. Immediately, my heart started to beat faster. I knew he was calling with either good or bad news.

Before I could say anything, he said, "Go buy your khaki uniform, Ensign Walker. You were selected for the DCO Program."

Becoming teary eyed, I gave thanks to God, and I thanked the recruiter for his assistance.

I went to his office to pick up my commission officer paperwork. He congratulated me and shared the selection results: two candidates each from the East and West coasts. I felt proud to know I was one of the two selected from the West coast.

He told me to bring my paperwork to VR-55 on my next drill weekend. My commanding officer would perform the swearing-in ceremony. I was told to buy my uniform and ensign bars but not pin the bars on my collar. The CO would pin them on after I was sworn in.

I called Uncle Joe to tell him the good news.

I could hear him yelling through the phone, telling Faye I'd been selected.

Then I called the rest of my family to share the news.

On drill weekend, I left home early for Alameda in my khaki uniform minus the ensign bars. I knew almost everyone in the squadron, yet no one knew I had applied for the DCO Program—let alone been accepted. That drill weekend would be like no other.

As I walked toward the hangar, it didn't take long for the other sailors to notice. Everyone was accustomed to seeing me in my enlisted-sailor uniform or navy dungarees. I was surrounded by at least a dozen sailors asking me questions faster than I could respond.

I heard one sailor say, "Are you crazy? Why are you wearing that uniform?"

They all assumed I would be thrown in the brig. They couldn't believe what they were seeing.

When I was finally able to tell them that I had been promoted via the DCO Program, no one would believe me. I was bombarded with questions. As I continued toward the hangar, the crowd grew. I had to fight my way inside.

The news traveled fast, and the CO stood in his doorway, waiting for me. He invited me to be seated. I gave him my DCO paperwork, telling him I had been working on this for years and had finally been selected.

He said it would be his pleasure to pin on my ensign bars. He'd perform the swearing-in ceremony in the presence of the squadron sailors at morning quarters.

By now, everyone was standing at attention on the hangar deck. I followed the captain and command master chief down the passageway and stood at attention next to the command master chief. After each division reported, all present and accounted for, the captain conducted my swearing-in ceremony. Then he pinned my ensign bars onto my shirt collar. He shook my hand, and everyone cheered and clapped.

The captain walked to the podium and started his speech. He said, "Last month, he was Petty Officer Walker, and he wore an enlisted uniform. This month, he's Ensign Walker, and he's wearing an officer khaki uniform. Ensign Walker is a role model for all enlisted sailors." Again, he congratulated me for a job well done. I wasn't just an ensign. I was a Mustang! That's military slang referencing prior enlisted service.

Everyone gathered around, offering congratulations and asking questions. When I tried to answer, others would interject with more questions. I stayed at least 30 minutes, answering their questions.

When I finally got away, I entered maintenance control, where I'd worked as a petty officer second class. The maintenance chief, who'd been my supervisor, said his enlistment had expired and he was ready to re-enlist. I felt honored when he asked me to perform his re-enlistment oath.

Because I was promoted to ensign, I was immediately transferred. I reported to the personnel office and received transfer orders to Mobile Maintenance Facility (MMF-0280).

Naval Reserve
Mobile Maintenance Facility (MMF-0280)
Naval Air Station Moffett Field, California
September 1989–November 1991

As a new ensign, on my next drill weekend, I reported to MMF-0280, NAS Moffett Field. MMF-0280 had five officers and approximately 100 enlisted. The unit supported an operation in Misawa, Japan.

As the lowest-ranking officer in the unit, I was assigned Admin Officer. My office performed the unit administrative and clerical duties. Highest priority was always given to publishing the unit Plan of the Month and processing enlisted evaluations.

Three yeomen reported to me. Senior among them was a petty officer first class, who supervised the junior yeomen. Mostly, I interacted with the petty officer first class.

As a new ensign, I wore all my prior service ribbons on my uniform, including the Navy Good Conduct ribbon, awarded to enlisted sailors only. It indicates prior enlisted service.

The petty officer first class in the office tried to test me. Needing my signature on a letter, he said, "Joe, can you sign this letter for me?"

Everyone in the office had heard him. I knew I had to nip this in the bud. I stood and asked him to step outside the office.

Once outside, I looked directly into his eyes and said, "Whenever you address me, you say, 'Ensign Walker' or 'Mr. Walker.'"

He immediately tried to give me an explanation, and I cut him short. "I do not want to hear your explanation; just remember what I said." I turned and walked back into the office and he followed.

After that incident, I never had further problems with him or anyone else working for me.

There was a chief initiation in progress on base. One of the chiefs had no sponsor. Someone put out the word that a new ensign was on base. I received a call requesting I come to the initiation as a sponsor. Everyone in the Chief Mess knew I was a prior enlisted. I was drilled to the fullest. It was all fun and games. At the end of the day, I was present for the chief-pinning ceremony. That was one of my most enjoyable days in the Navy.

One Sunday on a drill weekend, I was on my way home in uniform and stopped at Travis Air Force Base. As I got out of my car, two Air Force airmen walked toward me. I could see they were trying to figure out if I was wearing a Navy officer or enlisted uniform. As I approached, they didn't salute. If I were on a navy base, I would demand a sailor salute. But I gave the airmen a pass; sometimes they don't know the other service uniforms.

As I passed by, I heard them talking among themselves. I was about four steps in the opposite direction when I heard in a loud voice, "Excuse me, Sir!"

I turned around; both airmen were standing at attention in salute.

I rendered a salute and said, "Carry on!"

They responded, "Thank you, Sir!"

Newly commissioned officers were required to attend the Direct Commission Officer (DCO) School at Naval Air Station Pensacola, Florida. The comprehensive, intense course was divided into two phases, designed to facilitate introduction responsibilities as a Naval Officer. Civilians with special skills that are needed by the Navy, such as doctors and nurses, attend the course. With my prior military experience, I was called on by the instructor many times to provide real Navy experiences.

During my training, an anesthesiologist and I became good friends. We'd study together after class. During our training, it was Mardi Gras week. Rather than study the whole weekend, we decided to drive to New Orleans. We studied on the road by quizzing each other. After spending time in the French Quarter, we did no studying on our return trip.

The Navy required every sailor to complete a Physical Readiness Test (PRT). Most sailors in MMF-0280 couldn't pass it. I was assigned as PRT coordinator. With two petty officers under my direction, I implemented a monthly PRT. Every sailor who failed their previous PRT was required to report to the gym on Saturday after work. When the unit's next PRT was completed, MMF-0280 scores had increased substantially.

I received my orders for two weeks' active-duty training in Misawa, Japan. When I reported aboard, I was told I'd work in the Admin office and was invited to attend the morning briefing. One of the main discussions was an outdated Wang computer. The unit had been unsuccessful at transferring its critical files to a new computer. I was asked to assist. With the database administrator assistance, we successfully retrieved the files and stored them on the new computer.

The Years 1990–1999

Northrop Grumman
Sacramento, California
Computer Onsite Manager
January 1990–August 1998

As a program analyst, I still worked onsite at McClellan AFB. I managed the Automated Technical Order System (ATOS) Project's daily operations and performed hardware and software debugging, data conversion, software testing, and occasionally installed new hardware. I had become an expert operating the Kurzweil Optical Character Recognition (OCR) Scanner. Capturing and storing data was my expertise. For major system upgrades, I was invited to the San Diego main office to be trained on the new software, then I trained the government employees.

Northrop Grumman participated in a computer technology fair in Phoenix, Arizona. I was invited to accompany the team. I assisted with setup and demonstrated our software to potential customers.

I was becoming antsy and wanted another challenge. Sometimes after work, I'd go to the bars in Sacramento for happy hour. I mingled mostly with state employees, hoping to get a state contract. There were always other contractors at the bars, too. A man who worked at IBM encouraged me to apply for a job there. I gave him my resume, but my skill set didn't match their needs.

ATOS Computer Lab

I circulated my resume, seeking other opportunities. I realized mainframe computers were no longer in demand. The internet had been introduced and most people now used desktop computers. My computer skills were outdated.

Fortunately, each month I reported for my drill weekend and worked with officers employed at technology companies in Silicon Valley. Naval projects we were assigned to work on integrated the latest technology. Working alongside them, I gained a new skill set.

On drill weekends, the officers told me about job opportunities in Silicon Valley. Many of them were leaving their jobs and going to startup companies. I heard stories of a company going public and the employees becoming instant millionaires.

Sacramento, California
January 1990–August 1998

In December 1992, Li'l Sister passed away. I flew to Louisiana for the funeral. I saw my half-siblings, Gloria and Marcus. The last time I had seen them, we were all kids. After Lil Sister's death, Gloria and I developed a close relationship. She's a caring and unselfish woman with an abundance of love.

A Class of 1973 high school reunion was advertised in the local paper. I graduated in 1973 and had never attended a class reunion. Although I didn't attend that school, I called the reunion coordinator and requested a registration form, which I submitted along with the attendance fee.

On the night of the reunion, I drove to the hotel and walked up to the registration desk. I had registered as "Joe Walker." I knew after 20 years many of the people wouldn't look the same. The reunion committee had taken a photocopy of each person from the yearbook and attached the photo to a name tag. The name tag for Joe Walker had the photo of a white guy. The lady at the desk assumed it was a mistake and apologized. I told her it was fine. I didn't pin the tag to my jacket. As I mingled, many people tried to refresh my memory of certain high school events. Some were convinced they remembered me. I gracefully agreed with any remembrance being discussed. I was a reunion crasher and the real Joe Walker in that class didn't attend. I had a great time and made several new friends.

I called Uncle Joe and suggested a family reunion. He liked the idea, so I started planning. I contacted family members and assigned duties. We created a flyer that was distributed, and we dedicated the reunion to Uncle Charlie Pierre, who, at 94, was then the oldest living relative.

The Walker/Pierre family reunion was held in August 1994, at the Hilton in Baton Rouge, with about 300 in attendance. The majority of our family is Southern Baptist. Almost everyone can sing, and some play musical instruments. We had a Gospel Extravaganza. My uncles led the singing. We also have ministers in our family, so all married couples renewed their vows. The food was a Southern-style buffet.

A friend who was an elementary school teacher in Stockton, California, told me some of her students were from military families, and they'd expressed an interest in learning military time. She asked me to come to her school for a military time presentation.

I created charts and wore my dress uniform. I explained why the military uses a 24-hour clock. At the end, to add a little fun, the students quizzed me by asking specific time conversions.

I was seeking volunteer work in the community. As I read the newspaper classifieds, I saw a Naval Sea Cadet ad. I didn't know anything about the Sea Cadets, but I was willing to learn. I called the number in the ad and a pleasant-sounding woman answered. Her name was Norma von Dohren. She was a petty officer in the Naval Reserve. Starting a new unit, she was recruiting officers, so I signed up as a Sea Cadet officer.

Norma and I co-founded "Gold Country Division." She was the Commanding Officer and I was assigned Executive Officer. In addition, I functioned as Admin Officer, Training Officer and PRT Officer. During PRT, I ran along with the Sea Cadets.

The Sea Cadets drilled one weekend a month. Male and female cadets between 10 and 18 years old learned basic seamanship, patriotism, and self-reliance, among other things. When a cadet didn't have a ride home, either Norma or I drove them. We took the Sea Cadets on field trips and, each year, they participated in local parades in the Sacramento area. On Veterans Day,

Independence Day and Memorial Day, Sea Cadets marched in municipal parades. Over the Christmas holidays, we went to the Salvation Army to monitor the line as children were given free toys.

Norma and I rotated duties as Commanding Officer and Executive Officer. Norma was an outstanding recruiter with many connections in the Navy. She recruited many cadets and identified hard-to-find Sea Cadet uniforms. We enrolled Sea Cadets into the Naval Academy and Navy ROTC. Due to the many hours I devoted to the Naval Sea Cadet, I was awarded the Military Outstanding Volunteer Service Medal.

I saw an ad requesting a trumpet or bugle player for military funerals. I called and was told many funerals were held weekly. *Taps* was currently being played on a portable tape recorder because there was no live performer. I volunteered to play *Taps* whenever my schedule allowed. I reported to the cemetery in my Navy dress uniform. I stood at attention, away from the funeral ceremony. As the casket was lowered into the ground, I was given the signal to start blowing. I provided this service in the Sacramento area for at least two years.

I also went to a convalescent home in Sacramento. I introduced myself and told the director I was available for service and asked to be assigned to a resident with no living relatives.

I was assigned to a 90-year-old woman. I visited her once a week for an hour. She was talkative and full of energy. She couldn't walk and, due to a broken arm, couldn't feed herself, so I helped feed her.

Born and raised in Texas, she moved to Southern California at a young age. She married her husband, but they didn't have any children. Her husband had passed away many years earlier. She was the only one left in her family. She and her husband were the owners of a newspaper printing shop in Hemet, California. She'd worked as an editor and prided herself on being an excellent speller. We'd play a game. I brought a dictionary, gave her a word, and challenged her to spell it. She'd quickly do so, then wait for me to congratulate and praise her for being a good speller.

She looked forward to my visits and always pleaded with me to stay longer. After a year, her health deteriorated. When she could no longer remember who I was, I stopped my weekly visits. I knew what was coming, and I wanted to remember the happy moments we had shared.

My parents had long spoken of going on a cruise but never had a chance to go. I booked them a seven-day cruise to the Bahamas on a Princess Cruise ship. They were elated with the food and service aboard the ship.

JD and Julia Walker

I had become a veteran cruiser. I decided on a different vacation and went to Hedonism II in Jamaica, an all-inclusive seven-day resort with unlimited water-sport activities and nightly entertainment. Adult beverages and food were available 24 hours. Every night during dinner, the guests were entertained with a live show.

On my return home, in shorts, T-shirt, and flip flops, I flew through Los Angeles and had to clear customs. As I retrieved my luggage, a U.S. Customs officer detained me. We went into a room where two additional U.S. Customs officers waited. I had to put my suitcase on the table, and they inspected its contents. When they finished, one officer asked me to strip down to my underwear.

"Are you serious?" I asked, incredulous.

All three stood steadfast, without smiles on their faces.

I complied. They apologized for the inconvenience after seeing I was hiding nothing.

I dressed, grabbed my suitcase and left, feeling violated. Never, in my years of traveling had I undergone this kind of scrutiny.

I'd gone to New Zealand while in the Navy and always wanted to return, so I joined a tour group on a three-week trip to New Zealand and Australia. I flew to Auckland and stayed a few days before boarding the ship. I joined an American couple for happy hour at a pub. After they left to go back to the hotel, I stayed at the pub. Next to my table was a New Zealander. He was fiftyish and had been drinking, but wasn't drunk.

Hoping to strike up a conversation, I asked, "Where's the party tonight?"

He snapped, "Just sit back and behave yourself."

I was taken aback by his rude response.

The next day, I boarded the ship. We cruised around the North and South Island of New Zealand. I visited Tauranga, Rotorua, Napier, Milford Sound, Doubtful Sound and Dunedin. I cruised through the rainforest, with its beautiful scenery. On a farm, I saw sheep being sheared. I visited wineries for tastings. At every port, I was treated with the utmost respect. When we arrived in Christchurch, I checked into a hotel.

After settling into my room, I changed for dinner. I was told of a preferred restaurant within walking distance. As I walked along the sidewalk to the restaurant, a middle-aged woman on the other side of the street walking in the same direction stared at me. I stopped, pretending to look in a store window. She stopped, still looking at me. When I walked, so did she.

I yelled across the street, "Are you following me?"

She pointed her finger at me and repeatedly shouted, "Go back to your country!"

I had no idea what she meant. I continued walking and she followed me to the restaurant. I went inside and she stood on the other side of the street.

I sat and ordered dinner. After I finished eating, the owner came to my table and inquired about my dinner. I told him the service and food were excellent. He recognized I was American and asked, "How are you enjoying your stay in Christchurch?"

I told him about the woman I'd encountered on the street.

He said, "I'm sorry you had this terrible experience in our city." He sincerely apologized for her behavior and welcomed me to come back to New Zealand again.

When I left the restaurant, I looked across the street. She was gone. As I returned to the hotel, I thought about the man at the pub in Auckland, and now, this woman in Christchurch. I'd never experienced any negativity from the locals in 1977 when I was in the Navy.

My tour group flew to Sydney, Australia, for a two-day stay. With no scheduled tours, we ventured out on our own.

I toured the famed Sydney Opera House. When I was at the beach, the sun was intense. In a restaurant, I had the opportunity to try kangaroo meat. I found everyone in Sydney welcoming, and I enjoyed my stay.

Dan Krasnow and I were lieutenant junior grade (LTjg)

officers in the Naval Reserve. Total opposites, we were good friends. He was always fun to be with. I never knew what he'd do or say. He could create a commotion anywhere. Dan asked me to join him on a tour to Russia. His travel agent had made the arrangements. I'd never been to Russia, so I agreed to go.

I parked my car at Dan's house in the East Bay. We rode the BART train to San Francisco International. At the airport, Dan told me to give him my ticket. He wanted to ensure we were seated together. I watched as Dan did the check-in. To this day, I don't know what he told the check-in clerk, but when we left the counter, we'd been upgraded to first class.

In the first-class lounge, we drank wine and ate appetizers. He made jokes as we waited to board. I told myself that this was going to be a great trip. Finally, our flight was called and we boarded the plane. Seated comfortably in first class and receiving the royal treatment, Dan was on a roll. He joked about the people in coach on such a long flight. I was enjoying his company, but I thought he'd never stop talking. Once dinner was served, he fell asleep, and so did I.

After clearing customs in Moscow, we went to our hotel. We were told to meet the tour group in the hotel lobby at 8:00 a.m. It was midnight local time, so we went to our room. With the time zone change, we were jet lagged and wide awake. An hour later, Dan suggested we go downstairs for something to eat. The desk clerk said the hotel restaurant was closed. But through the restaurant window, we saw a cook in the kitchen who appeared to be cleaning.

Dan motioned for him to come to the door. When he opened the door, Dan walked into the kitchen, with the cook and me following. The cook spoke no English. Dan gestured and rubbed his stomach, indicating hunger. The cook looked puzzled, so Dan went to the refrigerator, took out eggs and put them on the counter, along with some sliced bread. Now, the cook understood. He cooked us omelets and made toast. We took the food back to our room, ate and fell asleep.

The next morning, we met with the tour group. The four other couples were all retired. We were the youngest in the group. Our Russian tour guide spoke fluent English. We went to many museums in Moscow. I was awed by the number of artifacts in the country.

We also went to the Russian Ballet and the Moscow Circus. The performances were fantastic. We ate most of our meals at the hotel restaurant. During dinner we were entertained by Russian singers and dancers. Also, the meals were small. One night, we ordered two entrees because we were still hungry. One day, we went to one of the largest McDonald's in the world. The line snaked out the door and around the building. I was shocked at the number of cashiers behind the huge counter. The food didn't taste exactly like American McDonald's food, but it was good, and we were filled that day.

When it was time to leave Moscow, we boarded a train to Leningrad/St. Petersburg. We weren't impressed with the overnight accommodations, and the cabin had a rank smell.

In the dining room, we sat with two American women from Texas. Later, two Russian guys joined us. We'd been drinking wine for a few hours, it was getting late, and the women went to their cabin. Dan and I remained in the dining room with the Russians, who couldn't speak English. We didn't want to go back to our cabin because of the smell, but it was time to go to bed. We said good night and retired.

I hopped onto the top bunk and Dan was on the bottom bunk. We turned the cabin light off and lay in our bunks, talking, until we drifted off to sleep.

We awakened to the sound of someone pushing open the cabin door. Dan jumped out of his bunk and yelled, "Get away from the door!"

I pushed against it, too, trying to prevent the intruders' entry. Through the crack in the cabin door, Dan recognized the Russians we'd been drinking with. They acted like they didn't know which cabin they were entering and thought it was theirs.

We concluded they wanted to rob us. After they left, we stayed awake. We watched the sun rise and were awake when we arrived at the Leningrad/St Petersburg station.

Drowsy from lack of sleep, we met up with the tour group in the terminal. We boarded the bus and slept from the train station to our first museum. It was a snowy day and touring museums the remainder of the day proved daunting.

Late evening, we left the group for the airport. We'd included a side trip to Warsaw, Poland. On our flight, Dan started chatting with the female flight attendants who lived in Warsaw. He said we were en route to America with a layover in Warsaw. The flight attendants invited us to a house party, even agreeing to take us there. We told them where we were staying.

Arriving at the party, we followed them into an apartment. There were about six people there. Soft music was playing and everyone was standing with drinks in their hand. They introduced Dan and me, and we were given drinks. Dan promptly became the center of attention, making everyone laugh. We left the party late. Later that day, we toured Warsaw; the next day we flew back home—and, yes, Dan got us upgraded to first class again.

I met Alton Jackson in Sacramento. His son-in-law was Eddie Murphy. Sometimes he was invited to Eddie's movie premieres. When he had extra tickets, he invited me. At the premier of *The Nutty Professor*, I was invited to Hollywood and walked the red carpet. After the movie, we attended a private party at Universal Studios. All the food from the movie was served. I met many celebrities and had a wonderful time. Alton passed away in December 2012. I still miss his friendship.

I decided to make Northern California home and sold my house in Mira Mesa for a 40 percent profit. The only downside was the humongous capital-gains tax.

Naval Reserve
Naval Aviation Depot 0187
Naval Air Station Alameda, California
December 1991–March 1995

I was happily drilling at MMF-0280. I was a lieutenant junior grade (LTjg), enjoyed my work, and I had established myself as a productive junior officer.

Captain Don Drudik was the CO at Depot 0187 and actively recruited junior officers with aircraft maintenance experience. I received a phone call from him saying he had traced my Navy career and wanted me to join his unit. I was hesitant to leave MMF-0280, but he assured me joining Depot 0187 would broaden my Navy career.

Once I transferred, I learned the unit consisted of officers only—mostly senior officers. I was assigned as Project/ Assistant Training Officer. As a junior officer, I was assigned grunt duties.

The unit supported Naval Air Systems Command (NAVAIR), Washington, D.C. Whenever possible, on a drill weekend we did offsite research. We flew to Colorado Springs, Colorado, and stayed at Peterson AFB. We were given briefings at North American Aerospace Defense Command (NORAD) and Cheyenne Mountain Complex.

The unit was assigned a project to support the Navy Depot-Level Maintenance at NAS Alameda. Since I was a contractor at McClellan AFB, I was assigned to spearhead an offsite briefing at McClellan. I coordinated with the Air Force, and the unit Naval officers were invited to visit the Air Force

Depot Maintenance Repair Facility. Air Force officers gave technical presentations.

As a unit, we explored new technology for the Navy. We had an offsite weekend in Carlsbad, California. The company developed virtual-reality headsets, and we were in search of new virtual-reality technology for the Navy. We were given a demonstration of their latest product and attended a Navy symposium in Washington, D.C.

I received my orders for active-duty training on the Maintenance Inspector General (IG) Team for the Unmanned Aerial Vehicle (UAV) Program. I spent the first week at Naval Air Systems Command Headquarters in Washington, D.C., for briefing. The second week, I reported to NAS Point Mugu, California. Assigned to the maintenance department, I performed the IG inspection of the UAV aircraft logbooks.

Before going home after a drill weekend in Alameda, I went to San Francisco for dinner. In my khaki uniform, I entered a fine-dining restaurant and ordered a prime rib dinner and a glass of wine.

While I was eating, an elderly gentleman walked past my table and said, "Thank you for your service."

I looked up and said, "You're welcome."

When I asked for my check, the waitress told me the elderly gentleman had already paid for my dinner. Then she added, "Your glass of wine is on the house."

Deeply touched, the only words I could utter were, "Thank you!" As I go through life, I constantly remind myself to pay it forward.

Throughout my tour in Depot 0187, Captain Drudik nurtured my career and ensured I completed all requirements and training for promotion. Under his leadership, I was promoted to lieutenant.

LTJG Joe Walker

Naval Reserve
Naval Aviation Depot 1187
Naval Air Station Alameda, California
April 1995–August 1998

Depot 1187 and Depot 0187 were sister units. I transferred to Depot 1187 for unique training and leadership roles. I was assigned the duties of Admin/Training Officer.

For active-duty training, I reported to the Chief of Naval Operation, Congressional Support, Navy Pentagon, Washington, D.C. I offered support and assistance during a period of heightened Congressional activity. The office work pace in the Pentagon was accelerated. The staff worked long hours. I was in the office at 6:00 a.m., and my workday often ended after 6:00 p.m.

As an admiral's aide, one of my proudest moments was being a Navy representative invited to the House Appropriations Subcommittee hearing for the Navy/Marine budget.

We were chauffeured in a limousine from the Pentagon to Capitol Hill. When we arrived on Capitol Hill, reporters stood outside with cameras. We made our way past the news media, who met us with questions regarding the defense budget. I had been briefed to say "No comment" to whatever questions were posed to me.

Congress members submitted questions to the admiral. I recorded communications between them.

Whenever the admiral didn't have an immediate answer, his response was, "I will get you an answer." That was our signal to ensure we understood the question. On our return to the Pentagon, we'd research the question and provide an answer to the admiral.

On another active-duty assignment, I reported to Naval Air Systems Command (NAVAIR), Washington, D.C. I was assigned to the Single Process Initiative (SPI) Project. I identified and coordinated four military branches (Marines, Army, Air Force and Navy) to implement SPI and consolidate processes to reduce cost. Because Depot 1187 was a technical unit, I got to serve in Chief of Naval Operation, Information Technology Configuration Management.

I enjoyed all my tours in Washington, D.C. Most of the time, I tried to schedule trips during the Cherry Blossom Festival, a beautiful time of year to be in the nation's capital. There is amazing history in the Washington, D.C. area. I visited most of the museums and memorials. I always stayed in Crystal City. It was convenient to walk underground from the hotel to the metro. I'd board in Crystal City and exit at the Pentagon escalator. Sometimes I'd walk via underground tunnel from the Pentagon to my hotel. The underground had many restaurants and I'd stop for dinner. It was common to see a member of the House of Representatives or Senate in a restaurant. Because I was in my Navy uniform, lobbyists often approached me.

I was involved with the NAS Alameda base closure. I was assigned as a Ground Support Equipment (GSE) Officer. Our mission was to prepare and transfer all on-station aircraft ground-support equipment.

Depot 1187 was slated for an annual audit. As the Training Officer, I spent hours ensuring the unit was ready. Upon completion of the audit, when we received "Zero Discrepancy" and a 99 percent readiness rating, I was awarded the Navy and Marine Corps Achievement Medal.

As I reported for a normal drill weekend on a Saturday morning, I reviewed the message board and was surprised to see the Navy was requesting a one-year active duty recall for a lieutenant as an Assistant Y2K Project Officer in London. I thought it was the perfect opportunity for me and I made a copy of the message.

At home, I read the message several times. I knew I could fulfill all the requirements. The next day, I called the job-advertising officer in London. I was told someone had already applied and was being screened for approval. The commander said I should submit my Officer Qualification Questionnaire (OQQ) and resume, and she'd keep me on the standby list.

The next morning, my phone rang, and it was the Navy commander from London. The officer who had submitted his application had canceled and I had been selected.

I told her I had to discuss this assignment with my civilian employer and would call back the next day with a confirmation.

Thoughts sped through my mind. *What am I going to do with my house? Who's going to do my job while I'm gone?* Despite my many questions, I wanted to go on active duty.

My first call was to Northrop Grumman Human Resources. I asked about their military-leave policy. I was authorized to go. When I returned, I'd retain my salary and job title. My next call was to my manager. I said I'd been selected for active duty in London. While he didn't want me to leave, he recognized it was a great opportunity and gave his approval.

My next call was to my friend, Chuck Neville. Chuck was a corporate pilot who had flown in and out of London many times. I told him I'd been selected for active duty in London, and he assured me I would enjoy my tour.

The next morning, I called the Navy commander and accepted. Then I called Uncle Joe. He was excited for me.

I didn't tell anyone else until I had my orders in hand.

My orders were faxed the next day. I told my parents and sisters I'd be going overseas for a year. I had so much to do, and limited time to do it. I scheduled a date for the Government Housing authorities. The Navy would store my household goods. I had to change my mailing address and update my monthly expenses. Sometimes, I felt like I didn't have control of my life. I reminded myself the confusion meant a sign of growth.

Leaving Sacramento, California

I went to the Naval Reserve Center at NAS Moffett Field, completed the Depot 1187 check-out procedure, and received a one-way ticket to Seattle, Washington. I stayed overnight at NAS Moffett Field and flew to Seattle the next day.

From Seattle International, I went by shuttle bus to Naval Base Bangor for active-duty activation.

The next day, I reported to the base admin to start my active-duty check-in procedures. In the Navy Legal Office, I learned about the Soldiers and Sailors Civil Relief Act. Because I was going on active duty, I qualified for a lower interest rate for any outstanding loans, including my mortgage. And the legal officer assisted in drafting my will.

The next morning, the shuttle bus took me to Seattle International Airport. On the flight, I thought about my new job. The only description was what I had read in the Naval message. I'd read it so many times, I had it memorized. But I still didn't have a good grasp of the requirements. Reading it again didn't help. After dinner. I thanked God for allowing me the opportunity to take on this new endeavor and fell asleep.

Active-Duty Navy
Commander in Chief,
U.S. Naval Forces Europe (CINCUSNAVER)
Assistant Year 2000 (Y2K) Project Officer
London, England
August 1998–August 1999

Once I had cleared immigration, I retrieved my luggage and entered the terminal, and saw massive numbers of people waiting for arriving passengers. I'd been told to exchange American dollars for British pounds for the taxicab. I made the exchange and found a waiting cab.

The driver assisted with my luggage. I told him I wanted to go to Selfridges Hotel in Central London. I sat in the back seat and noticed the driver sitting in the right side of the cab. This was odd for me. The driver was very chatty and answered any questions I asked. I got the feeling I'd enjoy my stay in London.

I was impressed with the appearance of the hotel. I was escorted to my room. It was mid-morning on Saturday and I was jet lagged, not ready to sleep. I showered and went to lunch. Then I walked Oxford Street, admiring the city and the people. I noticed the British people walked looking straight ahead, avoiding eye contact. When I made eye contact and, said "Hi," they'd look at me strangely, saying nothing. Tired, I went back to the hotel to take a nap.

I had been sleeping for at least two hours when the phone rang. It was the commander (my new boss), welcoming me to London. She suggested we meet the next day (Sunday) to get acquainted, and we agreed to meet in the lobby of the office building. The office was a few blocks from my hotel. Across the street from our office was the American Embassy.

The nearest Catholic church was within walking distance from my hotel. After 9:00 a.m. Mass, I walked to my appointment with the commander. I sat in the lobby, talking to the building security officer, until she arrived. We greeted with a handshake.

She was a single mom and had brought her 3-year-old son along. She was sizing me up; I did the same. She gave me a tour of the building and an overview of the work environment. All work done in the building was classified and I had to get my security clearance upgraded. I was shown my office desk. We'd share an office. She gave me a manual to read to familiarize myself with the Y2K Project mission and goals.

We spent about two hours in the office, talking. As we left, I offered to walk her to the tube station. When I left the station, I went back to my room, changed and went jogging in Hyde Park. On my return, I stumbled into Speakers' Corner. I stood around and listened to a few speeches and debates, then I returned to the hotel and read the Y2K Project manual until I fell asleep.

Monday morning, I reported for duty. I was introduced to the CINCUSNAVER, London staff and was briefed on my duties. Six European commands reported to us, and our mission was to ensure they were in Y2K compliance and readiness. I was given more reading material.

As the Assistant Y2K Project Officer, I reported to the commander; a senior chief reported to me. A database administrator, he was a reservist who'd been activated for active duty, and he performed debugging and testing. One of our first tasks was to develop a Y2K contingency plan. Heightened priority was compliance of embedded systems and building infrastructure (sprinkler systems, fire alarms, elevators, etc.). We also focused on repositioning Navy ships offshore for the hospitalization of patients on life-support equipment.

Y2K representatives throughout the European command

reported to us daily. Our office assisted with resolving Y2K software issues via the senior chief. When a command did not report its Y2K compliance status, I engaged with the Y2K representative for updates and issues. Once a week, the commander or I gave a Y2K compliance briefing to the admiral and his staff.

I learned my way around London and familiarized myself with the tube stations and British Railways. I found the London Underground Network efficient and easy to learn. One of my difficult adjustments was crossing streets. I instinctively looked left instead of right. Many times, as I stepped into the street, car horns blew and people grabbed me by the arm. I started meeting people outside work and I found the British people friendly once they got to know you.

I stayed at Selfridges Hotel at the Navy's expense. In my second week there, I was told I had to move. With my demanding work schedule, I didn't have time to search for a flat. However, I did pre-survey two flats. Both had one small bedroom and limited living space. The bathrooms had the essentials with standing room only. The living rooms and kitchens were combined. I lost interest in looking at any more flats.

My senior chief also had to find a flat. During his search, I asked him to find one for me. I described the kind I wanted, within walking distance of the office.

After a few days, he came to me and said, "Lieutenant, I found the perfect flat for you."

When I went to look at it, he was right; everything about it was perfect. It was a block from a Catholic church, two blocks from Marble Arch Underground Station, and within walking distance of the office.

My flat was a furnished two-bedroom, with bath, kitchen and living room. Included in the lease was a maid. It was on the second floor; the first and third floors were attorneys' offices. I left for work early and returned home late. I rarely saw the attorneys, who didn't work weekends. I had all the privacy I wanted. My only complaint was the refrigerator and washing machine were small. The washer-dryer combo ran for hours, and still my clothing never dried completely.

Many locals shopped daily and carried grocery bags home every evening. I wondered why. I later realized they also had miniature refrigerators.

I'd been working for a month and had received no paychecks. The Navy disbursing office encountered a problem transferring my record to active-duty status. The disbursing officer was very apologetic and offered to lend me money until the problem was resolved. I assured him I wasn't in a hardship position. I had access to my account in the United States. Plus, I used my credit card to pay for purchases. Credit card purchases were cheaper than converting American dollars to British pounds.

Another problem was my passport would expire in 30 days. I went across the street to the American Embassy and was issued a new American passport the same day. It was the quickest and easiest experience I ever had renewing my passport. The only difference was the issuing authority was listed as U.S. Embassy, London, United Kingdom.

The more I learned about my job and what was expected of me, the harder I worked because I knew we had a limited time to complete all the Y2K compliance. I worked 12-hour days. Some were stressful and demanding. I never complained. I was developing new skills and invoking leadership skills. My senior chief was challenging. He had assumed coming on active duty would be a vacation. He'd tell me I was working too hard, and I'd say he wasn't working hard enough. We still had a good working relationship. During lunch, I'd jog around Hyde Park, then go to the office gym and work out with him.

One morning, I walked to work in blowing snow. Despite many gray, cloudy days in winter, London's weather didn't make me feel gloomy. I didn't give much attention to it, probably because I was always busy.

I enjoyed living in Central London. I visited St Paul's

Cathedral, but when I was home on a weekend, I attended Mass at the little Catholic church a block away. Everything was within walking distance. If I needed to go further, the underground was easily accessible. I'd never eaten Indian food before I moved to London, but once there, I ate it often.

While in London, I learned I had been promoted to lieutenant commander, along with two others on staff. The captain held a promotion ceremony for us.

We were required to travel to military bases in the European Command. My first trip was to Naval Station Naples, Italy, where I managed all the administrative duties. We held a Y2K workshop for all the Y2K representatives.

During the Christmas holidays, our workload lessened. My British friends invited me to go skiing. The ski club had access to a Swiss chalet in Bourg-Saint-Maurice, in the French Alps. They'd planned to stay two weeks, but I was only authorized a one-week vacation. As I traveled through France and the train stopped at stations along the way, I saw signs with names I'd seen in Louisiana: Breaux, Landry, Iberville, Orleans, Bordeaux and Pierre.

Snow skiing in France

I was impressed with the accommodations at our chalet: breakfast, dinner and maid service each day. After dinner, we'd sit by the fireplace and play Pictionary, Password or other games as we drank wine.

Each morning after breakfast, we hit the slopes. We skied the entire day and returned to the chalet after sunset. Our leader was a ski instructor. He led us up and down huge mountains. The snow was perfect, and the slopes were wide but challenging. We skied around the mountain into Italy.

I was chosen to attend a Y2K conference in Stuttgart, Germany. Before leaving London, I mapped out directions from the airport to the hotel. According to the map, the drive to the hotel was within 30 minutes. It was about 10:00 p.m. when I landed in Stuttgart and retrieved my rental car. As I drove out of the parking lot onto the main street, a policeman was redirecting traffic because of a car accident. I was detoured in the opposite direction, to a side street. My written directions were now useless. I was driving on a dark country road, with the signs all in German, and it had started to snow. I'd driven so far out in the country I could no longer see the airport lights.

I didn't know my location and I hadn't passed a single car. After I'd been driving in the snow about an hour, I saw city lights in the distance. I drove toward them. With the help of those lights, I found my way to the hotel in the early morning. I checked in and got in a few hours' sleep before having to drive to another location for the conference. By then the snow had stopped and it was easier to drive in daylight.

Another business trip took me to Switzerland. I was supposed to return to London the same day, but the meeting went long. I had to stay overnight. I was disappointed because it was my birthday and I wanted to be in London. After checking into my hotel, I went down to the bar in the lobby for a glass of wine.

Other people were having a joyful time. Soon, the people at the next table engaged me in conversation and invited me to join them. They were eating fondue. I don't recall how or why I mentioned it was my birthday, but at that point, the party escalated. They ordered more drinks and more fondue. They even sang *Happy Birthday to You*. I had a great 44th birthday celebration.

We weren't allowed to wear military uniforms outside the office. Whenever I participated in offsite meetings, I wore a suit and tie.

I was chosen to attend an Allied Y2K conference in London at the Houses of Parliament. I was escorted to the large conference room, where other people were chatting before the meeting. At each chair in this conference room's long table was an assigned name plate with a miniature flag of the respective country. As I approached my seat with its United States flag, I saw on the name plate, "Lieutenant Commander Joe Walker, United States of America." I paused and gave thanks to God, feeling privileged to represent my country.

Every Thursday night, a singles mixer was held in Covent Garden. There was a cover charge, but all beverages were free. Stereo music played in the background as everyone talked. I was a regular, and usually the only American. I met Barry Coleman at an event and we became friends. I got to know many people and only ever had one bad experience. One night, as I talked with a lady, a guy who'd had too much to drink grabbed me from behind and attacked me. I broke his grip and kneed him in the gut. While he lay on the floor, two guys rushed over to drag him out. The owner apologized and the evening resumed.

Sometimes, mixers were held on a riverboat cruising the River Thames. The city lights were always breathtaking. Music played, and people danced. It was always a great party on the riverboat.

I went to musicals and Broadway shows. With so many shows available, I got to see plays and shows I wouldn't have seen in America. One night after a show, I crossed a small bridge spanning the River Thames. It was the London Bridge.

I'd expected it to be spectacular, but it was just an ordinary bridge. I visited many castles. I saw the Changing of the Guard at Buckingham Palace, along with all the other touristy activities in London.

One weekend, I went to the seaside town of Torquay and visited Plymouth, the Mayflower's departure port for America. After I returned to America, while on the East coast, serving in the Naval Reserve, I visited Plymouth, Massachusetts, the site of the historic ship's disembarkation.

I was invited to a charity ball in Cardiff, Wales, to benefit the local high school. I visited many cities outside of London. I was invited to Southampton. I went to the Royal Navy Museum in Portsmouth. In Nottingham and Norwich, I had the best roast beef and Yorkshire pudding ever at local pubs.

A friend in London invited me to go to Grasmere, where her family had a cabin in the lake district. We hiked up a beautiful mountain, then ate authentic fish and chips at a country pub. On our return, we stopped in Liverpool, the birthplace of the Beatles. On a Beatles tour, I went down Penny Lane to Strawberry Fields and to the Cavern Club.

I went to Amsterdam. One of the best ways to see the city is on an Amsterdam canal cruise. I had a close-up view of Amsterdam's iconic canal houses.

With St Patrick's Day approaching, I went to Ireland. On exiting the Dublin airport, I hailed a taxi. The driver talked non-stop, welcoming me to Dublin. The friendliness of the people was the same at the hotel. After scanning the local newspaper in my room for nightlife, I left the hotel and hailed a taxi to a singles mixer.

The place was lively. I walked to the bar and ordered a glass of wine. A man beside me engaged me in conversation. He spoke openly of Dublin. Soon he said, "The women in here like colored men."

I did not take offense; I was positive he meant well. We became friends and everyone I met was friendly. At the end of the night, when people learned I'd come via taxi, several of them offered to drive me back to my hotel.

The next day was St Patrick's Day. The seemingly endless parade featured marching bands from all over the world and cheering crowds on both sides of the street.

As I maneuvered through the crowded street, I passed an Arab family. As I continued my fast-walking pace, I looked to my side and saw a little Arab boy, about 10 years old. He'd broken rank with his family and was walking in stride with me.

"Are you Arab?" he asked.

I said nothing and continued walking.

He kept stride and repeated his question.

I continued to ignore him.

Finally, he left and reunited with his family. I never figured out his reason for singling me out on the crowded street.

Later that evening, I went into the hotel bar to order a drink. I'm not a beer drinker, but as I was in Ireland, I had to try a Guinness. The bartender retrieved a glass and began pouring but didn't complete the pour. Instead, he served other customers.

Feeling ignored, I asked as to why there was a delay with serving my beer.

With a pleasant smile, he told me there was a process to serving Guinness. He told me more than I cared to know about Guinness. Apparently, it had to settle before filling the glass completely. He assured me I wasn't being ignored. When he served my Guinness, he flashed a bright smile and he talked with me the whole time I sat at the bar.

The next morning, when I entered the hotel restaurant for breakfast, I noticed many vacant tables. As I ate my breakfast, other people (mostly Americans) came in, and they sat together. Then an Irishman stepped into the restaurant. After he'd filled his breakfast plate, he sat with me, despite still-vacant tables. I watched people as they entered. The Americans sat with people they knew; but the Irish people sat at any available chair, which I found refreshing.

I invited my family to come and tour London, at my expense. Audrey Mae and Josie took me up on the offer.

I couldn't meet them at the airport because I had to work, but I emailed them detailed travel instructions from Heathrow Airport to my flat. I told them how to navigate the Underground. They had no problem finding their way around the city.

On the weekend, we went to Paris by train, through the underwater tunnel. They got to see the Eiffel Tower and the city of Paris.

I had to use my vacation time before leaving the Navy. I booked a trip to Stockholm and Helsinki, where I saw the Northern Lights. I stayed two days in Stockholm. I was impressed with its cleanliness. The cruise ship from Stockholm to Helsinki was huge. Passengers' cars were stored in the bottom of the ship. I stayed in Helsinki two days. I met a lady from Portland, Oregon, and we toured around together.

Still having unused vacation time, I booked a seven-day trip to Greece with a group. Each morning after breakfast, we toured the island. On one tour, the entire group was from Austria. I was the only English-speaking person. The tour guide had to translate everything. We went to a market in Turkey and to Rhodes. Later that night, after eating dinner and drinking Greek wine, we were all singing, holding hands and dancing around the tables.

As Assistant Y2K Project Officer, I was approaching the end of my active-duty tour. I was told I could extend my tour if I wanted to stay longer. I declined because I felt obligated to return to my civilian career. I was confident I'd helped prepare the Navy for the millennium transition.

I had presented my last briefing to the admiral. At the end of my briefing, the captain told the admiral I was returning to the United States. The admiral asked why I was leaving.

The captain said, "Lieutenant Commander Walker is a reservist, and he's returning to his civilian job after one year of active duty."

The admiral replied, "I didn't know you were a reservist. I thought you were regular Navy."

I felt honored to get such a compliment from the admiral. Upon departing, I was awarded the Navy and Marine Corps Commendation Medal.

While living in England, either for work or leisure I visited Italy, Switzerland, France, Wales, Belgium, the Netherlands, Ireland, Greece, Turkey, Sweden, Finland and Germany. Ireland was my favorite country. I met the nicest people, and it was easy to make friends. When I talked with people there, it was like meeting up with an old friend I hadn't seen in years.

Leaving London, England

I emailed Northrop Grumman to let them know I was returning to America. I said I wanted to remain in Northern California.

Due to the closure of McClellan AFB, my job had been transferred to Utah. They offered to move me to Salt Lake City or to a position in Los Angeles. I wasn't interested in either assignment. I decided not to contact Northrop Grumman again until after I'd been discharged.

During my flight home, I reflected on my time in London. I felt blessed to have gotten to live and work there. Part of me didn't want to come back, but I felt returning to America was best for my civilian career.

Upon my return to Naval Base Bangor, I completed the deactivation and was reassigned to active reserve status. I called family and friends to let them know I was back in the United States.

I wasn't ready to move back into my house in Rocklin. The tenant's lease had been extended another year and all I wanted to remove from storage was my car.

I'd never taken extended time off from work, and I wanted to relax. I drove to Napa and spent a day in the wine country. Then I drove to San Francisco and Monterey for a few days. I drove down the Pacific Coast Highway to Santa Barbara and Hollywood. I stayed a few days in Orange County and San Diego. Then I drove to Las Vegas, with a side trip to the Grand Canyon. After that, I drove to Yosemite National Park.

Back in Sacramento, I called Northrop Grumman for an

update. The only available jobs for me were in Salt Lake City or in Los Angeles. I asked about opportunities in San Diego. They said nothing was currently available.

I gave serious thoughts to my career at Northrop Grumman. I'd left my job to go on active duty because I wanted a change and growth opportunities. Northrop Grumman's job offers were not growth opportunities. I updated my resume with my recent Navy project management experience and started my job search.

At a job fair in San Francisco, I talked with many companies and distributed my resume. When I gave Chrome Data my resume, they were interested and I was told I'd get a phone call the next day. I hadn't planned on leaving California, but Chrome Data was a small family-owned company in Portland, Oregon, planning to expand and go public. Their going public interested me. I'd known people who joined small companies and were given stock options. When the companies went public, they did quite well.

Chrome invited me to Portland for an interview and sent me a round-trip airline ticket.

They were hiring four project managers. My interview went well and I was offered a job. The offer included a 30 percent salary increase, a bonus, company shares, relocation expenses, 30 days' accommodation, and a standard benefit package. I said I'd give them an answer within two days.

Back in Sacramento, I called Northrop Grumman again to ask about possibilities other than Salt Lake City and Los Angeles. Those were my only options. It was clear to me that it was time for me to seek other opportunities. I resigned from Northrop Grumman. My 401k had been fully invested in stocks with excellent growth. I had Northrop Grumman stock, too.

I called Chrome Data and accepted the project manager position. A few days later, I made the nine-hour drive from Sacramento to Portland. I decided to leave my household goods in storage until I was settled. Driving north on I-5, I knew I was starting another new chapter of my life.

When I approached Portland, it was night, with light rain. As I crossed the Willamette River, the city lights and high-rise buildings looked beautiful. Chrome Data had reserved a fully furnished apartment for me downtown in a new building with an enclosed garage. The next morning, I found a Catholic church. After Mass, I drove around Portland to get familiar with the city.

Chrome Data Incorporation
Portland, Oregon
Project Manager
November 1999–August 2000

The office in Oregon City was small, with about 10 employees. On my first day, folks were packing boxes. The company was moving into a larger office.

The next day, I went to the new office—a high-rise building in downtown Portland. Fewer than 20 people were there. Mostly, everyone was unpacking and setting up cubicles.

Chrome Data pioneered the technology behind electronic vehicle configuration on the internet. Chrome Data PC Carbook allowed users to configure and order vehicles in the U.S. As a new project manager, I was told the office reporting structure had not been confirmed. Everyone on the technology staff reported to the Chief Technology Officer (CTO).

I didn't know much about Portland, but I learned quickly that its winter weather was horrible. Rain, snow, cold and little or no sunshine. In winter, the whole day was gray and overcast, with light or heavy rain. By 3:30 p.m., it was dark. I'd leave for work in the early morning. It was dark, cold, and wet. When I returned home, it was the same. Dark, cold and wet.

I moved into a secluded complex in West Linn. It was a gated building with a gym, pool and tennis courts. I got to choose which building and apartment I wanted to live in. But it didn't matter because I was at work more than at home.

Each morning, I noticed a police car at the end of my

street. One morning, the officer pulled me over and asked to see my license and registration. He asked if I lived in West Linn. When I said I did, he said I should change my license and registration to Oregon. I told him I'd been working long hours and hadn't had the time.

He never stopped me again. Nor did I change my registration.

Most Fridays after work, I flew to the Bay Area. Or I drove to Seattle. Tacoma had military bases I frequented. If I stayed in Portland, I went to a bar that had live bands. I got to know some of the locals. I toured Portland and visited Multnomah Falls and Mount Hood.

My half-brother, Marcus, lived in Seattle; one day, he drove to Portland while I was at work. He left a note with his address at my door. We hadn't seen each other since Li'l Sister's funeral. That weekend, I drove to Seattle and we went to lunch.

Within a month, more employees were hired company-wide. Four project managers were now on board. We managed software releases, performed team management, and conducted training sessions. With limited history and best practices to reference, we frequently relied on previous work experience to guide us. It was a fast-paced environment. Office processes changed daily.

I was in the office before daybreak and didn't leave until dark—even during Thanksgiving and Christmas holiday periods. From the 18th floor, on rare clear days, I could see Mount St. Helens from one side of the office and Mount Hood from the other. Both were beautiful snow-capped mountains.

Sometimes, my colleagues arrived before me. When I came in, the overhead lights were off. Employees sat at cubicles with their desk lights on. As I walked past, I switched on all the overhead lights. Then I'd hear someone yell out, "Joe's here!"

I'd tease them by saying they'd lived in Portland too long without sunshine.

I liked my job, I liked the people I worked with, and I liked

Chrome Data. But it was hard to adjust to the lousy cold and rainy days.

I strived to do my best work. Working with smart people, I soaked up as much information as I could. I wasn't always verbal, but when I had valuable input to contribute, I spoke up.

Everyone was looking forward to the millennium. Many programmers had feared computers would stop working after December 31, 1999. Computer programs were coded only to handle years with two digits, not four. The U.S. Government and businesses had spent billions to update their computers. People were still unsure what would happen at midnight. Would planes fall out of the sky or traffic lights malfunction? The speculation was endless. We were in a wait-and-see period.

At midnight. I was in Bellevue, Washington, at a New Year's Eve party, unconcerned.

Most new employees at Chrome were granted pre-Initial Public Offering (IPO) stocks. The company was hopeful the stock would open at $10 per share or higher. In anticipation, employees envisioned becoming instant millionaires. I overheard two product managers discussing how they'd drive to work in matching Mercedes convertibles.

Every day, I encountered unexpected changes at work. I'd believed the upper management was in accord, but one day, most of the senior management staff was let go, due to disagreements—including the CTO. I was sorry to see him go. The rest of the management team was re-organized. That same week, some recently hired employees were let go.

After the shakeup, I was involved in additional projects. I helped build the company intranet and assisted sales staff in creating sales processes. I wasn't worried about being fired because I knew I was productive. However, I was concerned about the IPO. I held out hope the company would go public, as I'd been given a substantial number of shares. Plus, a company memo stated the board had approved a four-for-one split on Chrome Data's stock. With this news, I was on track for early retirement.

Although I was working hard to get things done, I had a gut feeling my colleagues and I weren't aware of the company's full IPO status. I believed it was being stalled. Because I was in the Naval Reserve, I flew monthly to the Bay Area to drill. Most of my colleagues in my unit worked in high-tech in Silicon Valley. I started networking and made it known I was actively seeking work.

Commander Mel Abueg worked for Informix as a manager. After one drill weekend, he emailed me to say they had a job opening for a technical account manager and was I interested? I'd known Mel for years; he knew my capabilities and qualifications. I faxed my resume. He scheduled an interview at Informix's office in Menlo Park. When I arrived, we went into his office and he briefed me on the job expectations. Then he introduced me to the first interviewer.

We had a cordial interview. After lunch with Mel, I met the department vice president. She knew Mel and I worked together in the Naval Reserve. During the interview, we talked about my time in the Navy and my current job at Chrome Data.

Mel said he'd contact me after he had a discussion with the interviewers. I drove to the airport and flew back to Portland.

The next day, Mel called to say all the interviewers were impressed, and the job was mine. We discussed salary and benefits. They offered me a good package, including company shares, a 25 percent salary increase, the standard health insurance and 401k. I thanked Mel and said I'd set a start date after talking with Chrome Data. I wanted to ensure I was fair with them, because they'd been good to me. Plus, I wanted to bring closure to the projects I was working on.

Later that afternoon, I met with my manager in a private office. Before I could speak, he said, "You have another job and you're leaving the company."

I told him I was resigning and moving back to California.

He offered me a salary increase to stay.

I declined, saying I'd enjoyed working at Chrome and liked

all my colleagues, but my main reason for leaving was the Portland weather. I didn't say I was concerned about the IPO.

He and the HR manager encouraged me to stay. I held firm, saying I wanted to move back to California. I thought I could give the standard two weeks' notice. But the HR manager reminded me I'd been granted stock options when I was hired—plus more shares since then. The stocks had already split four times. To retain my stock options, I had to work an additional week.

Soon after our meeting, word got out around the office. People came to my desk asking, "Is it true, are you leaving the company?"

I assured them I was leaving because I couldn't adjust to the weather, and I missed sunshine.

I called Mel and gave him my start date. Although I'd begun bringing my projects to closure and transferring my workload to another project manager, I still came in early and worked until late evening, plus I offered to help anyone who needed additional assistance.

The three weeks flew by. On my last day at Chrome Data, the project management team took me to lunch. After we returned, a department-head meeting was called. Project and product managers and some salespeople were told to meet in the conference room. I didn't have to attend. I continued cleaning out my desk.

About twenty minutes later, everyone returned, holding large brown envelopes. Their expressions were sad and subdued.

I asked, "What happened in there?"

"We've all been fired."

I was shocked!

Someone asked me, "Did you know there was going to be a layoff?"

I had no such knowledge. I immediately thanked God I wasn't included in the layoff. I said a prayer for them, because they were unprepared for this news. Now they had to search for new jobs.

Chrome Data never completed its IPO, and all my stock options became worthless.

Naval Reserve
Naval Air System Command 1187
Naval Post-Graduate School Monterey, California
December 1999–September 2003

While living in Oregon, I didn't realize my body was missing sunlight until I returned to California and walked out into it. It was like I'd awakened from a deep sleep. I felt alive!

My first drill weekend after returning from London, I went to NAS Moffett. The base was in the process of closing. My assigned unit, NAVAIRSYS 1187, had been transferred to Monterey. I was in the admin building where the yeoman was packing admin boxes for transfer. I asked for my service record. He couldn't find it. Nor could he find any paperwork indicating I'd been attached to the unit. Eventually, we discovered when I left for active duty, someone assumed I was being discharged, so all my records were sent to Washington, D.C. for archiving. I received many apologies, but apologies didn't resolve my problem.

I went to Monterey to join NAVAIRSYS 1187. We had a new CO, and several new officers.

I was assigned as Project/Admin Officer. Each month I was responsible for publishing the unit Plan of the Month.

During my two weeks' training, I was assigned to work on the AH-1Z/UH-1Y Helicopter Project and Multi-Mission Maritime Aircraft Project. My job consisted of research. I met with the maintenance staff to discuss technical issues. I also made trips to the Pentagon Library for additional research.

I was authorized to attend the Joint Military Operations

Course at Navy War College, Newport, Rhode Island. I was required to write a research paper. In my class were officers from all branches of the military. On the weekend, we toured the U.S. Naval Academy in Annapolis, Maryland.

On a drill weekend, I left work and went directly to the Portland Airport. While boarding the aircraft, a man yelled out, "Hey, Joe Walker!"

I waved and continued boarding. He sat next to me and asked if I remembered him. He said we were stationed together at NAS Fallon, and he mentioned other people stationed there. I recalled all the others, but not him.

During the flight, we reminisced about our days in Fallon. He said he was married, had kids and was a pilot at Delta Airlines and a commander in the Naval Reserve. I congratulated him and told him I was also in the Naval Reserve. I purposely didn't reveal my rank.

That weekend, all reservists on base were required to attend an All-Hands meeting. Everyone was told to report to the base theater. I was wearing my lieutenant commander uniform. From the corner of my eye, I saw the guy I'd met on the flight from Portland. He wore a Navy Chief uniform. He pretended not to see me. The expression on his face said it all. He was embarrassed because he'd said he was a commander. I wondered what else he'd lied about, but I never saw him again.

I had a conversation with my father about my recent promotion to lieutenant commander. He told a friend who was the same age as him and had served in the military. During the friend military service, Blacks were only allowed to serve as cooks and cabin stewards, so his friend convinced him I wasn't a lieutenant commander. The friend insisted Blacks weren't allowed to be officers and I'd lied about my rank. My father was so convinced he called me for confirmation. I reassured him I was indeed a lieutenant commander and his friend's information was outdated.

Leaving Portland, Oregon

Informix's office was in Menlo Park, so I planned to find an apartment near there, as my Rocklin house was still rented.

I had some free time before reporting to work, so I took a quick trip to Louisiana. I hadn't seen my parents since my return from England. My mother cooked my favorite red beans and rice. Bobbie and I attended Mass at The Madonna Chapel. I saw Brother Pasqua there, in a wheelchair. After Mass, I talked with him. Months after I returned to California, I was told he passed away.

Informix had authorized me to stay at the San Francisco Embassy Suites until I found an apartment. From my room on the top floor, I enjoyed a spectacular view. I watched airplanes landing at San Francisco International, and each morning I jogged around the bay seawall before going to work.

The Years 2000–2009

International Business Corporation (IBM)
Menlo Park, California
Technical Account Manager
August 2000–July 2016

I joined Informix Corporation in August 2000. IBM acquired Informix in April 2001.

My first few days on the job I familiarized myself with the company operations. Mel Abueg was my manager and mentor. My second week, I took a database administration course at the Informix Education Center in Denver.

When I returned, I looked for an apartment. I wanted to avoid a long commute in Bay Area traffic. I knew rentals in the Bay Area would be expensive, but I was still shocked when I was told the monthly rates. I rented a one-bedroom apartment in Belmont, 10 minutes from my office. I brought only my clothing and a sleeping bag. I went there to shower and sleep. Then I was back in the office.

My job title was technical account manager. I handled Informix Elite/Premium customers in the United States and overseas. I managed system upgrades, certifications, software engineers' daily production, project post-mortems, and facilitated the team agenda.

Within months of my arrival, Mel left the company, so I was assigned a new manager. Our team supported several hundred customers and we had serious problems stabilizing their systems. We would fix one problem and accidentally generate new software issues. Customers were operating on various versions of the Informix software, and not one version was stable. My job was to stabilize their database systems. Relying on all my previous work experience and skills, I scrambled to find solutions for the customers' complaints and the instability of their database systems.

My new manager gave me a crash course on database software. On a whiteboard, she diagrammed problems and resolutions. In the middle of the diagram, she identified the "software bugs." The bugs were not my friends. Rather than chase each bug daily, she introduced me to a concept of rolling all known software bugs into a master software release. We identified the master software as a Jumbo Patch that was delivered to customers as a certified tested, bug-free software release. Once I mastered the Jumbo Patch concept, I was able to stabilize all our customers and ensure their next upgrade was successful. I give the credit to my manager, Cindy White, and grateful for her guidance and direction.

Informix was a small company, and I got to know people personally. I enjoyed the excellent working relationships with colleagues and customers. I carried a beeper, and when customers called in with problems, I was engaged until it was resolved. After cell phones became available, I slept with my cell phone by my bed.

Within Informix, I managed my own enterprise. The team included two software engineers in the U.S. and three in Germany. We supported all Informix customers worldwide. My manager gave me the freedom to excel. However, if I needed assistance, she was there.

Daily, I resolved customers' escalation problems via conference calls. Occasionally, I went onsite to domestic customers. Annually, I reported onsite in Germany to interface with customers and software engineers. I flew into Frankfurt and drove to Heidelberg, a beautiful university town.

Our team flew to the Informix Lenexa, Kansas office. After our team-building meeting, we boarded a bus to Big Cedar Lodge in the Ozarks for a company-paid weekend retreat with breakout work sessions, nightly entertainment and free drinks. We stayed in private accommodation log cabins. Breakfast, lunch and dinner were served daily.

During the weekend, we heard whispered rumors of IBM acquiring Informix. Those in the know didn't confirm or deny the rumors, so everyone assumed it was true.

Months later, the merger was confirmed; we'd become IBMers. We were issued IBM ID cards and continued business as usual. In the IBM Toronto, Canada lab, IBMers did similar work to what I did for Informix. I was authorized to go there for job sharing and to learn IBM work processes. While in Toronto, I had a chance to visit Niagara Falls.

My Rocklin tenants gave notice and moved out. I wasn't happy paying exorbitant monthly rent for an apartment I was in less than eight hours a day. I painted the interior and had new carpet installed, then moved back into my house. I had a long commute to Menlo Park. To avoid traffic, I left home on Monday at 4:00 a.m. and was in the office by 6:30 a.m. I never left work early. Because I was in the Naval Reserve, I stayed overnight at NASA Ames Moffett Monday through Thursday. If NASA Ames Moffett had no vacancy, I slept at my desk and showered in the office.

On Fridays, I drove home. To avoid traffic, I'd go out to dinner and drive home after 10:00 p.m. Many times, on my commute, I'd stop along the side of the highway to resolve a customer issue or join a conference call. I never complained because the work was exciting and rewarding.

The following year, I was authorized to work from home Mondays and Tuesdays, so on Wednesday mornings at 4:00 a.m., I was back on the road. I worked in the office Wednesday through Friday. Again, I stayed overnight at NASA Ames Moffett when they had vacancies. Late Friday night, I'd drive home.

Customers often called in for support on weekends. I never referred them to the weekend duty manager; I worked with them personally.

When a large customer in Mexico suffered a database crash, their system was down for weeks. I dedicated my time and all the resources I could find to resolving their issue. Once it was resolved, I received a special thank you letter from the company president.

I attended a two-week first-line manager training course at the IBM Learning Center in Armonk, New York.

Informix served free ice cream on Wednesdays and free doughnuts on Friday. Friday afternoon, our team met in the parking lot, and from the trunk of a car, they dispensed free beer and wine. After socializing, we went back to work. Working at Informix was enjoyable and fun!

Menlo Park / Rocklin / Cameron Park, California

Uncle Joe was Catholic but converted to Baptist. He recorded a gospel CD and asked me to assist with marketing. I'd learned the power of the internet and built and designed a webpage for him. It included his photo and bio. Potential buyers could sample the CD by clicking on a song title link to hear 15 seconds of each song. Transactions were completed via credit card.

My father came to visit for a month, and I scheduled delivery of my household goods from storage. I was at work when the truck arrived. My father supervised the unloading of the truck. When I came home that weekend, he'd already unpacked the boxes.

He liked Rocklin and said he'd consider moving to California. I said he and my mother were welcome to live in the Rocklin house, as I had plans to buy a second home. He called her to discuss a move, and she wasn't interested.

When I was at work in the Bay Area, I called my father every night to ensure he was okay and to see if he needed anything. When I stayed at NASA Ames Moffett, I went jogging each morning before work. One morning, I turned on the TV and couldn't believe what I was seeing. It was September 11, 2001, and New York was under attack. Commercial airliners had flown into the World Trade Center buildings. As I watched, the news reporters were confused, and no one could grasp what was happening. I called my father and told him to turn on the TV. I showered, dressed and went to the office. All my customers' business was on hold; no one was working. Everyone was told to go home and look after their loved ones. I called my father and told him I was coming home.

Once I decided to purchase a second home, I found an interesting condo in the newspaper's real estate section. I called the realtor, who invited me to take a walk-through. I wasn't impressed with its layout. When Joni Becker, the realtor, shared the MLS listings, I changed my search parameters from a condo to a house.

We viewed many homes in El Dorado County. One day, as she drove past one house, I commented, "That's a very nice house."

Her response was, "That's my house."

At that moment, I felt certain I'd buy a house from her.

Weeks later, she called me and announced, "I've found the ideal home for you."

It wasn't far from her home. After viewing it, I immediately made an offer. In December 2004, I took ownership of the Cameron Park house. Before moving in, I had both bathrooms remodeled, new carpet installed in every room, and wood flooring put in the kitchen. I spent the Christmas holidays painting the interior. Months later, I painted the exterior. My Rocklin house again became a rental property.

I religiously followed the financial market and saw a swing in real estate. It was prime time to buy, and banks were issuing mortgages with little scrutiny. I encouraged Josie to buy a second home. She found one in Temecula and, after the close of escrow, I flew to Southern California to assist her with the move. Not long after she was settled, the housing bubble burst and the real estate market crashed.

Uncle Joe's 65th birthday was approaching. I discussed a surprise party with Faye. We planned a catered meal at the Officer's Club at NAS Miramar. I told Uncle Joe I had to attend a Navy award ceremony at Miramar and wanted him to go with me. I picked him up wearing my dress white uniform. Family and friends had gone to the club ahead of us. I told him the ceremony was in a private room. I opened the door and let him go in first. When he did, everyone shouted, "Happy Birthday!"

He was overwhelmed at seeing his children, brother, sisters, nieces, nephews and friends.

Before long, I was working from home full time. I'd converted my dining room into an office, but I wanted a designated home office. I drew rough blueprints for the new addition and hired a contractor for the demolition and remodeling. After the construction, the house was 2700 square feet.

In August 2005, Hurricane Katrina stormed the Louisiana coastline and flooded New Orleans. All my relatives evacuated, except my 92-year-old uncle. I called him the day before the storm and tried to convince him to go to my parents' home. He refused to leave. He lived alone and was in good health. Before we hung up, he asked, "Will you call me tomorrow?" I promised I would. The next day, after the storm had passed, I called several times, but the power and phone lines were down. The storm was over, but the levee breached and water rushed into the city. An IBM coworker lived in New Orleans; I gave him my uncle's address and he told me that neighborhood was underwater. Days later, the rescue team entered my uncle's neighborhood. Searchers believe Uncle Sam survived the hurricane itself, but not its aftermath. His body was found floating in the attic.

I wanted to improve my presentation skills, so I joined a local Toastmasters club, where I presented timely speeches weekly. I earned the Toastmasters Competent Communicator Award and was nominated to serve dual duties as treasurer and vice president of membership and public relations. I mentored new enrollees. After receiving the Toastmasters Advanced Communicator Bronze Award, I served as club president.

The stock market's performance had been superb over the years; I was heavily invested in the market. Through the years, I'd faithfully contributed to my 401k and was on track for retirement. I'd set a goal to retire from my civilian job at age 55.

In 2008, the stock market crashed. Rather than ride out the

downturn, I withdrew my 401k. My portfolio was hit hard, and I rebalanced my 401k for future investments. While we were in a bear market, I purchased additional stocks outside of my 401k at a cheaper price. I knew I'd have to prolong my working days to recoup the hit to my 401k.

I'd just gotten into bed when my telephone rang. It was Josie. Uncle Joe awakened during the night coughing up blood and was rushed to the hospital. I asked her to call me back with any news. Millions of thoughts poured through my mind. Uncle Joe was 70, but he was physically fit and healthy. I'd never known him to be sick, other than a cold. I said a prayer for him. The rest of the night, I couldn't sleep, anticipating a call from Josie.

By morning, there was no change. The whole family had sat in the hospital lobby overnight. I called my manager and said I had a family emergency and wouldn't be online full time, but I'd still monitor and manage my workload. I booked a one-way ticket to Los Angeles and packed my laptop so I could work while I was there. I arrived before noon and drove directly to the hospital. All the family and his closest friends were present. He lay in the bed with tubes in his nose. I touched his arm and called his name, knowing he wouldn't respond. He was breathing with the assistance of the machine.

As night approached, there'd been no positive updates. Because everyone had stayed at the hospital the night before, I recommended they go home and rest. Faye and I remained in the lobby overnight.

The next day, the doctors gave us the sad news. He wasn't breathing on his own, and they'd done all they could do. After some serious family discussions, we made the difficult decision.

I had a heavy heart. I wasn't ready for his death, but I was grateful he didn't suffer. I never thought he'd leave us so soon. I tried to imagine life without him. Then I focused on the good times we had together. He was never too busy to talk. We'd spend hours on the phone. He'd shared with me the discrimination he encountered in the Navy in the 1950s. He'd served 22 years, not all of them enjoyable. Opportunities for Black sailors had been limited. That's why he felt so proud of me each time I got promoted. When I told him my job assignments, he'd smile. I didn't take my Navy career for granted. I knew people like Uncle Joe had paved the way for me.

A military funeral was held for Uncle Joe. I gave a special tribute, talking about how he not only had a positive influence on me, but on everyone in our family. He felt strong love for his family and taught us by example. He inspired me to dream *big*. I'm thankful he was in my life and I cherish the years we had. Every time I visit Southern California, I deliver flowers to his grave. I still miss him dearly.

Joe Louis Pierre

Uncle Bill and I were also close. At Christmas, he'd bring fruit baskets to the elderly. I drove him to people's homes and helped him give out the baskets. A retired cook, every New Year's Day, he made gumbo and invited me over. As he aged, he stopped driving. Once a month I drove him to Sunday service to receive Communion. He'd tell me which streets to take to avoid the traffic. One Sunday morning, following his directions, we ended up in downtown Sacramento, miles from the church.

I said, "Uncle Bill, we're downtown."

His response was, "I guess I gave you the wrong directions."

We discovered he was developing Alzheimer's. The disease hit him fast, but he was a fighter. He read the newspaper daily, morning to night, trying to activate his brain. He was in good health, but after a while, all he did was sit and stare. Uncle Bill passed away at the age of 91. On Memorial Day and Veterans Day, I go to St. Mary's Cemetery to put flowers on his and Aunt Vickie's graves.

Naval Reserve
Air Test and Evaluation Squadron
(AIRTEVRON) Three Zero (VX-30) 0376
Naval Air Station Point Mugu, California
October 2003–January 2006

Captain Rick Chambers was VX-30 CO. I'd served with Rick in a previous command and he recruited me for VX-30. The unit had five officers and about 50 enlisted sailors. Rick knew I possessed strong organizational skills, so he assigned me multiple jobs. I was assigned Admin/Training Officer and PRT Officer.

On my first drill weekend with the unit, I learned the CO wouldn't be at Saturday morning muster. Instead, he'd attend a meeting aboard the Naval Air Station. So, the Executive Officer conducted the unit morning muster on the hangar deck. Everyone huddled in a circle as he casually gave updates. I was disturbed with this style of briefing. After muster, I suggested to the Executive Officer that Saturday morning muster be formal. I wanted to see sailors standing in formation, so he delegated me to establish the morning-muster formation. I submitted in writing the new procedures, and he approved. The following muster, the Executive Officer stood front and center. Each officer reported and rendered a salute as the enlisted sailors stood at attention. This procedure was carried out the remainder of my tour in the unit. Also, I immediately drafted an organizational chart for the unit.

As Admin Officer, I managed all the unit administrative duties and coordinated completion of backlogged enlisted evaluations. As Training Officer, I tracked and ensured all enlisted sailors completed the requirements for the Navy-wide Advancement Exam. Serving as PRT Officer, I ensured the unit's physical fitness readiness increased. For my efforts, Captain Chambers awarded me the Navy and Marine Corps Commendation Medal (Gold Star in lieu of second award).

Many times, I performed extra duty in the Navy. Rather than request additional time away from my civilian employer, I used vacation days to serve. Once I was on a special assignment at NAS Point Mugu and was invited to attend a Navy retirement ceremony dinner at The Ronald Reagan Presidential Library.

For one of my active-duty trainings, I attended a two-week course at Navy Supply Corps School, Athens, Georgia. I completed the Joint Aviation Supply and Maintenance Material Management (JASMMM) Course.

I'd entered the Navy at the end of the Vietnam War and served during the Gulf War, Desert Storm/Shield, and the Iraq War. I saw many men and women return home from war not the same as when they left. I prayed for these people. Although I enjoyed serving in the Navy, I'd set a goal to retire at age 50, since I'd joined at age 18 as an airman recruit. Over the years, I'd traveled the world, made countless friends, and been promoted beyond my wildest dreams. I felt blessed to be a lieutenant commander. With eight years of active duty and 24 years active reserve, I'd achieved my goal and had the time of my life. Given the opportunity to relive my life, I'd do it all over again. I *love* the Navy! In January 2006, I submitted my retirement papers. I was asked if I wanted a Navy retirement ceremony, but I chose to go out quietly.

Upon my retirement from the U.S. Navy, I was presented with an American flag that had flown over the U.S. Capitol Building October 20, 2005. The flag remains in a frame in a place of honor in my home.

During my military service, I was assigned the following duty stations and awarded the following military decorations:

Retirement Rank: Lieutenant Commander (Grade - 04)
Duty Stations Included:

- Congressional Staff Duty at the Pentagon, Washington, D.C.
- Commander-in-Chief, U.S. Naval Forces Europe (London, UK)
- Naval Air Facility Misawa, Japan
- Yokota Air Base, Japan
- Naval Air Station Cubi Point, Philippines
- McMurdo Station, Antarctica (South Pole)
- Christchurch, New Zealand
- U.S. Naval Forces, Korea
- Stuttgart, Germany
- Naval Station Rota, Spain
- Naval Air Station Sigonella/Naples, Italy
- Assignments at various Naval bases throughout the United States including Guam, Alaska and Hawaii

Military Decorations Awarded:

- Navy Commendation Medal (2)
- Navy Achievement Medal
- Meritorious Unit Commendation Medal
- Good Conduct Medal
- Naval Reserve Medal
- National Defense Medal
- Antarctica Service Medal
- Global War on Terrorism Service Medal
- Outstanding Volunteer Service Medal
- Sea Service Deployment Ribbon
- Navy Overseas Service Ribbon
- Armed Forces Reserve Medal

I'd recently retired from the Navy when Audrey Mae and Josie called saying they'd planned a retirement party for me. The weekend getaway was held in Laughlin, Nevada. My whole family, including cousins and friends attended. Even my Navy friend, Chuck Neville, flew in from Chicago.

The Years 2010–2020

International Business Corporation (IBM)
San Jose, California
Technical Account Manager /
Educational Enablement Manager
August 2000–July 2016

I supported customers throughout the United States and overseas. Working from home full time, I no longer commuted in the pre-dawn hours. What I liked most about working from home was not having to hear people talk about their weekends or ask me about mine. As far as I was concerned, the weekend was over. I'm social and outgoing but I'm a loner at heart, and I neither need nor want to be around crowds of people all the time. If I had to visit a customer, I flew to my destination and returned home when my business was completed. IBM also had an office near downtown Sacramento, where I occasionally went for office supplies.

I normally started work at 6:30 a.m. If a customer escalation required my attention, I started earlier; most days, I did. I never had a designated quitting time. I worked weekends, too. I was always available for my customers. Throughout my career, I'd always made my job priority one.

January 15, 2010, I decided I'd never work on my birthday again. Every subsequent birthday was a vacation day. I did what I felt like doing and went where I wanted to go. It was my special day.

Many years ago, I'd worn braces. When they were removed, the orthodontist instructed me to wear my retainer at night. I didn't and, through the years, my teeth slowly shifted position. I used my IBM dental plan to have braces installed a second time. I wore them for a year. Now, I faithfully wear my retainer at night.

IBM sponsored an annual Engineering and Technology week. In support of it, employees were asked to visit local public schools in Silicon Valley, to encourage students to consider careers in software engineering. Each year, I volunteered. I went to junior high schools in the San Jose area to deliver a PowerPoint presentation. Then, the students could ask questions. I found them to be very enthusiastic.

I never expected anything extra for my work. However, one day my manager said, "I have good news for you. You're being awarded IBM stock options."

Plus, I got special bonus pay. I enjoyed my work and always wanted to do my best. When I went to bed at night, it felt good to know I'd earned my pay for the day.

Already a huge company, IBM continued to absorb other small businesses. As those smaller companies merged into IBM, I made myself available to learn their products. At the same time, I still considered myself an Informix employee. But, as my fellow Informix employees integrated into the IBM environment, all traces of Informix began to vanish. When this happened, my passion for the work diminished as well. I yearned for the Informix days.

As years passed, I lost interest in my job. I didn't hide this from my manager. To pacify me, I was given extra projects. I was assigned to create and maintain the department contents for the intranet webpage. I volunteered to learn the office working tools, so as to train other employees. I took on these responsibilities to become energized in the IBM environment. Still, I'd preferred working in the Informix environment. I was still productive, but the job excitement I once had at Informix was fading. I was also thinking of retiring soon, so seeking employment with another company wasn't an option.

I'd always felt energized about my job and gave one hundred percent. I didn't feel good about making only minimal contributions.

I discussed other opportunities with my manager. He was supportive and advised me of a management opening on the Educational Enablement Team. I applied and was accepted. Involved with IBM Big Data Analytics, I assisted IBMers with qualification of IBM products. At the outset, it felt interesting because it was new. But I soon lost interest and no longer volunteered for extra projects.

Increasingly interested in retirement, I called Human Resources to determine my eligibility. I learned I could retire at age 62 or after 15 years of service at IBM. I had 14 years and 6 months of service. The earliest I could retire was January 2017, or on my IBM anniversary in July 2016. I chose July 2016.

I thought about when I was in college and had dreamt of working at IBM. Now, I realized, I didn't like working for a large company. Too many layers. In my dwindling months, I continued to work with diminished enthusiasm. I couldn't regain the excitement I'd enjoyed at Informix.

With the Christmas holidays over, and six months remaining until retirement, my 401k had rebounded nicely.

I don't recall ever taking a sick day while at IBM. Because of my number of years with the company, I was authorized 30 vacation days a year. Many years, I didn't take all my vacation days; whenever I lost them, it never bothered me because I preferred working.

I didn't tell anyone I was planning to retire. I still had many vacation days remaining, so once a month, I took Thursday and Friday off. I'd have a long weekend out of town. I no longer felt obliged to answer my cell phone or work weekends.

I took a road trip to Death Valley. I started on the western side and drove to the eastern side, stopping at the lowest point (below sea level). Other trips were to California coastal towns or a western coastal state (Washington or Oregon).

In May 2016, with two months left, I still hadn't announced my retirement plans to anyone. I took a seven-day all-inclusive resort vacation to Cancun. My room's balcony overlooked the Caribbean Sea. Each morning, I woke before sunrise, jogged on the beach and went to the gym. In the afternoons, I'd take a nap. I read. After dinner, I socialized and drank wine with new companions. I reflected on my retirement preparation and life after IBM. I'd invested wisely and was financially prepared. It was a relaxing vacation. I decided to share my July retirement date with IBM the first week of June.

On my first day back, my manager requested a conference call. After welcoming me back from vacation, she said IBM was downsizing and my position had been eliminated. At hearing the news, I felt relieved. Now I didn't have to tell them I was retiring. I was told my last workday would be in August, and I'd be given a severance package. She said I could search other openings within IBM.

I said I wasn't interested in another job, and I'd wait for receipt of the severance package. After I reviewed the package, I asked to be transferred to IBM retirement status because I qualified for retirement on July 31. My second request was that I not work through August. I requested July 15 as my last workday. Because I still had vacation time, the rest of July would be granted as vacation days.

Several other employees were also let go. Because they weren't ready to retire or prepared to be unemployed, many panicked and wondered what next steps they should take. Some applied for other jobs within IBM, but I don't know of anyone who was successfully reassigned.

I'd worked from home the previous 11 years. I had to go to the San Jose Office to turn in my badge, laptop, and American Express card. It gave me a chance to say goodbye to people I knew in the office. I had an exit conference call with my manager to finalize my severance package and pay. After I turned in my work items to the mailroom to be shipped back to headquarters, I chatted with a few people, and we went to lunch.

I'd started working professionally at age 18. I was never unemployed and never collected unemployment. I never feared being fired. I never required direct supervision. I knew how to work and how to remain employed. I'd completed 15 years of service at IBM and felt good heading into retirement. My official retirement date was recorded as July 31, 2016.

Cameron Park, California

Whenever there was a major upgrade to the Yamaha keyboard, I'd buy a new one and donate my old one to local high schools for underprivileged children.

I was thankful to God to have both parents still living. While they were in good health, I knew they wouldn't be as mobile as the years went on. I wanted them to be comfortable in their golden years. Before I retired, I offered to buy them a new low-maintenance home in Louisiana that would give them greater freedom in retirement. They chose to stay in their current home.

So, I took them on a seven-day cruise. We boarded a Royal Caribbean ship in New Orleans, cruised the Eastern Caribbean, and had a grand time.

I organized a 2010 family reunion at Drusilla seafood restaurant in Baton Rouge. Its theme was reflection. We had over 225 family members in attendance. A family memorial wall featured photos, names, and the date and cause of death for each deceased.

Years later, my sisters suggested our family celebrate Christmas at my home. My parents flew to Sacramento; the rest of the family drove from Southern California. Audrey Mae and Josie cooked dinner at their houses and brought the food to my home. We had turkey and all the trimmings.

Afterward, we drove up the mountain so my nieces and nephews could see snow for the first time. When we left, it was sunny and 65°. Twenty minutes later, in the mountains, the temperature was 30° and it was snowing hard. They'd never experienced such a rapid weather change. I explained the further up we went, the more snow we'd see. I stopped to let them play and throw snowballs at each other. As we drove back home, they were amazed at the quick change of weather, because it had turned sunny and clear again.

On Christmas Eve, we went to downtown Sacramento to see the Christmas lights. At an outside ice skating rink, Christmas music was playing. The kids ice skated for a couple hours. Then we went to Christmas Eve Mass.

I enjoy living in the foothills of California. It's an ideal location. The summers aren't too hot, and the winters aren't too cold. I enjoy skiing and I'm only an hour away from South Lake Tahoe. Now that I'm retired, my former neighbor, Alberto Recendez, and I ski as often as we can.

In June 2013, I went to my 40th high school reunion. On Friday night, we met at a restaurant in Baton Rouge for dinner in a private dining room. The next day, we met at Julia Harris-Johnson's home for a picnic. She served red beans and rice, along with many other Southern favorites. I hadn't seen some of my classmates since graduation. It was refreshing to reconnect with everyone.

A few days later, Julia and I invited our first-grade teacher to lunch. Miss Wisher remains a role model for me—as she is, I'm sure, for the innumerable students she taught.

I'd always wanted to visit China. A colleague at IBM was from China and told me she had a friend who could be my tour guide. She gave me her friend's email and we began corresponding. She was a high school teacher, and we agreed my travel plans would have to align with her schedule. We exchanged photos via email so we'd recognize each other at the airport.

In Beijing terminal, as I walked through the crowd, I felt someone grab my hand. It was Ying, my tour guide

I said, "Hello."

With a friendly smile on her face, she replied "Hello." I quickly learned this was about the extent of her English. In our emails, she'd communicated exceptionally well. However, she never indicated she couldn't speak English.

As we left on the train, I tried to talk with her; she only smiled and said, "Okay."

Terrific. My life was now in her hands and all she could say was "Hello," "Okay" and "Yes."

Everywhere we turned, I was shocked to see so many people. We arrived at the train station and changed to a train bound for her village.

Again, I couldn't get over the number of people I saw. The taxi driver drove us to our destination, and we walked down a dirt road. I was still amazed at all the people. Many of them sneaked a peek at me; others stared, with smiles on their faces. I assumed many were seeing a Black person for the first time. Plus, I was taller than most of them. I saw some resemblance to the Philippines. We seemed to be in a slum area, with many small stores and people selling all sorts of things. The air was filled with smog and I could still smell Chinese cooking. The homes looked like shacks. In the distance I saw several tall apartment buildings. One was Ying's building. They were ugly and everything in the area was dusty.

We entered the basement of her high-rise building and she led me up the stairs. No elevator. We had to walk to the 15th floor. I was thankful I had only one suitcase. Entering the apartment, I followed her lead, removing my shoes at the door. I looked around; it was almost empty. Everything was dusty. The kitchen had a miniature stove and refrigerator, a table and two wooden chairs. The bedrooms contained wooden bed frames with bamboo mats. The bathroom lacked the standard American fixtures. There was a toilet, but to flush, a bucket of water had to be poured into the bowl. In the middle of the bathroom, a shower sprinkler with an attached string hung overhead. When you pulled the string, room-temperature water spilled out.

By now, we'd learned how to communicate. Ying had a

writing tablet and pen. Whenever I wanted to ask a question or if she wanted to ask something, we wrote on the tablet.

It was hot, day and night. Her small fan was on constantly, but I only felt hot air blowing.

Ying was a good tour guide. I visited Tiananmen Square. It was hot the day we went to the Great Wall, and we walked miles along it. During our tour, we met a group of touring Chinese high school girls. I don't know who they thought I was, but they all insisted on taking a photo with me. Ying took me to her local school, where the students were excited to meet me. Again, everyone wanted a photo with me. I felt like a celebrity.

On our return to the airport, Ying hailed a taxi as I stood on the sidewalk. The taxi stopped, and the driver opened the trunk. It appeared Ying was negotiating a price. Then she beckoned for me to get in. When the taxi driver saw me approaching the car, he slammed the trunk. Ying's voice went up several notches. I didn't understand what they were saying. They pointed at each other, screaming in Chinese. I gathered it had something to do with me. The driver drove away, and we were left standing on the sidewalk.

Ying flagged another taxi. This driver was much kinder. Seated in the back seat, I tried to ask Ying what had occurred with the first taxi driver.

She only said, "It's okay," despite a still-angry look on her face. At the Beijing Airport, we said good-bye and I checked-in for my return flight.

I had learned about the National Senior Games, but never found time to participate. Now that I was retired, I registered for the track and field events. I flew to Las Vegas, rented a car and drove to St. George, Utah. A couple in the parking lot engaged me in conversation. He asked what I was competing in. I said long jump and triple jump. As I checked in, we continued talking in the hotel lobby as though we had known each other a lifetime. Their names were Leo and Xie Tricase.

The next morning, I went to the track field, my first time

on a track field since high school. I stretched and did warmups. Soon my age category group was called for the long jump. I watched intently as the other jumpers performed. When it was my turn, I blasted down the runway and made my jump into the sandbox. It was a great jump, even though I hadn't jumped in years. I placed third with my best jump at 15 feet, nine inches.

Long Jump

By now, I had warmed up, and my jumping techniques were replaying in my mind. My first triple jump was easy. Still, the competition was challenging. I placed second. My best triple jump was 29 feet, five inches. Both jumps qualified me for the 2017 World Senior Games in Birmingham, Alabama.

Triple Jump

After my events, I met up with my two new friends, Leo and Xie. We went to the track and field social for dinner. Leo and I discussed our performances. He was a runner and a coach and gave me pointers to improve my jumps.

After competing in the Senior Games, I took a seven-day Caribbean cruise. When I returned, my retirement gift to myself was a 30-day vacation across Asia. I went to Singapore, Vietnam, Hong Kong, Philippines, Malaysia, Thailand and back to Singapore, which is a clean city and easy to navigate. The streets were always crowded with pedestrians. There were countless underground and above-ground malls and stores. After dark, I went to Clarke Quay, along the Singapore River, where I enjoyed the many restaurants and live music.

In June 2017, I participated in the World Senior Games in Birmingham. I watched guys high jump, which looked easy. I'd never high jumped, but I thought I could do it. I was allowed a few practice jumps. At the start of the event, the bar was mounted at three feet. I cleared it easily. After the bar inched up higher, everyone was eliminated except three of us. The bar was now at four feet ten inches. On my first attempt, I ran toward the pit, but as I approached, I stopped. A second time, I stopped before reaching the bar. On my third try, I positioned myself and started running. Approaching the pit, I planted my left foot on the ground. As I sprung up, I heard a loud "pop!" and I fell to the ground. People came over to pick me up. I limped off the field and was out of the competition. I finished in third place; my best high jump was four feet five inches.

High Jump

I toured Birmingham. I went to the Civil Rights Institute, 16th Street Baptist Church and the Civil Rights District.

Before returning to California, I visited my parents. While in Louisiana, we talked about them being the oldest married couple in Bayou Goula. I wrote an article for the local paper. The "Oldest Couple" article was published in the *Plaquemine Post*.

While at IBM, I made annual donations to various charities. The nonprofit Sacramento Loaves and Fishes was one of my favorite charities. After retiring, I contacted the director, told her I was a keyboard player and said I wanted to volunteer there. She was thrilled to have me entertain the guests. I perform twice a month in the Loaves and Fishes park. People gather around to listen to the music. Some sing along, and some dance. Over the years, I've added many new songs to my repertoire.

Now that I'm retired, I've pledged to honor the Lord's Day and not work on Sunday. I also promised myself I'd take daily naps. I'm still working on that.

In July 2017, I returned to London. I toured the city, visiting old friends. Strolling along the South Bank of River Thames, I joined the line for a ride on the London Eye observation wheel. At the top, I enjoyed a panoramic view of London. I browsed at Harrods and later that evening, attended a social event.

I spent the second half of my trip in Warwick. I went to the home of my friends, Barry and Corina Coleman. Barry kept a busy schedule and, while touring the city, he ensured I had a chance to have my favorite English fish and chips. We visited Shakespeare's birthplace, the theater and museum. Another day we spent in Oxford and at Christ Church University.

We went to the British Motor Museum; we saw many makes and models of vintage British cars. Among the many Royal automobiles on display was Princess Diana's Jaguar.

Back home, Josie called to say Faye had been hospitalized with a recurrence of cancer. She'd undergone chemotherapy in the past and its side effects were difficult. She died July 9, 2017, at age 77. A giving woman who always tried to fulfill others' needs, she was one of my favorite aunts.

The following January, I took a seven-day Caribbean cruise to Cuba, Key West and Nassau. After the cruise, I drove to Sarasota, Florida, to visit Ellen and George Colliard. They surprised me with dinner and a birthday cake.

One Sunday morning in August 2018, I dressed for Mass, as usual. I didn't feel anything out of the ordinary. In fact, I felt great. I got in my car. As I turned the key in the ignition, I immediately felt an odd spinning. The entire garage looked like it was moving. I shut off the engine and tried to exit my car. As I tried opening the door, the car seemed to tilt. I didn't know what was happening, but I was determined to get back in the house. As everything spun, I managed to get out. Holding on to the car to keep from falling, I remember walking as if I were drunk. I couldn't take a step without holding on to something.

As I staggered into the house and sat in a chair, the spinning slowed. I wondered what was going on. I tried to stand but couldn't walk straight. I thought I'd better go to the emergency room. I called 911. About when the Emergency Medical Responders arrived, the dizzy feeling had stopped. As I described my experience, I began gagging as if I needed to throw up. But nothing came up. The EMRs insisted on taking me to the emergency room. I didn't want to go, but I agreed because the gagging wouldn't stop.

When we arrived, I was still gagging and the EMRs explained my situation to the doctor. She gave me some pills and the gagging subsided. I was now coherent enough to communicate with the doctor. She asked if I'd ever experienced this problem.

I never had.

She explained I had experienced vertigo, the sensation of feeling off balance and like everything is spinning. I was given a prescription to fill and was released from the hospital. I called a taxi for a ride home.

When I got home, I felt fine, so I drove to the pharmacy to fill the prescription. The pharmacist said the store computer was offline and he couldn't fill it for another hour. I decided to go back the next day and I drove home feeling fine.

About three hours later, I was watching TV and suddenly the TV and the room started to spin. It was happening again. I called my neighbor (Byron) and asked him to take me to the emergency room.

He came immediately, and I explained what was happening. The spinning had stopped, but I was gagging and nothing came up. I sat in the back seat of Byron's car, gagging into a plastic bag all the way to the ER.

Because I hadn't been brought into the emergency room by EMR, I had to fill out medical forms and wait to be seen. Byron sat patiently with me. Finally, I was seen by the doctor. Because I hadn't gotten my prescription filled, the pills they gave me earlier that day had worn off. The doctor gave me more, and soon I stopped gagging. It was after midnight when we left. Byron drove to a 24-hour pharmacy, where I was able to fill my prescription. I finished taking the prescription, and I never had another occurrence of vertigo.

The theme for our 2018 family reunion in Louisiana was "finding our roots." I created a family tree booklet for each family. Prior to the reunion, I'd gone to Salt Lake City to the history museum for family tree research. In my research, I learned that data for many slaves was not recorded. But I found census records for our immediate family.

The reunion was at Bayou Plaquemine Waterfront Park in Plaquemine, with a Southern-style barbecue picnic. Each family brought a dish to share. We sold raffle tickets and awarded cash prizes. Proceeds from the raffle were donated to the Plaquemine Nursing Home. Our attendance count was 325 family members.

Family Reunion

During my visit in Louisiana, I visited my half-sister, Gloria Collins, who has natural talent for cooking. She cooked a large pot of delicious Creole gumbo. I ate two large bowls of it. She also gave me a set of rosary beads.

In October 2018, I participated in the Senior Games in St. George, Utah and Las Vegas. At the Vegas games, I long jumped 15 feet, and triple jumped 30 feet, seven inches. I finished in first place for both events.

After those games, I went on a cruise across the Atlantic. The Queen Marry II departed New York for Southampton England.

In June 2019, I participated in the National Senior Games in Albuquerque, New Mexico. Of 26 long-jump participants, I finished in the top five. I also finished in the top five of the 14 triple-jump competitors. Before returning home, I drove to the Four Corners Monument, the only place in the U.S. where four states (Utah, Colorado, Arizona and New Mexico) join.

I'd scheduled a cruise on the Grand Princess. Destination Hawaii, its port of departure was San Francisco. We were due to embark March 7, 2020. But the day before, an email from

Princess Cruises stated the ship was returning to port with sick passengers. The 15-day cruise was canceled, my money refunded, and I was issued a credit for a future cruise.

Earlier that year, I'd heard of a coronavirus originating in China. I hadn't given it serious thought because everything I'd heard was China-related. Now that my cruise had been canceled due to coronavirus, not only I, but everyone in the United States, was paying attention.

We learned the outbreak's epicenter was Wuhan, Hubei Province, China. The virus spread quickly and was classified as a pandemic. Many people were dying. People across the world were told to shelter in place to slow the spread. We were only allowed to leave our homes for emergencies and to buy food. Restaurants, bars, schools, sports venues, churches, and many other places were closed. We were told to wash our hands, wear masks and practice social distancing. When exposed to the virus, people were told to quarantine for two weeks. Manufacturing of masks, ventilators and personal protective equipment occurred around the clock. Hand sanitizer was in high demand.

This was unprecedented. People were stranded on cruise ships or abroad. As businesses closed, people immediately became unemployed. Some could work from home, while students were home schooled. Mass was celebrated online. It was my first time not receiving Holy Communion for months. After adjusting to such radical changes, the closing of the country affected the economy badly. Millions of Americans were infected and thousands died.

The stock market tumbled. Before the coronavirus, the Dow Jones Industrial Average was a few points shy of 30,000. When the coronavirus appeared, the market tanked, closing as low as 18,200. I took advantage of the decline and purchased stocks at a bargain.

Also in 2020, SpaceX became the first private company to launch astronauts for NASA. This was an important step for our path to expand human exploration to the moon and Mars.

Meanwhile, protests around the country escalated, with national anger sparked over the death of a Black man by a White police officer. Police brutality against Black men has been recorded countless times, and history continues to repeat.

My Thoughts

Black Africans were taken from their homeland in shackles, crammed in slave ships and brought to America. Theirs was an unwilling voyage with no knowledge of their destination. Amid harsh conditions, starvation, dehydration and violence, many died before reaching America. Once on American soil, the enslaved Black Africans weren't recognized as people, but viewed as commodities to be bought, sold and exploited.

Slavery was inhumane, and I wish it had never occurred. I don't fault people today for what their ancestors did in the past. Also, I am not entitled to take credit for the pain and suffering my ancestors endured. The Black slaves did not live peaceful lives. However, they were true heroes. Without them, I wouldn't exist.

I initiated a trace for my family history. I learned tracing Black ancestors could be difficult because not all slaves were documented. Many were given their master's surname. Records show slave owners who arrived in the Albany, Louisiana area brought slaves with them to work the fields.

Albany, Louisiana is about 16 miles from Walker, Louisiana. It's not far-reaching to believe the Walkers had slaves. Those slaves who lived with and worked for the Walkers inherited their last name. This is my belief: Over the years, slaves in that area who were my ancestors drifted across the Mississippi River and settled in Iberville Parish.

Many years after slavery, during the spring, it was common for people in Iberville Parish to go to Albany to pick strawberries on the Hungarian families' strawberry farms. My parents, uncles and aunts picked strawberries on these farms for many years. It was a tradition they'd followed through the years.

I met a lady in San Francisco, who told me, "I am an African American."

I looked perplexed. I knew my eyes weren't deceiving me. She was clearly white skinned.

She said, "I was born and raised in South Africa. After graduate school, I moved to America. Years later, I applied for citizenship to become an American citizen. Therefore, I'm an African American."

A light bulb went off in my head. I can't assume people's origin by the color of their skin. I recognize that my ancestors can be traced back to Africa. If they were alive today, they'd rightfully be African Americans. My origin is America because that's where I was born. I identify as a Black American.

When I was an adolescent, the word "nigger" was tossed around lightly. I was called "nigger" more times than I can recall. However, the word never fazed me. I always knew who I was, and I knew I was never a "nigger." My birth certificate identifies me as "Negro."

Through the years, the word "nigger" became powerless in my world, but I was amazed when I first heard someone refer to it as "the 'N' Word." In my mind, whenever someone says, "the 'N' Word" that person is murmuring, "nigger." If "nigger" is not acceptable, it shouldn't be replaced with a code word. These words are not in my vocabulary. But, if someone says "nigger," I don't feel offended; it simply tells me where that person's heart is, and I have less respect for that person. The people I fear are the phonies who shout "nigger" behind closed doors but in my face reservedly say, "the 'N' Word."

God has commanded we love one another. As we advance, we still have difficulty learning how to live together and love one another. Some people show more love for animals than humans. A stray dog or cat on a busy street gets more attention than a homeless person lying on the sidewalk. We were all born with a skin color, and we didn't get to select which skin color we preferred. Each of us should be proud of our skin color. Our skin color may be different, but our internal organs are the same. Organ and tissue transplantation defies racial boundaries. I've heard when a transplant is needed, ethnicity isn't a concern. Some of the most religious people I know insist they want to go to heaven when they die. But if you can't love your brothers and sisters on earth, what will you do in heaven?

We all will face death. We were born and we'll all die. No one gets out of life alive. We came into the world naked and with nothing, and we'll leave this world with nothing. All we have is on loan. The mystery is not knowing the precise date or time of our death.

Every one of us was uniquely fashioned by our Creator. Not even identical twins have the same fingerprints. Because of our uniqueness, I believe everyone has been blessed with at least one talent. Some people discover their talents early on; others find theirs later. Some go through their entire life and never discover their hidden talent.

When seeking out a hidden talent, examine the things you do better than others. When those things seem effortless, and you enjoy doing them, you've probably found your true talents. Also, pay attention to your passions, because those may lead you to your talents. If you're fortunate enough to get paid to do what you enjoy doing, consider it a bonus.

Poor people have been around all my born days. Today, many people lack the necessities in life and they live in poverty. Regardless of how someone falls into poverty, I believe we, as a society, are obliged to help. Many lack jobs that enable them to care for themselves. I believe specific federal, state and county jobs should be granted to these people.

As a society, we should take care of any person living in poverty who does not qualify for a job because of mental, medical or other handicaps. Reaching out to help should constitute more than writing a check to an organization. Taking time out of our schedules or volunteering to mentor will contribute to the reduction of the poverty problem. And our focus should be to fulfill people's *needs,* not their *wants* or *desires.*

Everyone goes through life's ups and downs. One key to handling the swings is during the up times not to let the wins go to your head. Be grateful and appreciate the upswings because they won't last forever. When downswings arrive—and they will—don't let the failures go to your heart. Examine the situation and accept it as a lesson learned. Failures make you stronger and prepare you for the next roadblocks.

I wanted to be in the Navy so badly, I never considered a backup plan. After I entered the Navy, I learned I was average compared to other recruits my age. I'd heard all my life I was smart, and I believed it. I was only as smart as the people I was being compared with. I was subsequently compared to young men not only my age, but from a wider population across the United States. Rather than accepting being average, I tried to become a smart person according to my environment. Because I had many transfer duties within the Navy, I had occasion to put this comparison to the test many times, and I tried to ensure I stayed on a learning curve.

One of my many teachers in life was failure. Each time I failed, I looked for the lesson and learned from my failures. Failure gave me strength and enabled me to advance. Even when I had confronted failure, I still had to conquer the fear that smothered me. Failure and fear were my motivators, but my main ingredient was always faith. I couldn't simply say I had faith until I got past the failure and fear. Faith is what always carried me to the finish line.

Hoping and believing are also powerful motivators. But they must be executed. Execution is to do something. The doing engages the activator, faith. Therefore, faith is acting on what I believe.

The Bible gives us the example of Peter walking on water (Matthew 14:25-31). When he was told, "Come," he did something, and the doing part was getting out of the boat. He walked on water through faith. However, when he focused on the wind, he took his focus off faith, and that's when he started to sink. Peter walked on water with little faith; with great faith, I can only imagine what he could have done.

As a Catholic, my character is important to me. Character and skill are equally important. At times, my skills are underdeveloped, but my character is solid. Character is who you are. Character doesn't change daily. I define my character as the things I do when no one's watching. Because of my character, I know I was given opportunities above and beyond my skills.

I concluded I don't believe in luck for myself. I believe luck is for people going through life without a specific plan, goal or purpose. When good things happen to them, that's luck. As I've traveled through life, I've tried to do the right things, along with planning and having goals. I believe blessings were bestowed upon me—and blessings should never be confused with luck.

The years go fast, and we have a limited amount of time on this earth. Today, I give greater value to my time and my use of time. I have no specific regrets in life, but if I had a chance for a re-do, I'd make a few changes: 1) I'd sincerely study harder and strive to achieve better grades in high school. I attended every class and never missed a day of school. However, I did minimal work, studying only enough to make passing grades. 2) I'd study music as a profession and play a variety of instruments. 3) Without a shadow of a doubt, I'd join the Navy with the goal to become an admiral.

For most of my life, I was my worst critic and measured my success against someone born the same year as me. Granted, we didn't all start on a level playing field or in the same environment. I believed, if we were born in the same year, we started life together. I wanted to know what someone did to advance that I didn't do. Sometimes, I found the answers; sometimes not. A foreigner my age who came to this country unable to speak or write English always posed a challenge. As I conducted my comparisons, I was often satisfied with the result. Someone will always be more advanced than me and someone behind me. I tried to be grateful because I always knew I was right where I should be at any given time.

I traveled extensively during my career. My quest now is to visit every state in the union, and every continent. With five more states to visit, I'll complete my quest; my missing continents are Africa and South America.

I was born at a good time in history. I entered the world after slavery in the United States, and experienced the following:

- Jim Crow Era
- Civil Rights
- Vietnam War
- Computer Software Technology

Jim Crow Laws in America enforced legal racial segregation, a codified system of racial apartheid that dominated the American South. The laws affected almost every aspect of life, mandating segregation in schools, parks, libraries, drinking fountains, restrooms, buses, trains and restaurants. "Whites Only" and "Colored" signs were constant reminders of the enforced racial order.

Personally, living under Jim Crow Laws was the norm. I had no reference or life comparison. Living separately but equally was the rule for Blacks. When my cousins from Michigan came to Louisiana for the summer, my aunt would tell me to look after them before we went to the store; they weren't accustomed to associating with White people as we did.

While serving in the Navy, I interacted with people from all over the world. We'd compare our childhood years of the 1950s and 1960s. Most people I spoke with hadn't lived in the South. When they mentioned harsh treatment in the North, I'd tell them my experiences. They said when riding the city bus in the North, they had to sit in the back. I told them where I lived, there was no bus, and we walked everywhere. When they went to a movie theater, they had to sit in the balcony. The nearest theater to my home had a sign that read, "Whites Only." The first time I went into a Black theater, I was 18. Even the Catholic Church I attended was segregated.

"White" and "Colored" water fountains confused me. That people couldn't drink from the same water fountains was appalling.

I believe in Dr. Martin Luther King, Jr.'s quote, "We should be judged by the content of our characters and not the color of our skin." I believe we're making progress, but more must be done. Everyone has a part in making this world a better place.

The Civil Rights Movement was a struggle by Black Americans to achieve civil rights equal to those of Whites. These are: the right to vote, the right to a fair trial, the right to government services, the right to a public education, the right to use public facilities and more. Although Black people paid taxes, we were not allowed to enter public facilities such as libraries, city parks and many more.

After many years of injustice for Black Americans in the United States, courageous people fed up with unfair treatment took a stand. During this movement, blood was shed and many lives were sacrificed for our civil rights. With resistance, American laws were revised for the inclusion of Black American citizens.

I participated in the Civil Rights Movement in America. I was one of the first Black students to integrate an all-White school. Due to the disproportionate number of Black students to White students, it wasn't a smooth transition. I felt unwelcome, and I endured verbal abuse daily.

Even with all its complexity, I believe living in the South was easier because I knew what to expect. I lived in an all-Black community, and we knew our social limits. We always knew who we could trust. Whenever we encountered White people, they either liked you or they didn't. But living outside the South, I was randomly caught by surprise. People I thought were genuine were lacking, yet they still smiled in my face.

The Vietnam War was a long, costly, and divisive conflict between North Vietnam and South Vietnam. North Vietnam was communist and supported by the Soviet Union, China, and North Korea. South Vietnam was supported by the United States, South Korea, and other anti-communist allies. It was believed, if communist North Vietnam prevailed, South Vietnam and other countries in Asia would become communist.

At the time, I didn't understand all the politics of the war. While still in high school, on my 18th birthday, I registered with the Selective Service. Although the Vietnam War was coming to an end, and troops were being transferred back to the United States, I still wanted to join the Navy. I was young, fearless and naïve. I'm grateful my guardian angels were watching over me, and I didn't go to war.

Computer Software Technology is the amalgamation of computer science, information technology and computer engineering. Software programs and devices include programming, networking, database design and development to ensure computers function properly. Networks of networks became the modern internet. The online world took on a more recognizable form known as the World Wide Web. This field has evolved dramatically over the last decade.

I was introduced to computer technology in the 1980s. As the technology advanced and the internet grew, I discovered my niche in database management.

The work I've done affected lives, standards of living and various aspect of life. The Internet of Things and product barcodes were included in my work as well.

I pretended I was given a puzzle box at birth. On the cover was the picture of the completed puzzle. Inside were many small pieces, but not all. It was my job to assemble the puzzle and find the missing pieces.

As a child, I was assisted in filling in the puzzle when I learned to crawl, walk, talk and other youthful milestones. When I started school, I was assisted with completing more of my puzzle. My progress wasn't difficult because I was told where to place the pieces. Once I entered the world as a young adult, many of the pieces in the box had been positioned in their proper places. Vacant areas were for the puzzle pieces I didn't have.

It was time to get out of my comfort zone. As I ventured out into the world, I learned other people held my missing pieces. I had to find them. When I least expected it, people would come into my life and provide information I needed. Some became friends; others I never saw again. As I traveled through life, I did my best to treat everyone equally and with respect. I found many of the missing pieces to my puzzle by being nice to others. My puzzle is still in progress.

I once heard someone say, "There are things I know. There are things I don't know. There are things I know I don't know. And there are things I don't know that I don't know." I now know I will forever be learning.

As a child, I worked closely with my father, building and remodeling houses. He gave me a work ethic I cannot repay. During our hours of laboring, he'd rattle off quotes about work and life. Below are his famous quotes.

J.D. Walker's Quotes:
1) Money doesn't make me, I make money.
2) Don't dislike me; get like me.
3) It's hard, but it's fair.
4) Takes money to make money.
5) I work, work until work was tired and asked me to quit.
6) I'm ready if I don't get to go.

Acknowledgments

I want to thank my parents and siblings for their support. My father has an exceptional memory and was able to answer the many questions of my life before I could walk or talk.

Agnes Delone (deceased) played a major role in my life. She raised me from infancy to age four. Agnes was the first to tell me, I was "cute as a button" and referred to me as "My Button."

To my Uncle Reverend Briscoe Pierre, thanks for your prayers.

To my cousin, Beatrice Troxclair, thank you for collecting articles and photos of my high school track and field wins.

To the ATOS Team, Frank Blackwell, Tom Bower, Evelyn Brown, Emma Lou Cody-Bryant, and Connie Walters.

I owe a tremendous amount of gratitude to Margo Laverdure, Donna Pieper, Suzy Tunstall, and Norma Wooten (deceased).

To the White Castle High Class of 1973, I treasure your friendship.

I am grateful our life paths crossed, Katherine Bilanko, Ellen Barlow-Colliard, Lynne Eash, Dannean Farris, Alan and Maria Hurdle, Marilyn Kronabetter, Paula Meo, Mimi Nehse, Jerry and Joan Ontiveros, Joy Sheppard, Maria Sun, Leo and Xie Tricase, and Mary Warner.

I would be remiss if I failed to say a simple "Thank You" to Carol Berman, Sylvia Hurdle, and Sherreta Lane.

Author's Note

After years of collecting my thoughts, writing my auto-biography was challenging and rewarding. During the process, I learned more about myself and those who helped make me what I am. Some of the dialogues recounted are approximations. Stories from my childhood and adolescence were documented as best I could remember. My father told me many early stories, and I thank him for opening his heart to share difficult memories. Any factual mistakes in this book are my responsibility.

I think of my story as the culmination of the work I put forth and faith in my God. I feel privileged to have benefited from opportunities created by those before me and I hope my story can help people following me. I profoundly thank all relatives and friends who touched my life in countless ways.

And, finally, to the woman who brought me into this world and made me the man I am today—my mother, Julia M. Walker—I sincerely thank you, and I love you.

My Immediate Family

Father: Joseph Dave "J. D." Walker, Sr.

J.D. Walker was born in Plaquemine, Louisiana, in 1932 and raised in Bayou Goula, Louisiana. He was an only child. His biological father was Joseph Walker. His mother, Lorenza Bowzer-Carter, married Riley Carter. His stepfather raised him and treated him as his own son.

J.D. quit school in the 8th grade. He worked in his stepfather's sugarcane field alongside his mother. He worked as a planter and hauled sugarcane to the sugar mill with a mule and wooden cart. Years later, when his stepfather bought a tractor, he hauled larger loads of sugarcane, generating more income for the family. Eventually, J.D. graduated to a working position in the sugar mill.

Many years later, he joined the labor union and worked on various construction jobs. After gaining more work experience, he became qualified to work as a maintenance/laboratory technician at Exxon-Mobile for 24 years, until his retirement in 1994. A self-taught carpenter, he built several houses in Bayou Goula.

Mother: Julia Mae "Mick" Pierre-Walker

Julia Mae Pierre-Walker was born and raised on Tally Ho Plantation in Iberville Parish, Louisiana in 1934. Her parents were Samuel Pierre, Sr. and Florestine Johnson-Pierre. They bore 10 children, of whom Julia was the sixth. She was a young teenager when her father died of kidney failure. Her mother was forced to raise the children on welfare.

Julia completed elementary school in Bayou Goula and received her high school diploma by attending night school. She enrolled in vocational school for office administration and received a certificate of completion.

In her early years, she worked many days in the sugarcane field, harvesting and planting from sunrise to sunset. Later, she became a housewife and worked as a maid, cleaning homes. Because she could drive, other maids relied on her for rides to and from work. Julia now lives a happy retirement life.

Sister: Audrey Mae Walker-Lott

The first-born daughter was born in 1950. Audrey Mae graduated from Bayou Goula Elementary, Dorseyville Junior High, Iberville High and Westside Vocational-Technical. She married Charles Lott, Sr. and had four children: Latasha Lott, Angelete Lott-Hill, Charles Lott, Jr. and Shakara Lott. These children gave Charles and Audrey Mae six grandchildren. Audrey Mae worked as a data-entry clerk and office administrator and retired from the University of California San Diego Bookstore Department.

Sister: Barbara Ann "Bobbie" Walker-Carter

The second-born daughter was born in 1957. Bobbie attended and graduated from Bayou Goula Elementary, Dorseyville Junior High and White Castle High. She attended Southern University A&M College and Louisiana State University. Bobbie holds bachelor's and master's degrees and works for the Iberville Parish School Board.

Sister: Josie Mae Walker

The third-born daughter was born in 1959 and graduated from Bayou Goula Elementary, Dorseyville Junior High, White Castle High and LaSalle University. Josie holds a bachelor's degree in business administration. She has a daughter, Jemetra Shanae Trotter, and a grandson. Josie worked for the United States Department of Veterans Affairs and is now retired.

Sister: Belinda Marie Walker

The fourth-born daughter lived from November 17 to December 28, 1961 and died of colic.

Sister: Judith Ann "Judy" Walker

The fifth-born daughter was born in 1964 and graduated from Bayou Goula Elementary, Dorseyville Junior High, White Castle High and Southern University A&M College. Judy holds a bachelor's degree, master's degree and minister's license. She has two children from a former marriage, Patricia Ann Franklin and Leon Robert Walker, as well as two grandchildren. Judy worked for the Federal Detention Center, Houston, Texas and is now retired.

Brother: William Samuel "Sam" Walker

The younger (second) son was born in 1966 and graduated from Bayou Goula Elementary, Dorseyville Junior High, White Castle High and Columbia Southern University. A recipient of a bachelor's degree in sports management, Sam is married to Scherrie McCarroll-Walker and has two sons: Christian Walker and Nicholas Walker. His other children are Jeremy Walker, Shakyra Coleman and Kumichell Richard-Jenkins. Kumichell has three children. Sam retired from the U.S. Navy after completing 20 years' service and works for the United States Department of Defense.

Half-sister: Gloria Walker-Collins

Gloria was born in 1953 and graduated from Reserve Rosenwald Elementary, Reserve Fifth Ward High and Tongue Point Job Corps Center, Astoria, Oregon. She's married to Eddie Collins, Sr. and has four children: Eddie Collins, Jr., Vincent Collins, Sr., Demetria Collins-Robinson and Spencer Collins, Sr. Those children have given her 14 grandchildren. Gloria worked as a Certified Nursing Assistant and retired from the Cancer Disease Center, Carville, Louisiana.

Half-brother: Marcus Sims, Sr.

Marcus was born in 1954 and graduated from Reserve Rosenwald Elementary, Iberville High and Westside Vocational-Technical. Marcus has four children: Marcus Sims, Jr., Marquisha Sims, Devona Sims and Catrena Sims; and five grandchildren. Marcus is retired.

Riley Carter
Lorenza Odrick-Carter
Samuel Pierre
F Johnson-Pierre
Joseph Dave Walker
Julia Mae Pierre-Walker
Audrey Mae
Joseph Dave
Barbara Ann
Josie Mae
Belinda Marie
Judith Ann
William Samuel